GOD
OUR SAVIOR

GOD
OUR SAVIOR

Theology in a Christological Mode

C. Norman Kraus

HERALD PRESS
Scottdale, Pennsylvania
Waterloo, Ontario

Library of Congress Cataloging-in-Publication Data
Kraus, C. Norman (Clyde Norman), 1924-
    God our Savior : theology in a christological mode / C. Norman Kraus.
        p. cm.
    Includes bibliographical references and indexes.
    ISBN 0-8361-3551-2 (alk. paper)
        1. Theology, Doctrinal.   2. Jesus Christ—Person and offices.
    3. Mennonites—Doctrines.   I. Title.
    BT75.2.K67   1991
    230'.97—dc20   91-6674
                                                                CIP

The paper used in this publication is recycled and meets the minimum requirements of American National Standard for Information Sciences—Permanence of Paper for Printed Library Materials, ANSI Z39.48-1984.

Except for the author's own translations or other attribution, Scripture is from the *New Revised Standard Version Bible*, copyright 1989, by the Division of Christian Education of the National Council of the Churches of Christ in the USA, and used by permission. Scripture designated RSV is from the *Revised Standard Version of the Bible*, copyright 1946, 1952, 1971 by the Division of Christian Education of the National Council of the Churches of Christ in the USA, and used by permission. Passages marked NIV are from the *Holy Bible, New International Version*, copyright © 1973, 1978, 1984 International Bible Society, and used by permission of Zondervan Bible Publishers. Quotations marked NEB are from *The New English Bible*, © The Delegates of the Oxford University Press and The Syndics of the Cambridge University Press 1961, 1970, and reprinted by permission.

99 98 97 96 95 94 93 92 91 10 9 8 7 6 5 4 3 2 1

To all my students
of the past forty years
from the six continents

Contents

The "Intermediate State" of the Soul
Death and the Essential Self
The Resurrection
Christ's Resurrection and Ours

Preface

When I first planned this theological project, I envisioned the present volume as based on my *Jesus Christ Our Lord* (1987, revised 1990). Therefore, I wrote the volume on Christology as an introduction to the more general discussion of theology. I have stayed by this plan. Questions of methodology and philosophical assumptions are more prominent in the first volume. Since I gave special attention to soteriology in the first volume, I have not repeated that material here. As I neared the end of the present essay, however, it became clear to me that a single volume covering the scope of theology would be a great advantage for use in the classroom. Accordingly, I added the chapter on Jesus Christ as an "overture" to the whole work. The introduction functions as a simple prolegomenon.

I have explored the implications of a christological norm for the theological task as I had envisioned it in the previous volume. My procedure is to treat the materials in the context of current issues, yet in light of the historical discussion. Also, I have focused on issues which impinge on discipleship and life in this world, rather than speculate about metaphysical definitions and future eventualities. Even so, I have not developed the practical ethical implications. This is not a "theology of discipleship," but a theology which will inform and stimulate discipleship. Finally, as one convinced that Christian doctrine must be based on a normative apostolic witness and record, I have tried to take the biblical materials seriously.

This volume was written in the context of ongoing intense discussion in the church concerning Christology. Although my theological approach has not gone in significantly new directions, I have taken special care to clarify some ambiguities in the first book. I am much indebted to colleagues at Eastern Mennonite Seminary and Associated Mennonite Biblical Seminaries who read the manuscript and discussed it with me in a series of consultations. They offered many stimulating and helpful suggestions which have helped me to clarify my presentation.

—C. Norman Kraus
May 1990

Introduction

Theology is not popular today. Indeed, one hesitates even to include the word in a book title. To laypersons, theology often seems unnecessarily technical and confusing. They wonder why the simplicity of Christ must be so complex. They view it as a speculative and polemical discipline. As one person wrote to me lately, "Why bother to write on the subject? No one will agree with you anyway!"

At the other end of the spectrum, academia has largely discredited the old claim that theology has a place as a *"science* of God." The claim that there is a normative revelation of God prescriptive for all human cultures is considered an arrogant presumption. The proper approach to the study of religion, many hold, is phenomenological and comparative. Some scholars hope that by this method a future universal community of theological discourse may be created. In the meantime, the major intellectual task is to carry on interfaith dialogue.

So one must explain, if not defend, the importance of theology for the church. This is especially true in a tradition like that of Anabaptist-Mennonites, who have always emphasized the biblical disciplines in contrast to the theological. On occasion I have been asked explicitly why I chose to write a theological treatise on Christ rather than take some other approach. Sometimes the question was simply one of wonder. Other times it implied that another approach would have been more appropriate.

The Function of Theology

The church is a community of shared experience and discourse. Like every other human community, it has its own system of meaning and its own terminology to explain and justify its understanding of things. Many who have grown up in the church are quite unaware how foreign are terms like *born again, kingdom of God, miracle, salvation, sin, lordship of Christ,* and *the world,* to those outside its community of discourse. Theology is an examination and elucidation of this system of meaning and discourse.

Theology is a dialogue carried on in the church and between the church and the world cultures. As a special discipline within the church, theology speaks both *to* the church and *for* the church to the world. To the church it speaks as a constructive critic examining the language the church uses to convey its message. In this role it is especially important to the teaching and preaching of the church. It also explores the implications of the church's experience of God in Christ for its ethical decisions, worship, organization, and mission strategy.

But theology is not only concerned with in-house matters. It is deeply involved in the church's dialogue with the world cultures. It concerns itself with the contextualization of the gospel message in order to convey its real meaning to those outside its boundaries. The church must couch its proclamation in terms that are understandable to those who know little or nothing of the Bible's message. At the same time, it must be faithful to the original message.

Along with this *kerygmatic* function, theology must also give a consistent and coherent defense of the truth of the church's message. This latter is its *apologetic* task. The more deeply the church becomes involved in the life of world cultures, the more profound and comprehensive must be its theological self-understanding.

Theology, then, has a rational and analytical role to play. This does not mean it must be speculative and rationalistic. It is, as Paul puts it in Romans 12:1, a rational service to God. Doing theology is praying in the rational mode, or "praying with the mind" (1 Cor. 14:13-15). As Anselm (1033-1109) put it, theology is "faith seeking understanding." It is a spiritual discipline in which we attempt to discern the "mind of the Lord" for the church. Its goal is effective proclamation and intelligent discipleship.

How we understand and talk about God has a direct bearing on how we think about ourselves in relation to the world and other human beings. For example, the corollary of the doctrine of God's unity and universality is the unity of the one human family. If the old polytheisms are correct, there really are multiple species of humanity, each of which is related to its own deity. But if God is the Creator of the universe, our ecological responsibility is grounded in more than a pragmatic sanction or the "laws of nature." Our care of the earth is a spiritual responsibility under God (Ps. 24:1).

The theoretical sciences provide *models* of physical reality which other scientists and engineers can use to extend scientific knowledge and create new products. Similarly, theology provides models for understanding spiritual reality which can enhance our experience of God and guide our ethical response. For example, if our model of God is that of a supernatural manipulator or celestial Santa Claus, our experience of prayer will be limited largely to asking and receiving. Our concept of fellowship with God will be quite different if we think of God as a just judge or a warm friend. How we theologize about Jesus as the revelation of God is directly related to the way we experience God and the way we understand discipleship.

Today there is much stress on the importance of spirituality and the spiritual experience. In an age of secular rationalism and moral relativism this is important. But we must never forget that knowledge enhances experience. For example, knowledge of aesthetics and musical theory can significantly heighten the experience of art and music. So theological reflection and meditation can heighten the spiritual experience. We are in need today of informed spirituality!

Theology and the Knowledge of God

At one time theology was considered to be a "science." Not an empirical science, to be sure, but a rational science which could give us direct and certain knowledge about God. Philosopher-theologians used human logic to draw conclusions from nature about God's existence, based upon the assumption that God is the Creator of the universe. They called this "natural theology." They viewed nature and the Bible as the sources of revealed theology. Information about God (e.g., the Trinity) could not be deduced with any certainty from the evidences of nature. It must be revealed directly by God. Using these sources, systematic theology built a logical system of truth about God—a rational *science of God*.

Today there are still conservative, or fundamentalist, theologians and biblical scholars who view the Bible chiefly as a source book of revealed rational information about God. For them theology is still a definitive statement of dogmatic truth. At the opposite end of the continuum, liberal theologians define theology as the science of *religion* rather than the science of God. They would say that theology is the data of religious experience. Thus they virtually reduce theology to the philosophy of religion. Is there no other option? I think there is.

Many agree that the process of deriving knowledge about God is not as direct and rational as the older scholastic orthodoxies assumed. They question whether theology can properly be called a science in the strict sense of the word. They view the Bible as the inspired record of Israel's revelatory experiences of God culminating in Jesus Christ. And they view theology as a reflective analysis of this revelational data in light of the ongoing experience of the church.

In this view the data of theology is God—*the God experienced in past history, and as still experienced in the church*. Thus theology is an objective intellectual discipline, but it is neither a science of God or religion. It is rather a descriptive faith statement, a confession of faith, based upon the firm conviction that Jesus Christ is the self-disclosure of God in history.

According to this latter view, theological reflection is based on revealed historical experience and not on revealed theological ideas. This is not to imply that the experienced data is not the result of divine interaction, or that ideas are excluded from the "historical experience." (See the chapter on revelation, pages 41-67.) But it does shift the primary locus of revelation from an oracular transfer of theological ideas to a historical personal expression or self-disclosure, which becomes the source for theological reflection. Therefore, our first major concern is to know how and where God has disclosed himself to us in our historical experience, and whether one can find a normative expression of God in history. The distinguishing claim of Christian faith is that there is such a normative revelational expression in Jesus Christ, who is the Word of God in history.

Theology is an existential discipline in the sense that it does not deal with God as a rational idea or object to be examined, but as a personal subject with whom we have had fellowship. Knowledge of God has its source in God's gracious self-disclosure, but it becomes known to us in our obedient response to the word of God, and not simply by our intellectual comprehension of information about God (John 8:31-32). To put it another way, we come to know God truly when we respond to him as Personal Subject in obedient faith to his commandment given in Jesus. In that moment of grace we are grasped by the truth of God as it has been disclosed in Jesus Christ.

Theological reflection is based upon such existential experience. It appeals for its validation as knowledge to the continuing possibility of such an experience of God in Christ through the Holy Spirit. In this sense it is a confessional discipline based on faith's perception and understanding of the rational empirical data of our lives. The difference between the philosopher and theologian is, as Tillich used to say, that the theologian begins from within the circle of faith. A person of nonfaith can report on the theology of others, but only a believer can *do theology* as spiritual contemplation.

Theology as Contextualization

From the time of the fourth-century creeds—Nicea and beyond—the ultimate purpose of theology was to formulate *dogma*. Dogma is the universally authoritative statement of Christian belief. It assumes that one can capture the experience of God in Christ in terminology that will be the same for all times and cultures. Such dogma then becomes the mold in which the biblical material is interpreted and cast. Dogma defines the revelatory data of the biblical record, and it becomes the final norm for theological orthodoxy.

This is the way the ecumenical creeds of the first centuries have functioned in the history of the church. The Ecumenical Councils stated officially that their formulations were "what had always and everywhere been believed in the true church back to the apostles." Thus by direct implication they claimed to be defining biblical revelation not only for their own time and place, but for every place and for all time. These creedal formulations became the norm for orthodoxy.

There were minority objections to these theological definitions—not everyone in every place and time agreed—but dissenters were coerced into submission or banishment by the power of the state. Our point here, however, is not that dogma and orthodoxy were enforced by the political power of the state (although that in itself throws some doubt upon the legitimacy of its claims to be the "universal" normative biblical teaching). Our point is that the church leaders did not recognize that their dogmas were contextual restatements of the apostolic experience and expressions. Thus, on the face of it, they should not have claimed a universal authority *equal to the biblical data*. They were necessary and helpful statements for their own time and place, and in some degree for other times and places, but they could not be universalized except by coercion.

This is, of course, only what the Protestant Reformers were saying when they rejected Catholic *tradition* and adopted the slogan *sola scriptura*. However, they did not apply this criterion radically. In effect, they stopped the process of critical assessment and reformulation with the ecumenical creeds of the fourth and fifth centuries. These remained normative for the interpretation of Scripture. It was at this juncture that the Anabaptist Reformers insisted that the *sola scriptura* principle must be applied more radically. The creeds can give us valuable guidance, but only Scripture has final authority for the reformulation of theological doctrine.[1]

The principle of theological contextualization has again become crucial for us in the twentieth century. By *contextualization* we mean the reformulation of theological statements in the context of the world's varying cultures so the message truly conforms to the original gospel of Jesus. As the church has moved into cultures that do not share the Greek and Latin heritage, it has become imperative to reformulate the biblical message. Even in the Western cultural context, so much has changed that new ways of conceptualizing and describing theological ideas are necessary.

The idea of contextualization is not new. In fact, it is inherent in the writing of the Bible itself. The Old Testament was written in the context of Hebrew and Jewish culture over a long period of time. Indeed, the prophetic literature is a contextualization of the Mosaic Torah (law). The ministry and teachings of Jesus also contextualize the "law and the prophets." The New Testament letters represent a crucial step in contextualizing the story of Jesus as Paul and the other apostles penetrated the Greek, Roman, and tribal cultures with the message of the gospel. In fact, the letters of Paul are an important guide for us in the contextualization of the gospel message today. The Christian teachers of the following centuries continued this process of reformulating theology in the languages and thought forms of the Near Eastern world. The conciliar definitions of Nicea and Chalcedon should be viewed as part of this process.

The task of theology is to contextualize the message of Scripture so its true meaning can be communicated. This is not a simple process. It begins by carefully examining the original message of the Bible in its own historical, cultural context. Then it must critically examine its own cultural setting, analyzing the way in which the original patterns and thought forms have been adapted to communicate the original message. Third, it must critically analyze the thought structures and language of the new culture into which the gospel message is to be cast. These steps are often reciprocally related. As we study another culture, we begin to understand our own better. At the same time, the distinctiveness of the biblical culture becomes clearer. Nevertheless, the theological process must recognize each of these three aspects in formulating its statements.

To say that theology is a contextual discipline means that its categories and language must be open to reformulation. This is true both as we move geographically across cultural lines and as we move across historical-cultural boundaries. Theology must consider new questions and new perspectives on old questions if it is to remain meaningful and relevant. It must take seriously the validity of various cultural perspectives if it is to be the nonimperialistic servant of Christ.

My own life pilgrimage has taken me across many cultural boundaries. I began in a sheltered Mennonite community where a naive commingling of biblical and Greek concepts provided the mold for theological thinking. My first introduction to Anabaptism was also within this "orthodox" context. Later I became acquainted with what Karl Barth called "the strange new world within the Bible." I became aware that biblical presuppositions and definitions were not necessarily the same as those of my Mennonite biblicism. Also, I began to see more clearly the implications of *modern* Western culture and how it differed from both the ancient biblical and Greek cultural concepts. When I lived and taught in Asian and African cultures, I observed the significant differences in their worldviews. One could not assume that biblical explanations which fit Asia would be relevant in Africa!

Finally, I spent a number of years in Japan, attempting to understand their culture and to make the gospel clear and relevant to them. I began to see a correlation between the fact that Christianity has never developed an authentic Japanese expression and the fact that so few Japanese people have become Christians. Even though it may be admired, Christianity is still viewed as a "foreign" (Western) religion. The dogmas of Chalcedon have little direct relevance or meaning for Japanese life. The Bible as translated and taught is a Western book. In this setting I was again challenged to think of theology not as a dogmatic formula to transfer to other cultures, but as a process of relating the original gospel message to the particular culture.

In that same spirit I offer this present volume as an attempt to understand the significance of the biblical message in our "postmodern" culture. Interestingly enough, our postmodern Western culture has growing similarities with the Asian cultures, so I hope what I have written may even help to be a bridge between the two cultural worlds.

CHAPTER 1

Jesus Christ and Theological Reflection

Introduction

Christian theology begins with the fundamental conviction that Jesus Christ is the normative revelation of God to us. What we learn of God through the life, death, and resurrection of Jesus of Nazareth is "final" in the sense that we do not expect a revision that would change our understanding of God's character and purpose for the world. It is not final in the sense that God has no more to teach us. The Spirit of *Christ* continues to guide Jesus' followers into all truth. The consummation of history (the *eschaton*) will be the final revelation, but it too is spoken of as a manifestation (*epiphaneia*) of Christ.

In the history of theology this normative centrality of Jesus Christ has been challenged in different ways. For example, those systems that make "natural revelation" the controlling context for understanding the Christ event have challenged it. While philosopher-theologians like Thomas Aquinas held that the revelation in Christ was "final," they did not make it the hermeneutical norm for understanding nature and history. Instead, they insisted that Christ be interpreted in the categories and framework of nature and reason.

In the seventeenth and eighteenth centuries, rationalistic movements like deism made human reason the final norm. They praised Jesus as a religious teacher, but they held that one must interpret revelation in Jesus in accordance with the norms of human rationality. This approach was continued in the liberal theologies which followed the philosophical leads of Hume and Kant and the modernism of empirical theologians in the twentieth century.

Much more subtly, a modern biblicism has also displaced the centrality of Jesus with the centrality of the inerrant Bible. This focus on the authority of an inerrant written text has much in common with the biblicism of Judaism in Jesus' day. The Pharisees were biblicists *par excellence*. They refused to acknowledge Jesus as Messiah in the first place because he did not fit the categories of Mosaic revelation as their scribal scholars had interpreted it. Modern biblicism accepts Jesus' messianic claim, but insists on making him conform to legal patterns of justice which it reads from Old Testament law.[1]

Ironically, like the Pharisees, these modern-day "biblicists" are offended at Jesus' claim to have authority over Moses and the prophets (Matt. 5:17, 22, 28, 32, 44, etc.). Instead of reading the continuity between Jesus and the prophets as Jesus himself understood it, they insist that he be understood strictly within their own theological categories of Old Testament interpretation. Thus the uniqueness of his new (*kainē*) covenant revelation as the true fulfillment of the Mosaic intention is subverted.[2]

Today in the broader Christian world, the centrality and exclusive normativeness of Jesus Christ as the self-disclosure of God is being challenged from yet another perspective. According to this view, Jesus Christ is the unique self-disclosure of God *for Christians*, but one cannot assert his universal normativeness without reservations. One must recognize the validity of other revelations and test the normativeness of Jesus for them in open dialogue with their claims.

Such a position raises the specter of relativism and challenges the church not only to assert Christ's exclusive authority, but to demonstrate the character and reason for that authority. What is there about this person that leads us to the conviction that he is the normative self-disclosure of God to the world? The exploration of this question is the task of Christian theology. In this chapter, we will examine how the church has understood the person and work of Jesus as the Messiah, and why it has always asserted his universality and finality as a norm for all revelation. In the following chapters we will look at the implications of this claim for an understanding of God at work in the universe.

Jesus as Revelation

Jesus' Character

What is it about Jesus that has convinced Christians that he is a normative self-disclosure of God? Certainly it is not some philosophical argument offered by Jesus or one of his apostles. Jesus and Socrates represent two very different approaches to knowledge of the truth. Jesus said, "I am the truth," not "I have a truth to teach you." Neither is it Jesus' mystical sainthood. He was no "Mahadevi" who achieved divinity through mystical visions. Nor was he a Guatama in search for enlightenment who achieved Buddhahood through ascetic discipline and meditation.

We must begin by asking what in the first instance led the apostles to confess that Jesus of Nazareth was the "Christ of God"? Was it the unusual circumstances that surrounded his birth? Was it John the Baptist's announcement that he was Messiah? Was it his miraculous power over evil? Was it the superiority of his teaching or the compassion of his ministry? Was it his execution as a martyr on the cross? Was it his resurrection from the dead? In a sense all these elements are part of the reason, but even their cumulative effect does not explain this confession.

It was Jesus' identity—who he was in the totality of his being for others—what I have elsewhere called his *gestalt*. It was how he related to other people, how he perceived and related to God as his Father. It was his compassion, transparency, and reliability. It was his inner strength, yet absence of egotism, which grew out of his absolute confidence in God. It was the consistency between his life and teachings—between his own behavior pattern and the demands he made of others. It was not so much that he had unusual powers, but the way in which he used these powers. Not only that he died as an innocent martyr, but that he died as the "righteous one" in solidarity with his people.

It was not simply the wonder of a resurrection, but the realization that the Jesus raised from the dead was the one who had been crucified as representative substitute for the people. All this is reflected in the kerygmatic description of him given by others, especially by those who had never heard of him. This identity could be revealed only in the personal relationships of historical interaction.

Self-Disclosure in Historical Events

In the life of Jesus, revelation moved beyond the normal boundaries of prophecy. He did not come with a prophetic oracle from God. Not once did he preface his pronouncements with "Thus says the Lord." He did not announce the imminent coming of the "Day of the Lord," as John the Baptist did. Rather, he announced the arrival of that day and kingdom in the introduction of his own ministry (Mark 1:14-15; Matt. 12:28). He demonstrated his authority over the demonic. He assumed authority to change Mosaic tradition and to forgive sin. He spoke of God as "*Abba*" and claimed an intimate family relationship. And when this assumption of divine authority was challenged, he appealed to the character of his ministry to authenticate his claims. In short, Jesus presented himself as God-at-work among humankind. That is, by implication, he was God's self-revelation to God's people.

This unique prophet so threatened the religious hierarchy that they collaborated with the Roman officials to execute him. Their own basic charge was blasphemy, but this blasphemy included messianic pretensions. They were convinced he would lead the nation to ruin both religiously and politically. So they urged the Roman governor, Pilate, to execute him as a political threat. His calm, dignified, and totally nonviolent response to his suffering impressed even the Roman soldiers (Mark 15:39). But not until his resurrection did his disciples dare announce that he really was the Messiah.

The resurrection itself was not a fully public event. Only the disciple band witnessed it in the form of an empty tomb and "appearances" (Acts 10:40; 1 Cor. 15:3-8). These appearances were more than mere visions. Luke called them "convincing proofs" (Acts 1:3). They established that the same Jesus who had ministered among them and was crucified was now alive and present with his disciples in power and authority. However, the exact nature of the resurrection experience remains mysterious. The apostles described it as Jesus' convincing presence (appearances) with them and his exaltation to "the right hand of God" where he now reigns with messianic authority (Acts 2:33, 36). They were convinced he would return momentarily, and in the meantime, he was among them in the power of the Holy Spirit, who came "in his name."

In this manner Jesus is revealed to be the Son of God. The revelation came in what had and was happening among them, and they were enabled to perceive and understand the events as revelation by the Spirit who prompted and guided them into the truth. John, the evangelist, begins his letter with just such a historical reference to what "we have heard, what we have seen with our eyes, what we have looked at and touched with our hands, concerning the word of life . . . the eternal life that was with the Father and was revealed to us" (1 John 1:1-2).

The impact of Jesus' life, death, and resurrection convinced his followers that he was more than a prophet. He was the self-expression, or Word, of God embodied in human existence (John 1:14; Phil. 2:7-8). As the writer of Hebrews put it, he bore the very stamp of God's nature and reflected his character (Heb. 1:2-3). John expressed this conviction in the words of Jesus to Philip, "Whoever has seen me has seen the Father" (14:9). The Christ event in its historical totality is the revelation of God.

On the basis of this historical experience, then, the apostolic church worked through the implications of all this for both faith and further action. Led by the Holy Spirit of Christ (John 16:12-14), the apostles proclaimed Jesus to be the messianic Son of God to whom God had delegated all authority.

A Surprising Disclosure

This conviction included two significant and surprising conclusions. First, *the Jesus of Nazareth who died on the cross and whom God raised is the true disclosure of the way God is present and at work in the world* (Mark 10:45; John 13:3-5). The Son of God did not come as a dictator, warrior, or judge, but as a suffering servant who washed his disciples' feet. He did not dominate or use others for his own purposes.

Previously, most people assumed God was a sovereign after the pattern of human kingship and would establish the kingdom by coercive force. But Jesus revealed that God comes to us as a servant, not a despot. God's pattern of presence in the world is death and resurrection, not violence and domination. God has made him who was the incarnation of *agapē* "the Lord of all." He is the one who will ultimately judge humankind.

As the Servant-King, Jesus demonstrated that the power of God is the power of love, not violent coercion. He did not use divine power to enforce his own will. Instead, as a humble son of peasant stock, he appealed to others' sense of goodness and right. If they did not respond, he did not resort to violence or force obedience. He taught that God treats the just and the unjust without partiality, and that his followers should love their enemies in order to be like God.

He not only taught it, he lived it. Such love is the fundamental meaning of his death on the cross. He showed us that God's way of dealing with evil in the universe is the way of crucifixion and resurrection, not violent revolution.

Second, they concluded that Jesus was the messianic *Savior for the whole world*. The religious and cultural barriers between God's covenant people Israel and the rest of the people of the world were completely abolished (Eph. 2:14-15). Consequently, his salvation was available to all on the same basis; namely, by faith (Gal. 2:15-17). We should note that this was a totally nonimperialistic announcement, that at long last God's salvation has been manifested in a universal Savior. Indeed, an explicit part of the good news was that Gentiles did not have to convert to religious Judaism in order to be disciples of Jesus.

We have spoken of this disclosure as a surprise, but we must hasten to add that it does not represent a change in God. This same Word which was embodied in the earthly Jesus of Nazareth had always existed in God. "Before Abraham" and even "in the beginning" as the word of creation, this same Word of "grace and truth" expressed itself. Jesus was no new, or novel, word about God, but rather the eternal self-expression of God now focused in this one life for the salvation of the world.

The Pauline letter to the Ephesians speaks of Christ as the revelation of the *mystery* of God's will and plan (1:9-10; 3:9-10). This mystery, or hidden purpose, he wrote, was hidden "for ages" in the God of creation, and was now disclosed in Christ. Therefore, revelation in Christ is not a novel addition. Instead, it is the uncovering of the inner ("hidden") meaning and purpose of God already in creation. Christ is in this way identified with God's eternal purpose and grace.

Jesus as God's Presence with Us

We have already said that Jesus is God at work in history. We must now examine further what this means and how the church came to this conviction. Theologians have spent much time and energy trying to explain metaphysically how and in what manner the man Jesus is God. After all the explanations, the mystery remains. Those who framed the Chalcedonian Confession were wise simply to point to the mystery with a series of negative metaphysical statements! If we want to make positive statements, we can only point to revelatory historical events.

A Historical Presence

The biblical concerns about the deity of Christ focus at a different point than do later metaphysical debates, and so do ours. Our problem is not primarily how to explain the possibility of incarnation in a philosophically credible way. In philosophical language the best we can do is to state the doctrine in paradoxical terms. Rather, our concern is to demonstrate that Jesus truly is the representative presence of the Creator-God revealed to Israel as Savior (*Yahweh*). Hence it is important for us to learn why the writers of the New Testament, in the face of opposition from certain religious authorities, came to the conviction that Jesus of Nazareth truly was the Son of God.

First, we should note that the conviction grew in stages. That is what we might expect in a historical revelation. According to John 14:26 and

16:13, one role of the Holy Spirit was to prod the disciples' memory and further enlighten their understanding of what had happened. This was clearly a historical process. One can trace the developing convictions in the pages of the New Testament. Only in the events which followed Jesus' resurrection, did they begin to understand the inner meaning and implications of what he had said and done during his earthly ministry.

The identity of Jesus as Son of God was not known from the beginning of his human life. The unusual circumstances and events that surrounded his birth raised questions about the significance of his birth (Luke 2:19). The appearance of the Magi in Jerusalem looking for a "king of the Jews" who had just been born, caused anxiety in political circles. The appearance of John the Baptist and his testimony to Jesus raised hopes that a messianic leader might be in the offing. But not until a few months before his execution did Jesus raise the question of his identity with the disciples (Matt. 16:13-17). And even after his death, the disciples on the way to Emmaus described him only as "a prophet mighty in deed and word." They had hoped he would turn out to be the Messiah (Luke 24:19-21).

It was not until after the events associated with the resurrection that the disciple band came to the firm conviction that Jesus was indeed God's Messiah sent for the salvation of Israel. Peter interpreted his earthly ministry as a work under the anointing and power of the Spirit (Acts 10:38-39). He understood the resurrection as God's vindication and exaltation of Jesus to be the Messiah who would soon return to establish his kingdom (Acts 2:32-33, 36).

Apparently, it was the manifestation of the Holy Spirit in the events of Pentecost which first convinced them that a new eschatological era had begun. They identified the Spirit as the messianic Spirit promised by the prophet Joel. They expected Jesus as God's Messiah to usher in "the day of the Lord" without delay (Acts 2:16-21). Early in their experience they identified the risen Jesus as "the Lord," and God's eschatological savior.

When Jesus did not immediately return as Messiah, they began to realize that in his humble earthly guise he was already God's Son, the Messiah. It was not only that he would return to establish the messianic kingdom. In his earthly ministry he was already the Messiah—Christ, the Lord—inaugurating his messianic reign. The way he had lived among the people was in fact the way God lives and works among humankind. As Paul put it, "in [and through] Christ God was reconciling the world to himself" (2 Cor. 5:18-19).

As they reflected on his life and death in light of the resurrection and Pentecost, they began to see with increasing clarity that he was God's self-revelation. Or as they put it, he was God's Son. Jesus had revealed God, as only one who is "in the Father" and in whom the Father dwells (John 17:21; Matt. 11:27) could reveal him. When viewed in retrospect, his life from beginning to end could only be explained as God's saving presence among God's people.

A further stage of realization came as they experienced Christ's continuing presence through the Spirit of God dramatically thrusting the movement forward. They experienced the Spirit both as the power of God and as the continuing presence of Christ. The authority and power of the Spirit were immediately associated with the "name" (authority) of Jesus. Through the power of the Spirit in the name of Jesus, they were given the same power that Jesus himself had exercised. And so they came to the realization that the risen Jesus was in the most intimate way to be associated with God. His authority, power, salvation, judgment, and love were God's authority, power, salvation, judgment, and love.

Describing the Presence

In order to express this new reality they experienced, they developed a new vocabulary. Among other Jews, they asserted that Jesus is the new name for Yahweh, God our Savior. Peter refers to him as "our Lord and Savior" (2 Pet. 1:11) and identifies him with God in the phrase "our God and Savior Jesus Christ" (2 Pet. 1:1). Especially in proclaiming the message to pagans, they were forced to expand their categories.[3] They asserted his lordship in contrast to Caesar's "divinity." Indeed, Paul said that God had given Christ preeminence and authority over all the principalities and powers. He was the "image of the invisible God. . . . In him all the fullness of God was pleased to dwell" (Col. 1:15-20). John speaks of him as the embodiment of the "Word" which is identified with God himself (1:1-14).

Paul says even now he is reigning over the affairs of nations. The destiny of humanity is in his hands. Ultimately, as the Lord of life, he will defeat death before he hands all authority back to God, who will then be "all in all" (1 Cor. 15:25-28).

This certainly is exalted vocabulary which strains at the limit of human imagination to describe Jesus' "equality with God." But it is a confession of the new reality of God experienced in Christ and not a philosophical explanation. That type of metaphysical formulation became necessary only in the centuries following, as the church became institutionalized and theologians attempted to describe the mystery of Christ's deity and humanity in the categories of Greek philosophy.

They used the metaphysical categories of subsistence or essence (*hupostasis*) and face (*prosōpon*) or person (*persona*) to state the relationship of Jesus to God in more rationally precise terms. God, they said, is one in *substance*, and three in *persona*. Jesus as the Son of God is one of the *personae* who has eternally shared God's essential nature or subsistence. Such language warded off heresies which on one hand described Jesus as a created being (Arianism), and on the other hand as a phase or temporary role played by the unitary God himself (modalism). This metaphysical language functioned in the ecumenical creeds to define the orthodox position. It thereby became normative for theology in the following centuries. The creeds declare that Jesus is truly God "of one substance with the Father," and truly man "like us in all respects, sin only excepted" (Chalcedon, 451 C.E.).

Today this metaphysical language of substance and *persona* has become problematic. Our word *person*, for example, says far more than the ancient church fathers intended by *persona*, which in the first instance referred to the masks a single actor wore to portray different characters on the stage. Today we think of reality in terms of energy and motion rather than static substance. But however we say it, the Christian conviction is that Jesus was "Immanuel, God with us."[4]

When we approach Christology from such a historical perspective—that is, "from below"—we recognize that our theological statements are a confession of faith based upon the historical experience of the church beginning with the apostolic eyewitnesses. They are not philosophical statements of a universally rational idea (truth) which can be demonstrated logically. Instead, they are attempts to make rationally coherent statements which help us understand our experience of historical reality in Christ. Inasmuch as the experience was and is an experience of the one universal God, it can be universalized—indeed, it must be universalized—if humanity is to reach its maturity in God.

The Person Disclosed

Because of our experience of God in Christ, we find it necessary to use more than strictly historical, "from below," categories to describe Jesus. When we confess our belief in the incarnation, we mean that in Jesus Christ, God was present and expressing himself within the boundaries of our historical existence. That in this one person, time, and place, God, who in every time and place has attempted to make himself known, has manifested himself to us in a unique fullness of disclosure.

Through his embodiment in Christ, we learn that God is among us as the healer and life-giver, as the reconciler, as the one who confronts evil and injustice with unfaltering love, even allowing himself to be crucified. We learn that he turns the crucifixion into resurrection victory, offering new life and hope. Only in Jesus can we find such fullness of self-disclosure of God, and yet we acknowledge limitation of our capacity fully to know God (1 Cor. 13:12; Exod. 33:19-20).

When we call Jesus the Son of God, we are identifying him as the historical self-revelation of God. We are saying that we know God as *Father* through his disclosure in the *Son.* The implied contrast is to revelation that has come through God's "servants"—Moses and the prophets (Heb. 1:3-4; 3:5). The servants spoke and acted as God's delegated messengers, but Jesus speaks and acts as the Son who shares God's authority because he shares his Father's character and life-giving power. This is the proper input for a Christology "from above."

The designation *Son of God* was primarily a kingly or messianic designation and denotes Jesus' position as Savior.[5] The Messiah was a special soteriological figure in Israel's destiny. He was to be the eschatological savior of the nation. Thus the title *Son of God,* or *Messiah,* focused attention upon Jesus as Savior. But what kind of savior was he? As we have noted, the new disclosure is that he is the Savior of the *whole world* (John 3:16-17). God is the universal Father—"the Father from whom every family in heaven and on earth takes its name" (Eph. 3:14-15). His Son, the Christ, is therefore the universal Savior.

We confess our faith in the Messiah-Son as the "Word of God." He is the authentic expression of that personal dynamic which informs the universe and moves it toward the ultimate expression of *agapē*—that love which seeks the ultimate good of every creature in God. The word *logos*, which John used, designates far more than a spoken verbal symbol. *Logos* is the rational dynamic that forms and informs the creation. In Jesus Christ, we learn that that form is *agapē.* The love was embodied in him as "the Good Shepherd" giving his life for the strayed sheep, as the compassionate judge forgiving a prostitute, or as the "Suffering Servant" loving his enemies. That love demonstrates to us the ultimate grace of God.

We confess our faith in the Christ as the "Light of God." The words of the Nicene Creed, "Light of Light," were meant in the first place to signify Christ as the radiance of the God who "is light and in him there is no darkness at all" (1 John 1:5).[6] In the letter to the Hebrews, Christ is described as "the reflection of God's glory" (1:3). John identifies him with the light which first illuminated the primeval darkness and created life. That light of God, he says, has ever since continued to penetrate human darkness, making life possible (John 1:4-5).

Light in this reference is associated with life-giving—rather than intellectual—illumination. Jesus is that light and warmth of God on the human scene, overcoming darkness and bringing life. Thus Jesus' claim, "I am the light of the world" (John 8:12), is set in the context of his creative restoration of sight to one who was born blind.

This image of light was a favorite of Athanasius (d. 373), who used it against Arius. He argued that as the light of the sun is identical with the sun, so Christ is one essence with God.[7] Actually, one can use the metaphor to argue both that Christ derived from God—as Arius used it—and that he is coequal with God. In its biblical setting, however, it probably was not intended to make either of these points. It is more fitting to see it as a figure of the life-giving nature and effect of God's salvation in Christ. In fact, John mixes his metaphors and says that the "life" of God in Christ is the "light of all people" (1:4), and that the "true light" offers salvific enlightenment to all who will receive it (1:9-13).

The image of light also speaks of Christ's power to dispel demonic darkness. So Jesus cast out unclean spirits and thereby was bringing deliverance from the darkness of ignorance and superstition. As the light of Christ exposes the evil in the human heart, it causes a *krisis* (judgment). When faced with the truth of God, people must make a decision (John 3:19). Their response becomes a self-judgment. Thus, as the Light of God, Jesus reveals the truth and gives life to the world. Or in the words of a related metaphor, he is the true and living Way to the Father (John 14:6).

Finally, the church also confesses that Jesus is *God's universal authority* when it designates him "Lord." From the New Testament perspective, his authority has been given to him by the Father (Matt. 28:18; John 5:19, 26; 7:17; Acts 2:32-33a; 1 Cor. 15:27). And by virtue of the Father's commission, his authority is equated with God's authority (1 Cor. 8:6; Eph. 2:20-22; 4:5-6). In the New Testament, his commandment fulfills and supersedes the Ten Commandments from God through Moses. (He is "lord even of the sabbath" Mark 2:28.) As Lord, he is the authority in the present era, and he will rule until "every [other] ruler and every authority and power" shall have been destroyed or dethroned (1 Cor. 15:24-25; cf. Rev. 21:24, 26). He is one with God in authority (1 Cor. 8:6), and he must be obeyed above every political divinity. To obey him is to obey the God of the universe.

If we ask how he exercises his authority in the world, we can only point to his cross and resurrection. His exaltation to authority ("the right hand of God") is via the cross, and the banner of his authority continues to be the cross. His followers are to take up their crosses and follow him (Mark 8:34; 1 Pet. 2:21). His authoritative *vicar* (agent) is the Holy Spirit, who convinces the world of sin, justice, and judgment (John 16:8). In their struggle against the false authority of the "authorities and cosmic powers," his soldiers are armed with "the sword of the Spirit" (Eph. 6:12-17). This does not provide a political platform or strategy, but it does imply a social mandate with political implications under his authority and leadership.

For Christian faith, then, Jesus stands at the center of the theological and ethical disciplines. Or to change the image, he is the nail from which the whole theological picture hangs. In Christology, we are concerned to clarify his position as the authentic historical presence and representation of God among and for us. In the broader theological discussion, we attempt to understand the implications of saying that he is a genuine self-disclosure of God.

Jesus the Clue to Human Nature and Destiny

For theological and ethical purposes, the humanity of Jesus is as important as his deity. Jesus not only reveals God to us, he shows us what it means to be fully human. Paul calls him the *eschatos adam*, i.e., the "last Adam," or the eschatological human being. He recognizes that all humanity shares in the "image of the man of dust," that is *adam*, but he says our destiny is to share in the "image of the man of heaven," that is, Jesus Christ (1 Cor. 15:49). This suggests that humanity did not reach its goal in the creation of Adam and Eve, but in the incarnation of the Christ.

Incarnation not only means that *God* came to us in a human form, but that God *shared our humanity*, thus revealing its true meaning and dignity. Through incarnation God placed the indelible stamp of his own image and nature on the one human, Christ Jesus (Heb. 1:3; 1 Tim. 2:5).[8] Incarnation was not a mere communication technique. The very possibility of a divine incarnation grows out of the special relation that the Creator has with humankind, whom God created in his image. Its realization means the consummation of that image. Or, to use the language of 1 Timothy 2:5, the human Messiah, Jesus, is the "mediator" of that image.[9] And Paul says that the whole creation moves toward the final realization of that image in the children of God (Rom. 8:22-23).

Definitive Humanity

The humanity of the Christ is everywhere taken for granted in the New Testament. He was the man from Nazareth whose family was well-known in the region. The ecumenical creeds also affirm his full humanity, although many of the patristic explanations of its nature tend to diminish its actuality to an "enfleshment." When the essential element of humanness was understood as "flesh," or animal body and rationality, it was enough to say that in Jesus the divine essence had assumed human flesh. The divine spirit or mind (*nous*) had limited itself to residence in a fleshly body. In the words of the twelfth-century theologian, Peter Lombard, the Godhead assumed the flesh and soul but not the person of a man.[10]

As the distinctively human characteristics came to include an expanding conception of the personal dimension of life, it became necessary to incorporate new elements into the definition of Jesus' humanity and to insist that he was human in every sense that we are human. The only exception is sin, which is peculiar to human existence, but not essential to it. Therefore, in theological parlance, it is standard to say that Jesus was fully human except that he did not sin.

The phrase "flesh and blood" in the Bible refers to the weakness, dependence, and vulnerability of humans. Using flesh in this way, Paul says that Jesus was "born in human likeness" (Phil. 2:7). Or again, he was "born of a woman, born under the law" (Gal. 4:4).[11] That means he fully shared our vulnerability and human handicap.

In the Apostles' Creed, Jesus' vulnerability is epitomized in the words *born, suffered,* and *died.* As an infant he was completely dependent upon a human mother and father. As a child he was socialized as a Jewish boy. He found his self-identity among the peasants and artisans in Galilean society. As a developing adult he was tempted as all humans are. He was limited in knowledge and power, and he knew the frustrations which are so much a part of our existence. He had to rely entirely on God for the fulfillment of his destiny. And Jesus was subject to death with only God's promise of resurrection.

What is extraordinary and even miraculous in all of this is that Jesus realized the full potential of the image of God within the existential boundaries of sinful humanity. He resisted the temptations to selfish pleasure and power. He identified with the oppression and weakness of the poor. He made *agapē* his life motivation and rule. *Agapē* determined his response to friends and enemies alike. Jesus made the Father's will the first priority of his life—even to the point of death. He found his self-fulfillment and self-identity in a theonomous rather than an autonomous relationship. Thus Jesus fulfilled the sinless image of God in and for humanity and became the paradigm for all humanity as "children of God" (John 1:12-13).

Christ's Humanity and Our Salvation

Theologians from Athanasius to Karl Barth have emphasized the necessity of Christ's humanity for our salvation. They all assume the corporate solidarity of the human race, and therefore what one person has done can affect the whole of humanity. For example, Karl Barth wrote,

> He [Christ] is an individual in such a way that others are not only beside Him and along with Him, but in their most critical decision about their relationship to God, they are also and first of all *in* Him. His individuality is such therefore that with His being and doing, with His living and dying, a decision is made about them.[12]

This is the correlate of the doctrine of human solidarity in the sin of the first parents.

Athanasius argued that God took to himself a human body in order to restore humanity to immortality. Jesus, he held, submitted to death in order to undo its power not only for himself but for the whole human race. "For the solidarity of humankind is such that, by virtue of the Word's indwelling in a single human body, the corruption that goes with death has lost its power over all."[13]

Anselm (d. 1109), sometimes called the father of scholastic theology, said that sin robs God of the honor and obedience that human beings owe him. So what must be given to God as a "satisfaction" must be *human* honor and obedience. Therefore, to satisfy this human obligation, Christ became fully human, and through the gift of his life and death in perfect submission to God, he paid our debt.

John Calvin (1509-1564) followed this familiar theme, but he first emphasized Christ's mediatory role as the reason why his humanity was necessary. He wrote that

> God's natural Son fashioned for himself a body from our body, flesh from our flesh, bones from our bones, that he might be one with us. Ungrudgingly he took our nature upon himself to impart to us what was his, to become both Son of God and Son of man in common with us.[14]

After that he adds the necessity of his obedience as a human being "to present our flesh as the price of satisfaction to God's righteous judgment, and in the same flesh, to pay the penalty we had deserved."[15]

All these explanations think of human solidarity primarily in physical and rational or mystical terms. When we think in personal and social terms, the imagery of the Bible takes on new meanings. The biblical writers clearly state that God's personal presence and power lived among them in the life of one particular man, Jesus of Nazareth. It was manifested to a degree beyond prophetic inspiration and beyond kingly or priestly anointing. They recognized this authoritative presence in his salvific activity. He had authority over the evil forces that hold humankind in bondage. Jesus of Nazareth was God-in-solidarity with us, sharing fully our existential situation of shame and guilt.

How then shall we understand his saving activity according to this paradigm? We must emphasize first that such a paradigm requires God's full humanity in Christ. It is necessary for him to be fully identified with us and recognized by us as sharing our sinful situation. If he is to overcome sin for us, he must do it within the limitations of our human weakness. If his sinlessness—which we affirm—is to have saving effect, Jesus must have achieved it under the restraints we experience. Only in this way can we be fully identified with him in his victory over the power of sin.

Second, we must understand that our sinful condition is far more serious than our guilt feelings might indicate. Guilt describes our sin as acts against the law of God. Guilt indicates a kind of naughtiness for which appropriate punishment can be assigned. Juridical penalty, or in some cases restitution, can right the situation and restore the status of "not guilty" before the law. This in turn may clear the way for reconciliation.

Guilt has provided the primary theological model for explaining how Jesus' life and death atoned for our sins. The cross has been seen as a penalty borne by a divine-human substitute who satisfies the justice of God and "justifies" the sinner before the law. According to this paradigm, the humanity of Jesus need only be spelled out in generic terms. He must be sufficiently human to pay a human debt to justice. But when our sinfulness is understood according to a shame model, Jesus' solidarity with us must be complete and personal.

Shame indicates a failure to achieve what we can reasonably be expected to achieve. Shame-anxiety stems from the realization that we have not fulfilled our potential.[16] We have not measured up to what God requires of us, nor have we measured up to what we require of ourselves. Hence we suffer inferiority feelings and shameful embarrassment. This is beautifully illustrated in the Adam and Eve story. They were "ashamed" when they realized that their attempt to achieve the potential image of God by their own means did not work. So they tried to hide! The result of shame is alienation and resentfulness. They tried to blame God for their own failure.

Human sinfulness is the failure to attain to God's image by our own schemes (shame) when we have spurned God's way to attain it (guilt). Our shame is a guilty shame, but because the shame element is so strong, its resolution must be effected in a sensitive personal way—especially when the sense of guilt is relatively absent. Since this is the case with the large majority of humanity, the resolution must begin with acceptance and reconciliation. This can happen only through identification with the one who feels the pain and animosity of shame anxiety. This God did when he identified with us in Jesus Christ, taking upon himself the humiliation and pain of our human alienation.

The cross represents Jesus' ultimate identification with humanity in its self-imposed estrangement and hostility. Execution by crucifixion was considered the most shameful death possible, reserved for slaves, foreigners, and people guilty of treason. (Incidentally, all of these characterize the human condition before God, and so the cross may also be spoken of as the symbol of God's wrath.) It was designed to strip a person of all dignity and expose him or her to public ridicule. It was a human symbol of worthlessness, failure, and rejection—the projected rage of a shame-ridden society. Consequently, in Jesus' death, which was in large part the result of his identification with the "accursed" multitudes, he took upon himself their humiliation as their representative.

Jesus, whom they knew to be innocent, voluntarily became a victim of those powers which degraded and humiliated the masses. He did this in solidarity with them, representing their cause when he might have escaped. In this way he made his cross the liberating symbol for the oppressed. That he died with dignity and compassion even for his tormentors, reversed the meaning of crucifixion. The cross, intended to be a symbol of failure and humiliation, became for believers the symbol of victory and a new self-identity. Thus Paul glories in the cross (Gal. 6:14), focuses only on the *crucified* Christ (1 Cor. 2:2), and proclaims the cross as "the power of God" for the salvation of humanity (1 Cor. 1:18; Rom. 1:16).

Jesus as a Present Reality

Jesus as Spiritual Presence

Jesus promised always to be present with those who meet in his name (Matt. 18:20; 28:20), and the church has always identified the Holy Spirit as that presence. In the experience of the earliest believers, the power of the Spirit and the name of Jesus are virtually identical. They experienced the presence of the exalted Christ in his body as the Spirit's courage, power, and guidance. This equivalence of the exalted

Christ and the Spirit is alluded to in many ways, as we will see in chapter five, but nowhere is it more explicit than in 2 Corinthians 3:17-18. Here Paul says "the Lord is the Spirit" and then refers to that Spirit as "the Spirit of the Lord." Finally, he calls this revelational presence "the Lord, the Spirit." This experience of the spiritual presence of Christ both convinced the apostles and helped them define the nature of Christ's identity.

The pattern of the identification of Christ with the Spirit moves both ways in the New Testament documents. In the Gospels the concern is to identify Jesus' authority and work with the Spirit of God. He was anointed by the Spirit (Acts 10:38). He was given the Spirit without measure so he might become the bearer of the Spirit and might baptize with the Spirit (John 1:33; 3:34). His salvific works were the work of the Spirit (Matt. 12:28). In him the messianic Spirit of God so far exceeds the Spirit's manifestation in the prophets that we may even speak of him as the embodiment of the Spirit of God.

In the postresurrection references, the pattern flows in the opposite direction. The Spirit's presence is identified with the presence and power of the exalted Christ, who is none other than the risen Jesus. According to John, the Spirit's role is circumscribed by the revelation in Christ. He will bring what Jesus taught to the memory of the disciples (14:26). He will speak only on Christ's authority, and he will declare only what he receives from Christ (16:13-15). The practical reason for this linkage is clear. The Spirit means "freedom." However, this is not the freedom of individual inspiration, but the freedom of Christ.

From one side, the Spirit's character and work coincide precisely with the character of the earthly Jesus. But from the other, the identity of the exalted Jesus is not limited to the human life of the preresurrection man from Nazareth. Jesus as the Christ shares in the authority, power, and freedom of the Spirit of God. And as the exalted Messiah, the Spirit "proceeds" from him as well as from the Father.

The later trinitarian language of the church also recognizes this identity as a "substantial" or "essential" unity of the Son and the Spirit. And although it caused controversy, the Western creeds suggested a certain subordination of the Spirit to the Son when they insisted on the *filioque* clause; namely, that the Spirit "proceeds from the Son" as well as from the Father. The Holy Spirit of God has come to be identified as the Spirit of Christ. Therefore, a full definition of Jesus as the Christ must include this spiritual reality.

Although the Holy Spirit is by no means limited to the organized ecclesiastical community, nevertheless it is primarily as the enlivening

Spirit of the church that the Spirit bears witness to Christ's identity (John 15:26-27; 1 Cor. 12:3b). In and through the Spirit's enlightenment and empowerment, the church is the "body of Christ." It thus bears authentic witness to Christ's true identity and mission.

Jesus and His Church

When we think of Jesus' relation to the church, we speak of him as *pioneer-founder*, "head" of the body, and *Lord* of the realm directly under his authoritative control. John Toews put it well when he wrote, "The fundamental concern of New Testament Christology as reflection on the person of Christ is peoplehood formation."[17]

Jesus did not organize the church during his ministry in the sense that he designed a community structure and appointed officers. But he was the pioneer-founder of a movement in history. He called disciples to learn his way and to live as citizens of the kingdom of God, which he inaugurated. And he commissioned them to continue as his representatives to proclaim his universal authority. John Yoder is quite correct when he elaborates a "politics of Jesus."[18] The covenant movement which he created was to continue the mission under his authority ("in his name"), and by the power of his Spirit.

The church began primarily as a movement and only secondarily as an institutional community. The movement finds its commonality, unity, and cohesion in its loyalty to Christ and his mission. Community is a gift to those who participate in the movement. It is a delightful surprise sustained not by ethnic cohesion, family relationships, or cultural tradition, but by the "unity of the Spirit [of Christ]" (Eph. 4:3-4). It is a community of grace, not law, bound together by the Spirit of Christ in pursuit of his mission.

Paul speaks of this unifying, enabling, directing function of Christ as his headship over his body (Col. 1:18). We must remember that the metaphor of the head's relationship to the body is more than one of rational direction. According to ancient psychology, the head is the source of nourishment and enablement as well as the organizational center of the body (Eph. 4:15b-16). Christ enables the members of the body with "spiritual gifts" for the continuing mission (1 Cor. 12:4ff.; Eph. 4:11). They find their unity in him (Rom. 12:5; cf. 1 Cor. 12:13-27).

To call the church the body of Christ suggests more than an organizational relationship with Jesus as president of the board. The incarnate Christ is in solidarity with his "body" in a way that affects his own self-identity and the world's apprehension of him as the Christ. This is the import of Jesus' high-priestly prayer (John 17:21). There he prayed that the church might share the same unity with God and himself that he has shared with the Father, so his own identity and mission might be validated.

The same concept is present in Ephesians 1:23, which refers to the church as Christ's body and "the fullness of him [Christ] who fills all in all." It is probably too strong to suggest that such language implies that the church is the extension of the incarnation. In both this and the Johannine passage, there is a clear and sharp distinction between the Christ and those who believe on him. But it does imply that the church shares in his embodiment of the presence and continuing mission of God in such a way that his identity as the Savior is integrally related to the identity of his body.

Thus the definition of Jesus as the Christ must include more than his individual relationship to God as a historical figure. He is Christ the Savior of the world, not merely by virtue of his death and resurrection as a historical individual, but also by virtue of his continuing bodily presence in the world. This involves the church in the responsibility to give an authentic witness to his way of being in the world. Only as the church bears witness through its life to the way of servanthood and the cross—in contrast to the political saviors of the world—can the true identity of the Christ be known to the world.

Jesus as the Eschatological Savior

Our theological picture of Jesus as the messianic Son of God must include the eschatological conviction that he is "King of kings and Lord of lords" (1 Tim. 6:15; Rev. 19:16). In biblical thought, both in the Old and New Testaments, the Messiah, or Christ, is understood to be an eschatological figure. It is he who ushers in the "day of the Lord." He is "the coming one" who brings in God's final salvation and victory over the powers of evil. For this reason the recognition of Jesus as the Christ was closely linked to his fulfillment of messianic expectations. His unprecedented power and authority to do the "mighty works of God" raised messianic hopes. But Jesus' disciples were not fully convinced and ready openly to announce his true identity as the eschatological Savior-Messiah. They were not ready until after the resurrection demonstrated his personal victory over death, and the Spirit, whom the disciples associated with the messianic era, had been manifested.

The title *Christos* meant far more than honored rabbi or even prophet. The Messiah was a royal figure anointed by God to play a special role in establishing the kingship of God. The disciples were convinced that Jesus had done just this. He had inaugurated a new administration in the reign of God. With his appearance on the scene of history, the "last times" (*eschaton*) had begun. His resurrection marked the introduction of "eschatological history" and the beginning of the end for the "history of death."[19] His resurrection was the harbinger and guarantee of final victory over death to all who accepted his messianic lordship (Rom. 8:11; 1 Cor. 15:57; Phil. 3:10-11).

It was precisely as the eschatological Messiah, the "Son of Man," that they first attributed the status of deity to Jesus. In his precrucifixion ministry, he was identified as a "prophet mighty in word and deed" who raised messianic hopes. But only in his exalted role as eschatological "Lord and Messiah" (Acts 2:36), was he "seated at the right hand of God," given "all authority in heaven and on earth" (Matt. 28:18), and given a name above every name (Eph. 1:21; 2:9-10). Henceforth he was associated in the most immediate and intimate terms with the divine presence, power, and purpose (Gal. 1:3; 1 Cor. 8:6; 1 Pet. 1:1). They attributed a divine identity and status to him which was proper to his divine role.

In his eschatological role as "Lord of all" (Acts 10:36), he is known as both *Savior* and *judge* (Acts 10:42-43; 17:31). As Savior, he sends the Spirit to continue his mission of inaugurating the reign of God (Acts 2:33). He frees us from the fear of death and empowers those who believe on him to "walk in newness of life" (Rom. 6:4). He carries on the battle against the powers of darkness until death itself has been defeated and all things have been united under the authority of God (1 Cor. 15:25-26; Eph. 1:10b).

In his role as judge, he is both the judicial person and the standard of judgment. He is the disclosure of God's plan and goal for history. In him are revealed the principles by which the nations will be judged. He adjudicates the destiny of humanity according to his own commandment and resolves the dilemmas and ambiguities of history by his divine decision, already revealed in the cross. Thus the eschatological prerogatives of Deity are attributed to him.

Jesus and Discipleship

Our theological definition of Jesus as the Christ includes an existential dimension. Our quest to know him and to understand the implications of his advent for our own lives is not merely intellectual or academic. As Paul wrote in Philippians 3:10-11, the goal is to share in his suffering in the hope of also sharing in his victory over death. To have *koinōnia* with the suffering of Christ means to identify with his movement (church) and to suffer the consequences of loyal engagement in his mission. This is what the Anabaptists called bearing the cross of Christ.

Such participation, or *koinōnia*, in Christ's life, death, and resurrection is also called *discipleship*, or following after Christ (Mark 8:34-35). Ultimately it is in following him that we learn who he truly is.

In our Western educational model, the concept of discipleship is not well understood. The relationship of disciple and master belongs to a different era and culture.[20] A *disciple* is an apprentice, that is, one who places himself or herself under the discipline of a *master* (a person who has mastered the art or craft one wants to learn.)

When such an apprenticeship involves a conscious quest for the source and meaning of life, the relationship between disciple and master is unique. The master (*rabbi*, *guru*) becomes an authority to whom the disciple freely submits in order to learn. Such learning involves one in absorbing the influence and style of the master by intimate relationship (*koinōnia*), observation, and imitation. In such a relationship, one learns to know not only the discipline but also the person of the master. In this way the follower of Jesus learns to know who he is.

Discipleship involves us in a response to grace and a relation to Jesus that in turn reveals new facets of his identity to us. It begins with *metanoia* (repentance), which is a change of mind about the validity of Jesus' claims and a willingness to adopt his lifestyle. In *metanoia* we recognize him as the *Prophet* and revealer of the true way. Discipleship continues in *submission* to Jesus as *Master*, to find life's integration and wholeness under his control (2 Cor. 5:14; Gal. 2:20). In the struggle to "take up the cross and follow," it becomes *dependence* upon his strength as *Friend* and Counselor. As we discover our lives being *transformed* through our relation to him, we recognize him as *Savior*, or Healer (2 Cor. 3:18). And as we "grow in [his] grace and knowledge" through koinonia with Christ (2 Pet. 3:18), we confess with Peter that he is "the Holy One of God" and the *Lord* of our lives (John 6:68-69).

In a theology for discipleship, then, we reflect upon the theological implications of our experience of Jesus as the Son of God, first to understand ourselves and our place in the world as disciples. Then we continue to explore the dimensions of Christ's authority and relevance to our world so we can more adequately confess him as Lord. Such theology is an offering of rational worship to God (Rom. 12:2). It is a form of spiritual contemplation—in the words of Paul, "praying with the mind" (1 Cor. 14:15).

CHAPTER 2

Revelation: The Word That Became Flesh

Introduction

The Christian faith teaches that the supreme and normative revelation of God to us has occurred in God's self-disclosure through Jesus Christ, the *Son* of God. God in Christ is the Source and Subject of revelation. The process of revelation is creation and incarnation. Incarnation is not simply one of a number of revealed doctrines. It is revelation in process—God making himself known to us. In John 1:1-2 the incarnate word—the Son—is identified with the creative Word. And that Word is the word of self-disclosure which imparts light and life.[1] Thus when we focus our attention on the subject of revelation, we are not simply looking at one doctrine alongside other theological beliefs. We are focusing on the process itself.

We certainly do not claim that the knowledge of God coming to us in the historical Christ is the first or only valid knowledge of God. Indeed, the Word spoken in Jesus is the same Word of creation spoken at the beginning. Creation itself is described as an act of revelation. It is an act of the "Word" of God bringing light, life, and order into existence. So creation is understood as the universal process of revelation, or what is sometimes called "general revelation," which biblical or "special" revelation presupposes.

Christianity is not the only religion which claims divine revelation.

Certainly, most religions claim some supernatural source of knowledge through oracles, mystical intuitions, inspired visions, or auditions. This is understandable since religion by definition relates human societies to that which transcends their ordinary existence. Whether this realm is thought of as spiritual, supernatural, or only as a transcendental dimension of life, its special knowledge is based upon communications or intuitions "beyond" normal rational processes.

In light of this we must examine precisely what we Christians mean when we say that God has revealed himself in a personal disclosure through Jesus Christ. How are our claims alike and how different from other religious claims? How do we get our knowledge of God? What kind of "knowledge" do we have from God? In what sense can we speak of "experiencing" God? Does God disclose himself directly to everyone? How is the disclosure in and through Christ related to the universal or general revelation? And how do we authenticate our claims of revelation in the Christian tradition? The answers to these questions are implicit both in the form and content of God's self-disclosure in Christ as it is witnessed to in the Bible.

Types of Revelational Claims

In our modern world the various religions are in close and constant contact. Their sacred writings are continually being compared. Virtually all the religions of the world claim to have knowledge from superhuman sources, or at least through supernormal experiences. The manner and content of these revelation claims vary according to their different cosmological views.

Christian theology views these claims as a reflection of general revelation, and theologians evaluate their validity from their own varied perspectives. Today the evaluative spectrum is broad, ranging from full acceptance of them as saving disclosures of God to almost total rejection of them as demonic. At one pole, God's saving revelation is held to be universal and available in many cultural religious expressions. At the other, the claims are viewed as false, idolatrous substitutes for the true supernatural revelation attested in the Bible. In light of this, we need first to review briefly the nature of other claims and then try to define the Christian concept in that context. Is the Christian understanding and claim the same as those of even its closest religious relatives, Judaism and Islam? If so, how is the revelation which has come in Christ related to them? Briefly, then, we will survey the different types of revelation claims before we look more closely at the Christian understanding of revelation.

Extrabiblical Types

The first type we might label *shamanistic*. In shamanistic religion, there is belief in an unseen spirit world in which dwell the gods, demons, and ancestors, who have superior knowledge and power. This world is vitally related to our historical life, but it is beyond the reach of ordinary people. The shamanistic medium has the special power to make contact and transfer information from one world to the other. In one type of shamanistic experience, the medium becomes the instrument through which the spirit speaks its message in oracular form. The ancient Delphic Oracle was such a medium. In another type, common among Eskimos and American Indians, the shaman goes into a deep trance and travels into the realm of the spirits to converse with them, and then reports back what he or she has learned.

One of the so-called "new religions" of Japan, called Oomotokyo (The Great Origin), claims to be based upon both of these kinds of revelation. It claims its founder was indwelt by the creator god, who spoke through her and caused her to write his divine messages. Her younger collaborator and son-in-law traveled into the spirit world and brought back much knowledge concerning its nature and relation to this world. These revelations have been written down in many volumes.

This kind of communication with the spirit world was contrasted to prophecy and condemned in the Old Testament as sorcery and magic. But its power has continued to attract Christians, and the concept has influenced some theories of revelation.

A second type—characteristic of Hinduism—might be called *mystical enlightenment*. Hinduism appeals to the sacred knowledge derived directly from the cosmic source of being. The original knowledge was heard (*sruti* means hearing) directly from Cosmic Reality or God. This cosmic reality is a neutral principle or activity said to have existed before the universe and is addressed as "That One Thing."[2] But since God (*Brahman*) is really not other than our interior self-consciousness (*atman*), one cannot speak of revelation in the Hebrew-Christian sense of the word. Truth came and still comes as a mystical intuition to those sages who learn the disciplines of meditation.

The original Hindu scriptures or *Vedas* are made up of prayers, hymns, magical incantations, riddles about the original mystery, and the like, recorded by the sages. The work of later philosophers and holy men, which expands and interprets this tradition of the original sacred truth, have been added at later times.

The original Buddhism, which began as a reform within Hinduism and then split off from it, was strictly agnostic about the supernatural. It interpreted religious knowledge simply as self-realization. The Buddha's teachings are the product of his own religious experience and enlightenment. Later tradition in China and Japan returned to a more Hindu conception of mystical enlightenment. Again, this is not revelation in the Christian sense.

Islam provides yet a third model or type, namely, *verbal transmission*. It is a "religion of the book." Its concept of revelation is strictly verbal. As one fourteenth-century source put it, the Koran, its holy book, "is the totality of the law of Islam (*shari'ah*), the pillar of the community, the fountainhead of wisdom, the evidence of prophecy, the light of the mind and eye. There is no path to God except through it, no salvation without it and no holding to anything that diverges from it."[3]

The Islamic view is that the original Koran is the words of God written in heaven and still remaining there. These words, it is claimed, were dictated to Muhammad by the angel Gabriel. He wrote them down in Arabic as a secretary. Since the sacred words were written in Arabic, full revelation resides only in the Arabic words. Even then the Muslim scholars argued whether the actual verbal symbols dictated by Gabriel were the utterance of God or merely their transmitted meaning. Words, after all, are human symbols. Today the society of Islam agrees "that the words of God are here with us and that we read them with our tongues, touch them with our hands, behold them with our eyes, and hear them with our ears."[4] Nevertheless, when vocalized by readers, the sounds produced by the larynx, tongue, and lips are not God's vocal syllables. This shows how strictly they adhere to the concept of verbal revelation.

Prophetic Inspiration

Some of the ancient Jewish rabbis taught a doctrine of verbal transmission of the Law similar to the pattern in Islam—indeed, that may be the source of Islam's idea. However, the Hebrew concept of *prophetic revelation* was distinctly different.[5] The Hebrew prophet was more than a shaman or oracle through whom a supernatural word was spoken. And he or she differed from a sage in that the word received was not understood as a mystical self-realization or enlightenment.

The prophet was able to control the prophetic announcement (1 Cor. 14:32). The message, or revelation, might come in an experience which we recognize as outside the limits of normal rational cognizance, but that was not the end or proof of it. The revealed "word of the Lord," as David Napier says, was "mulled over, reflected upon, wrestled with" in a process of rational discernment and testing.[6]

The process was far from a simple uncontrollable ecstatic pronouncement. There was no magic. The prophet prayed for counsel in the interpretation and announcement of the word. And the validity of the prophecy lay not in the mode of its reception, but in the veracity of its content.[7] Two tests were to be applied to prophecies, according to Deuteronomy 13:1-5 and 18:2-22. First, prophets must acknowledge and be faithful to Yahweh's covenant with Israel. Paul vigorously endorses this test in Galatians 1:8. Second, what they predict must come true. A third was added in the early church; namely, they must not prophesy to their own advantage. For example, they must not demand money by a prophetic word (Didache 11).

While the prophetic revelation might come in a variety of modes, such as dreams, visions, or signs, the predominant mode is described as "hearing God's word." It is a personal communication in which the message is heard and re-presented by the prophet. There are cases where the prophetic experience was an ecstatic seizure or frenzy and the utterances of the prophet were involuntary (1 Sam. 10:9-12). But the unique characteristic of the Israelite prophets' experience is the retention of prophetic self-consciousness. God speaks; the prophet listens, and then in turn faithfully reports the word to the people.[8] God is understood to be fully personal and effectively in communication with his people. As the king might speak to his people through a representative, so the prophet hears and represents Yahweh (Amos 3:7). He or she does not speak his or her own word, but the effective and authoritative word of God.

In this prophetic mode of revelation we have taken a long step toward the concept of self-revelation through embodiment of the word in Christ. To emphasize the personal intimacy of God with Moses, the writers say God spoke with him "mouth to mouth" (Num. 12:6-8, RSV and the Hebrew text). In this respect Moses is the foremost of the prophets, but the Christ has a position of even greater intimacy, "close to the Father's heart" (John 1:18; 5:20).

Personal Embodiment

The Christian concept of revelation which begins with Jesus Christ as the model of revelation, pushes the idea of personal self-disclosure one step further. We move decisively beyond the idea of the transfer of information from God. The God who spoke in a variety of ways through the prophets has now spoken through a Son (Heb. 1:1-4). God makes himself present to us in the life, death, and resurrection of his Son, Jesus. Hence, the personal revelation in Jesus transcends that of Moses and the prophets (the servants), both in mode and in content.

When we begin with Jesus, then, *personal embodiment* of the word becomes the definitive norm for both the mode and the content of revelation. What impressed the disciples was not just his prophetic words, although words and concepts were involved. Compared to the prophets of Israel, who heard and spoke the word of God, Jesus, the messianic son, embodies the word which the New Testament prophets and apostles heard and reported. This embodiment is a historical event—a totality of action, words, personal character, and presence. In its totality it is the image of "grace and truth"—what we have elsewhere referred to as a gestalt, or portrait, of Christ.[9]

The words *Christ event* have also been used to indicate the totality of Jesus' life impression on us. When we see the whole, completed Christ event, ending in cross and resurrection, we recognize who Jesus really was. And we recognize that God has identified himself with this Son in such a way that his very character (glory) is revealed through him. In the resurrection, as Pannenberg observes, God decisively identified with and vindicated the faith, life, and teaching of Jesus. God is one with Jesus in his revelation to us.[10]

In Christ, then, God reveals to us what kind of God he really is—what his intention is for human history, how he is at work in the world, and what he expects of us. God does this through a manifestation of his own personal presence and power in Jesus Christ.

The Christian Scriptures thus differ from the sacred writings of both Hinduism and Islam. They are not revealed *words*, as in Islam, and they are more than the sacred philosophy of the Hindu *Upanishads*. They are the prophetic witness and response to God's self-revelation to his people. They provide us with a historical record of that revelation which culminated in Christ. And inasmuch as they are a prophetic *re*-presentation of the revelatory "Word," they participate in the revelatory event and are themselves revelation in a secondary sense.

The Christian Concept of Revelation

Why Speak of Revelation?

The Christian concept of revelation is the corollary of its understanding of God as transcendent personal being. Jesus understood God to be transcendent Spirit (John 4:24). As such, one cannot discover God through empirical, rational, or mystical inquiry. God is not available to any kind of immediate objectifiable experience from which we can draw direct rational conclusions. (*Objectifiable* means a rationally controllable experience—one which can reproduce and demonstrate the known object.)

The *empirical* methodology of science is limited to observable phenomena. The *rational* methodology of philosophy is limited to logical extension of experienced phenomena. Human reason can work only by logical inference from observation or intuition. In strictly human terms, we can experience God only as the mysterious limit of experience and thought. Finally, by definitional assumption, the so-called *mystical* experience does not relate us noetically (rationally or intellectually) to the transcendent reality. In some traditions a descent into the interior depths of the self-conscious is identified with the divine (Atman-Brahman). In others it is an ecstatic communication with suprarational (therefore unknowable) Reality.

Thus, if there is such a transcendent Spiritual Reality as Jesus pictured, direct knowledge of it will have to come from the transcendent realm to us. Such a God will have to penetrate our sphere of ignorance because of our inherent limitation. However, once God reveals himself to us, belief in him becomes a reasonable response, and knowledge of him becomes a genuine possibility. Although we cannot discover him with our human methodologies, we can recognize him in his self-revelation.

Furthermore, if the transcendent Spiritual Reality is personal being after the analogy of human personhood, then God can be known only in self-revelation. To conceptualize this, we follow a personal analogy rather than a simple rational analogy. Our knowledge of the inner personhood of our fellow humans is attained indirectly through observation and inference and is then confirmed in "personal experience." In a similar way, God comes to us indirectly by way of historical manifestations which faith grasps. Experience, both rational and personal, then confirms it.

In human relationships, individuals are both observable objects and personal subjects. We can be studied as physical and psychological specimens. But more than detached scientific observation is needed to know us as *persons*. Other persons must share themselves with us, and we must become "personally involved" in what has come to be called an I-Thou relationship in order to have personal knowledge of the other.[11] The analogy is, of course, only that. As C. S. Lewis put it, God is "beyond personality." But we do want to indicate that the transcendent Spiritual Reality is not less, but more than what we call *personal*.

God is spiritual being and cannot be experienced like humans, who are physical beings with a personal dimension. In humans, the personal is known through its physical expressions. God, however, is the transcendent personal Subject who confronts us as an "Other." As the personal Other, God is the revelational Source and the cognitive Object of a personal experience. He confronts us as Subject after the analogy of personal confrontation by our fellow humans. Hence, revelation in the Christian sense, as we shall later discuss at greater length, is best understood as a self-disclosure.[12]

The Nature of Revelation

Largely through the influence of theologians in the twentieth century, revelation has come to be understood as God's *self*-disclosure.[13] Without doubt, the concepts of the individual self and personhood are quite modern. Consequently, the definition of revelation strictly as self-disclosure is also modern. However, this contemporary concept expresses very well the central meaning of the biblical concept. The God of Jesus Christ is presented to us in a mode, context, and categories that indicate personal self-disclosure.

First, the *mode* or way in which revelation comes is significant. Sometimes it is asked why God could not just proclaim from the heavens the message he wants us to hear. Or, as a Muslim scholar once asked me, "Is it not quite possible for God simply to reveal rational statements?" And, yes, he could, if it were merely information he wished to convey. But a rational transfer of knowledge alone would be quite an inadequate way for God to make himself known. Inasmuch as God is vastly beyond our rational comprehension, such statements would inevitably be ambiguous and paradoxical. The true meaning of ideas and words about God can be known only in the context of personal presence and communication. We all know from daily experience how inadequate written words are to communicate, even when we already know the writer!

Or, again, why does Christian theology reject the idea of mystical enlightenment as the ultimate way to experience God? The answer is that a mystical union of human spirit with divine Spirit does not convey knowledge of God as personal being. Self-disclosure involves us in an encounter with a personal other in a genuine act of communication, and such communication necessarily includes an exchange of conceptual content as well as mystical union.

Biblical revelation resides in a historical mode, disclosed piece by piece in the ongoing life of the people. It is not set forth in universal rational propositions or in mystical enlightenment. This fact is itself an important indicator of the personal nature of revelation.

Second, the *context* of revelation is the community of Yahweh worshipers. The Deity is specifically identified as "the God of Abraham, the God of Isaac, and the God of Jacob" (Exod. 3:15-16). God presents himself to the community which recognized these patriarchs with a self-introduction, "I am Yahweh." God names himself as the one who lives in covenant with them. He reveals his "glory" to them. His glory is the radiance of his essential character disclosed in its true light. But most fundamentally, he discloses himself as "the Lord" of the community of Israel. "God reveals Himself as the Lord; in this sentence we have summed up the way we regard the form and content of Biblical revelation," wrote Barth.[14]

Third, the biblical *categories* of revelation are the categories of a self-revelation. These categories are *promise,* the disclosure of God's intention toward us; *commandment,* the disclosure of God's will which lays claim on us; and *covenant,* the disclosure of his commitment to us. In these three forms God reveals his loving-kindness, righteousness, and faithfulness to us. The fourth and most comprehensive category is *salvation,* the disclosure of God's power at work among us.

All these categories find their purest expression in Jesus Christ, but especially as God's salvation, Jesus is the self-disclosure of God. In him we see the love of God for the world in its most profoundly personal form. In him we experience the power of God enabling us for new life.

"Personal" Revelation. In a word, then, we may define revelation as *a personal self-disclosure of God which culminates in Jesus Christ as the Word of God to us.* But this calls for considerable elucidation of concepts such as *self* and *personal,* as well as some explanation of biblical categories.

First, we must disavow several common popular meanings of *personal.* It does not infer an emotional relationship in which God comes to us in an intimate, chummy, or informal way. Nor does it mean face-to-face, direct exposure to God. The Bible is careful to deny the possibility of this kind of revelation.

Further, *personal* does not mean individual or private. Revelation is not private or esoteric. Instead, it is fundamentally public and social in its content and goal. It may come through an individual prophet, but it does not come to the individual for his or her private appropriation. Here we must make a distinction between an individual's perception of God's leading and revelation in the proper sense.

Personal means that revelation comes as an existential communication or disclosure, rather than as the transfer of scientific or speculative information. Revelation addresses us in the second person as responding subjects in a manner that requires a decision. It is a disclosure which demands personal involvement, not just detached observation and analysis. It requires a decision that affects our personal destiny—both individually and collectively.

This does not mean that only acts and not words are involved in revelation. Certainly, speaking is an act. But it does imply that words are not merely vehicles for the rational transfer of propositional knowledge. Words are part of a personal-relational disclosure and must be understood in that context. In those cases where it is informational, it gives knowledge of God's will, attitude, and intention toward us. It is a knowledge that reveals to us our destiny in God's future. Thus, it comes as an ultimate moral and spiritual demand upon our lives. In Emil Brunner's terms, it makes us "answerable" or responsible.[15]

Further, personal revelation is a disclosure that comes to us from a personal source. Christians understand revelation as a word spoken to humankind by God. The use of the auditory metaphor in this case is significant. The interior feelings and thoughts which disclose the person must be spoken in order to be known. A word can only be spoken by a person, and it can be heard only if and when it is spoken. Revelation, then, is an act of communication by the transcendent personal Subject, God. It is not a "discovery," or the product of human investigation and experiment.

This leads to a third aspect of the meaning of personal. It indicates an act of relating, and when it is truly heard it establishes a relationship. Revelation is a relational disclosure, a communication, a word that creates community. This is in sharp contrast, for example, to the Buddhist concept of *satori* (enlightenment), which comes as a silent dawning or recognition of truth. Enlightenment does not come to one as a communication *from* the Buddha. Buddhist enlightenment is an intuitive grasping of an elusive but ever-present reality gained by following the disciplines of the Buddha. Its goal is self-sufficiency, not community.

This concept of relational disclosure also contradicts the concepts of spiritism in which revelatory messages are supposedly spoken through an unconscious medium or oracle. Israel made a clear distinction between mediums and prophets. The latter received the word of the Lord as self-conscious servants of God for the people. Indeed, the biblical concept of revelation rules out any mystical experience of God which involves loss of self-awareness in the one being addressed.

Christ Our Clue to Revelation

We have constantly insisted that as Christians we should take our theological clues from Jesus Christ. This is no less true for the concept of revelation itself. What is implicit as well as explicit in both the manner and the content of revelation as it has come to us in Christ?

First, the *manner* of revelation in Jesus gives us our clue for understanding the relation of revelation and Scripture. Jesus is the climax of the historical succession of disclosures recorded in the Israelite Scriptures, beginning with Abraham and on through Moses and the prophets. He stands in this particular historical succession as "the one who is to come"; that is, the one who fulfilled and superseded what had gone before. Revelation in him adds a new dimension to the process and meaning of revelation itself. God's word came to Abraham, Moses, and the prophets, and through them to the people. It was a reported word. In Jesus, the Word was embodied (John 1:14). In his perfect response of obedient faith—not as reporter but as the one who received and lived the Word—Jesus was the manifestation of that Word which was heard, seen, and handled by the apostolic witnesses. Therefore, revelation reaches its normative climax in him.

That is why we must appeal to him as the ground of authority and hermeneutical norm for biblical revelation. Obviously, we come to the knowledge of historical revelation through the scriptural record. Nevertheless, the Scriptures themselves do not supersede Christ's authority, but only bear witness to it. Or to put it another way, the Scriptures do not stand in the historical succession of revelation—Abraham, Moses, the prophets, Christ—but only bear witness to it.[16]

Second, revelation in Christ is the basis for a Christian doctrine of "general revelation." In the Christ event we learn that God's self-revelation is universal in its scope and intention. Although Jesus came within and as the climax to a particular historical tradition, he did not come as its champion and preserver. On the contrary, he was perceived as a threat to the continuing nationhood and religious tradition of Judaism. This was a major reason for his execution. But in God's providence, it was precisely through his crucifixion and resurrection that he became a saving disclosure to all humankind. As Paul saw so clearly, this climactic revelation of God was not circumscribed by the Mosaic revelation. Although it had been given through that historical tradition, it presupposed and appealed to a revelatory activity as universal as creation itself.

This is certainly the understanding of John's prologue and the Colossian letter. The "Word" which has enlivened and enlightened everyone coming into the world, has now been embodied in Christ. He is the one in whom, through whom, and for whom creation exists (Col. 1:15-16). This, and not a doctrine of universal human reason, is the basis for a Christian concept of general revelation.

A third insight relates to the second. Revelation is an act of God's grace calling and enabling humankind of every culture and tradition to salvation. The immediate intention and potential of every revelatory disclosure is always and in every place salvific. A genuine faith response to God's self-revelation, at whatever level of understanding, is saving faith. Here the classic example is Abraham, who becomes the New Testament model of salvation by faith.

The classic Calvinistic doctrines of election and limited atonement—and the accompanying distinction between "supernatural" and "common" grace, "special" and "general" revelation—have obscured and distorted this point. According to the Calvinist system, salvation is limited to the elect through special revelation and supernatural grace. Therefore, general revelation and common grace serve to make humankind inexcusable for sin, but still leave them outside the pale of salvation. Some argue that God's *intention* in general revelation is salvific, but the results of inherited "original sin" in the human race make it ineffective.[17] Only revelation in its "biblical" or supernatural mode both communicates knowledge and imparts saving grace.

Certainly this goes beyond the intention of New Testament—and even Old Testament—Scripture. The gracious enablement of God for a saving response is a part of every authentic self-manifestation, whether in nature (creation) or history. Salvation is by grace, and by its christological definition, revelation is an act of divine saving grace.

Finally, the heart and substance of revelation as disclosed in Jesus Christ is *agapē*—that kind of love that was manifested in the cross and resurrection. It is precisely in Christ that we learn that God is pure holy love, or "grace." God is not a mixture of love *and* some other characteristic, such as justice. All other characteristics or attributes must be appended to love as adjectival modifiers, or subsumed under love. His power is the power of love. His law is the law of love. His judgment, wrath, and justice are all simply aspects of his grace. We have already spoken of this in *Jesus Christ Our Lord*[18] and will return to it in the discussion of eschatology. But here we want to note the implications for understanding revelation itself.

The human difficulty with God's self-disclosure is not so much its ambiguity, but its scandal (1 Cor. 1:23-25). The *agapē* of God which allows itself "to be pushed out of the universe," to use Bonhoeffer's imagery, is a scandal. Only "children" and the "poor"— those who have nothing to lose—can receive it, Jesus said. Thus revelation must be received "by faith." It cannot be understood simply as a rational datum, or rationally incorporated into a religious or political response. It can only be reflected to us in a "sinless" human life ("full of grace and truth"), and it must be experienced by us to become credible!

The reason for this is quite obvious. A revelation that requires the response of unilateral self-sacrifice is not credible in any form that excludes the revealer from the requirement. Until God manifested himself in unstinting grace and demonstrated the power of love in the resurrection, the implied demand of *agapē* was both ethically and rationally incredible. Even then it has continued to be considered "foolishness" and a "stumbling block" by most of the human family (1 Cor. 1:23).

The human proclivity for self-justification through self-defense, makes a full revelation of God's *agapē* impossible outside of a personal embodiment such as we have in Christ. The problem is already evident in the Law of Moses itself, which Jesus said had made concessions to the peoples' hardness of heart (Matt. 19:3-9). Although love is the true intention and fulfillment of the Law, law as such is quite inadequate to convey the meaning of love as *agapē!*

But the problem manifests itself in every religious system, including historical Christianity. Every religion embodies a distorted human response to revelation. Thus, by the very nature of the case, Jesus, the sinless Son of God in whom *agapē* triumphed, remains the norm for all revelation, general or special. This, as we shall see at greater length in the following section, is the reason we must insist on the lordship of Christ over every religion.

The Universality of Revelation

We have observed that it would be impossible to know God if he did not reveal himself, and that in Christ we learn of God's universal concern for and self-giving to all humankind. Now we must look more closely at some of the issues involved in this christological insight.

The Idea of General Revelation

Both the classical Roman Catholic and Protestant systems of theology have recognized the universality of revelation. What is at issue is the nature and status of revelation outside the Hebrew-Christian tradition as recorded in the Christian Scriptures.

Protestant scholastic theology followed the Roman Catholic precedent and differentiated between "natural" or "general" revelation on the one hand, and "supernatural" or "special" revelation on the other. For our purposes we need not go into the subtle differences between the two types of classification. In either case, "supernatural" and "special" revelation were viewed as the exclusive channels of salvation.

Natural (general) revelation, according to this classification, is that information about God which is universally available through creation and historical experience. It is recognizable and verifiable by human reasoning. Such revelation demonstrates the Creator's power and wisdom. It is enough to show humans that as creatures they owe worship and obedience to the Creator (Rom. 1:19-20). Even so, Calvin wrote, special or supernatural revelation as recorded in Scripture is required to "direct us aright to the very Creator of the universe. It is not in vain, then, that he [God] added the light of his word by which to become known unto salvation."[19] In other words, God can be known as Creator but not Redeemer through natural revelation. Even Adam, Noah, and Abraham knew God only as Creator, not as Redeemer.[20]

Today this idea that salvation is possible exclusively through special or supernatural revelation is being seriously challenged from several different perspectives. On the one hand, the phenomenological approach to religion views revelation merely as an intuitive dimension of human nature. Religion is defined as an experience of the transcendent and is viewed as the cultural manifestation of revelation. By definition, all revelation is "natural." Accordingly, the revelation through Christianity is merely an expression—at best, the highest expression—of the religious quest. And salvation is possible through many religious paths.

From within evangelical Christianity itself, the older orthodox position has also been challenged, not on the basis of reason but of revelation. Barth resolutely rejected the rationalistic approach and with it all possibility of natural revelation.[21] Religion, he held, is a human creation by which the race attempts to justify itself in its autonomy and rebellion. Religion as such is not the human matrix of revelation. And no one can find salvation through religion. In his later work he did hold that the self-revelation in Christ presupposes God's universal concern and engagement with humankind.[22]

This latter position recognizes some truly revelatory element in creation, but it does not go so far as the post–Vatican II (council) Roman Catholic position which stresses the idea of the "Cosmic Christ"; namely, that Christ is the "Word" of creation and thus the ground of natural revelation.[23]

This last approach offers the most fruitful possibilities for developing a truly christological view of revelation. Otto Weber summarizes it well when he says that "in view of the divine self-disclosure in Jesus Christ, which has reached us effectively in the Holy Spirit," we must now recognize a "continuity" between divine revelation and the human capacity to receive it. However, this continuity is not based upon an innate human ability, but upon the "affirmation which God in his activity has imparted to our humanity, our history, and our world."[24] That is, through God's universal self-disclosure, God has created the universal possibility of salvation.

General revelation is admittedly an ambiguous term, but as Hendrikus Berkhof observes, a more satisfactory one does not lie readily at hand. By general revelation we mean that revelation which comes to the human family outside the historical tradition which reached its climax in Jesus Christ and was recorded in the Christian Scriptures. It should not be equated with "natural revelation," for by definition revelation is not a natural phenomenon. The "truth" of revelation is never a *discovery* of human reason, but a *disclosure* by God to us.

Furthermore, it should not be contrasted to "special" (biblical) revelation, as though it is a different species of disclosure unrelated to and unfulfilled by Christ. It is general in the sense that it lies outside the recorded tradition which is the specific history of Jesus Christ. The Bible points to this general disclosure of the Creator God in its reference to the pre-Mosaic revelation to Adam, Noah, and Abraham. In this setting Jesus' words, "Abraham saw it [my day] and was glad" (John 8:56), are theologically significant since Abraham is clearly on the boundary of biblical revelation.[25]

The Limitations of General Revelation

As we have already noted, God's self-disclosure in Jesus Christ clearly implies that revelation always comes as a genuine and potentially effective offer of salvation, and that it is universally accessible. If God is the God whom Jesus revealed, then certainly he has not hidden himself from anyone. He has made himself universally available. The New Testament explicitly states this in a variety of ways. (See John 1:1-10; 3:16-17; Acts 14:15-17; 17:14-27; Romans 1:19-21; 2:14-16; and Hebrews 1:1-4.)

But we must be clear what this does and does not imply. It does not mean that every revelation is equally comprehensive, profound, and final. If we understand revelation after the analogy of personal encounter, it follows that the nature and quality of the encounter is in part dependent upon the recipient's capacity, inclination, and development. The historical character of biblical revelation itself clearly indicates this principle. God's approach is appropriate to the capacity of each recipient.[26] He is limited by the alienation of our hearts. He does not overwhelm us with impossible disclosures of his love, majesty, or law. Instead, after the analogy of wise and loving parents, he adjusts his self-disclosure to the capacity of the children to understand. So, from the historical perspective, one can observe levels or stages in the revelatory process.

We should not, however, construe these differences in revelation as differences of source, purpose, or effect. The source, and therefore the character and intention of God's self-revelation, is at all places and times the same. The cosmic source of revelation is the "Word" first spoken in creation, God "working salvation in the earth" (Ps. 74:12-17). And this same Word is most clearly spoken in its personal embodiment in Jesus Christ.[27] Again, the variation is due to the human reception and degrees of understanding.

Conversely, this means that Jesus is not the *exclusive* revelation of God, but rather the *normative* one who came at a particular time and place in human history.[28] He came in a historical succession at the right time (Gal. 4:1-7) to fulfill and supersede all that had gone before. Now that he has come, all humankind is called to a new stage of maturity, so they might "receive adoption as children [of God]" and call him "Abba" (Rom. 8:15; Gal. 3:25-28a; 4:5-6).

But what of the potential effect of revelation before or outside the historical incarnation of Christ? This question has been debated in several forms. For example, was it possible for the Old Testament saints effectively to be saved before the historical death of Christ? Or is it possible for anyone outside the historical stream of biblical revelation, such as Plato, to be saved by "natural" revelation? By direct implication, this raises the question whether those presently outside the pale of witness to the historical Christ, can be saved.

The issues in this debate are complex, and Christian theologians continue to argue the questions. However, our beginning postulate is clear. We must insist that God's genuine intention in revelation implies the genuine possibility of salvation wherever God discloses himself to humankind. If salvation is by grace through faith, we must conclude that the gracious act of self-revelation is at the same time an enablement to faith. Otherwise we make mockery of God's grace.

Further, "salvation by faith" and "not by works" implies salvation by a faith response at whatever level of capacity and understanding the revelation is received. Paul's argument in Romans 2 clearly indicates that his concept of salvation through faith excludes attainment to certain moral or intellectual standards (works) as a precondition to salvation.[29]

Perhaps the most significant indication in Paul's writings that salvation through faith is possible for those on the boundary of biblical revelation, lies in the fact that he chose Abraham as the paradigm of salvation by faith! Abraham was not saved by faith in a God different from the one revealed in Jesus Christ. Indeed, Jesus said of him that he saw my day and rejoiced (John 8:56). But he was before Moses and the Christ and stood on the boundary of that revelation. Paul clearly implies that all Gentiles stand with Abraham on that boundary where salvation is possible by faith in the God who has now been disclosed in Jesus Christ.

Again, we must be careful to note what this does and does not imply. The concept of universal revelation does not imply that *religion* as such is revealed and thus becomes the matrix of revelation. There is no "revealed *religion*," and the practice of religion is not the means of salvation. Salvation is by grace through faith in the God who is most fully revealed in the biblical tradition.

Religion is the human response to revelation, and such response varies greatly, depending on many cultural and historical factors. No religion, including Christianity, has come close to a full understanding and perfect response to God's self-disclosure. God's revelation is even now being hindered and obscured to the degree that it is misunderstood through ignorance, rejected through anxiety and weakness, or perverted for selfish purposes. Therefore, we must be prepared to recognize both the authentic responses and the idolatrous perversions in all religious systems. And the revealed norm for this is Jesus Christ himself.

Furthermore, the concept does not imply that every religious system is a direct response to God's authentic self-disclosure, or that every act of piety is an equally valid response to revelation. This clearly rules out the notion that every religious system offers an equally valid way of salvation. We do not say this by way of judgment on "non-Christian" religions. All our observations apply equally to the many versions of Christianity as well.

We do not attain salvation through religious works or through the ministrations of any religious system. We receive salvation only by grace through faith in the Word of God as it was finally and normatively revealed in Jesus Christ. In this sense there is salvation only in his name (Acts 4:12). Only he is the true and living Way (John 14:6).

Revelation and Scripture
The Primary Meaning of Revelation

When we move beyond the categories of mystical experience or rational transmission of ideas to historical experience as the mode of revelation, the process of disclosure must be understood according to the personal analogy. In the *primary* sense of the word, revelation is an act of self-communication.

Even in simple human communication, the act is a highly nuanced one. For example, it involves attitude, tonality, demeanor, body position, and body movement, as well as the actual words spoken. All these finely integrated aspects of communicating make direct vocal interaction much more effective than written words or even a telephone conversation.

Therefore, when we speak of revelation as God's action, we are not referring to bare movement or happening in history. The bare act is no more adequate for revelation than the bare words. On the other hand, we cannot simply equate words with revelation. The *meaning* of words does not lie in the words themselves.[30] The circumstantial and historical context, the expression of the speaker, and the effect of the words upon those hearing them, are all part of meaningful communication.

For example, Jesus would not have been the revelation of God's love and power without *disciples* who responded in faith. He *revealed* himself to them and not to the world (John 17:6-8). The "poor" and the "despised" heard his word gladly. He did not avoid the regions "beyond the Jordan" because of fear or lack of concern, but because he could not be "revelation" in that situational context. It was not incidental that the resurrected Jesus appeared only to his disciples (Acts 10:41). Only to them was it a revelation. The religious leaders could see only trickery and the work of Satan in Jesus' life and ministry.

Revelation, like *love*, is primarily a verb and only secondarily a noun. God's love is God loving. God's revelation is God expressing himself to us. We must speak of the primary meaning of revelation as God's dynamic action toward us and for us in history. God's revelation is primarily God relating, God communicating, God giving. Only in a secondary sense is it the established relation, the resultant communication, or the remaining gift. Luther was quite correct with his insight that revelation should be identified with the "living voice" (*viva vox*) and not written words.[31]

In this primary sense, Jesus Christ is recognized as the revelation of God to us. His life, death, and resurrection—sometimes collectively referred to as "the Christ event"—was a revelatory manifestation of God's presence and power among us. The disciples experienced their association with Jesus as a *revelatory* experience, not simply as a heightened spiritual experience. Thus they referred to him as the embodied Word of God.

Jesus *was* the Word of God spoken to us (Rev. 19:13). The disciples, like the prophets before them, *heard* the word. It is this interconnectedness and interdependence between the word spoken and the word heard, that gives the apostolic witness to Jesus as the Christ its character as "revelation," even if it is so only in a secondary sense.

Scripture as Revelation

Protestantism has from the first made a threefold distinction in its doctrine of the Word of God. In this it took its clues from the New Testament itself. In its pages the phrase *word of God*, or *word* is used in different ways. Primarily, Jesus Christ is called the "Word" (John 1:1-14; cf. 2 Tim. 2:8-9). But 1 Peter 1:23, 25 refers to the message of the gospel as the "living and enduring word of God." Paul refers to this same word as "the word I preached to you" (1 Cor. 15:2, NIV; cf. Gal. 1:8ff.). Again, Scripture is referred to as the word (2 Pet. 1:16-21; 3:2; 2 Tim. 3:15-16).

Protestant doctrine has thus always held that God's word comes to us first in Jesus Christ, then in Scripture, and lastly in preaching. Or, in Otto Weber's catching phrase, it is "the Word of God happened, witnessed to, and proclaimed."[32]

These three are dependent upon one another in a descending order. Scripture is a witness to Jesus Christ, and preaching is a proclamation of the scriptural message. Hence, in a secondary and tertiary sense, Scripture and the continuing proclamation of Christ may be included in our understanding of revelation. However, strictly speaking, only Jesus Christ may be spoken of as God's self-revelation.

Since the historical revelation in Jesus Christ comes to us only through Scripture, and since preaching depends upon Scripture for its validation as God's word, the Scripture itself has unique significance for theology. This has special importance in Protestant theology, where the normativeness of church tradition is denied. Precisely, then, in what sense can we properly refer to Scripture as revelation or the Word of God?

Scripture is faith's witness to God's self-revelation by people who participated in the disclosure. Revelation as a communicative encounter has two sides: disclosure and faith recognition. "Apostles and prophets" are those to whom revelation was given and through whom it was recognized. They are, therefore, participants in the original revelational events. Their record of the event, preserved for us as Scripture, gives witness to its character and meaning as a saving word of God. And through this Scripture, we too may participate in God's original self-revelation in Jesus.

It should be obvious that what we have called a "faith witness" is the same as the witness of the Spirit referred to in John's Gospel (15:27-28). The *Spirit's inspiration* is first the enablement of the disciples to perceive and understand the significance of the disclosure. Second, the Spirit preserved accurate memory and reporting of the original revelation (John 14:26). And third, the Spirit prompted authentic reflection upon the experience and application of it across cultural boundaries. This certainly is the meaning of Jesus' promise that the Spirit "will guide you into all the truth" (John 16:13). Because the Scriptures are a Holy Spirit–inspired response to God's disclosure in Christ, we may properly refer to them as a part of the revelatory event itself.

But Scripture is not only an inspired witness to past revelation. It is the vehicle of the Spirit for the communication of God's saving power in the present time. The Spirit's ongoing witness makes Scripture "gospel," which is "the power of God for salvation" (Rom. 1:16). Scripture continues to participate in God's ongoing self-disclosure through the witness of the Spirit (John 15:26).

In this manner, then, we think of the Bible as revelation—because it is part of the original revelational events climaxed in Jesus Christ, and because it continues to be the vehicle of authentic disclosure through the witness of the Holy Spirit.[33]

Hermeneutical Implications

This understanding of Scripture as witness to Jesus Christ has several implications for interpreting the Bible.[34] First, it is generally acknowledged that not all teachings have equal weight in the theology and practice of the church. But what is the criterion for decision through the ages and across cultures? What is our guide for contextualization?

If we make the standard of judgment for any writing its relationship to the central event of historic revelation in Jesus Christ, then not all the writings in the Bible have the same significance as witness to revelation. This is the obvious ground for making a distinction between the authority of the Old and New Testaments, which was a basic Anabaptist tenet. It is not that the New Testament revelation cancels out the Old, but that, as Pannenberg puts it, "in view of Jesus everything previously thought about God appeared in a new light."[35] The Hebrew Scripture becomes the "old" or preliminary revelation. Clark Pinnock has put it well:

> Most importantly, the bipartite Bible is structured in such a way as to identify the Old Testament as prefiguring narrative, not the last word on

the purposes of God. The messianic age has dawned in Jesus the Christ, and the revelation associated with that age takes precedence over the premessianic material. Scripture, thus, is not leveled in the way it is in the Judaic Scripture principle but is searched and interpreted in terms of a Christological presupposition. Naive rhetoric about biblical infallibility could easily lead to a tragic [distortion] of the Christian faith.[36]

But carrying the principle further, books like Proverbs, Ecclesiastes, Lamentations, or Esther in the Old Testament have less "revelational" significance than Isaiah and Genesis. Or in the New Testament, Jude, 2 and 3 John, or 2 Peter have less significance as witness to the revelation in Christ than the Gospels, Romans, or Ephesians.[37] Hence, if some books are only relatively significant, then we simply do not have a "flat Bible" of equally authoritative theological information.

Second, the centrality of the Christ event gives us a criterion to determine the meaning and relative applicability of individual statements or teachings within the various writings, both Old and New Testaments, for the contemporary life and thought of the church across cultures.

Two examples will help us see the importance of this hermeneutical rule. Romans 13:1-2 has been used generally to justify war and killing by Christians in obedience to "the governing authorities." But how can such an interpretation be right if we read the passage as a witness to the crucified Christ, and follow Paul's own admonition to imitate him as he imitates Christ (1 Cor. 11:1)?

There certainly are technical textual matters to be taken into consideration, such as the meaning of the word *hupotassō* (to be subordinate). All Christians would agree that it does not infer absolute obedience (Acts 5:29). But how are we to decide what are the exceptions? Only when such a passage is viewed as an independent verbal revelation by virtue of inspiration—and is separated from any immediate witness to Christ—can it be used to justify the traditional Protestant just-war ethic. The final hermeneutical criterion here is not literary or historical-critical, but theological.

To take a different kind of example, Galatians 3:28, 1 Corinthians 11:3-16; 14:30, and 1 Timothy 2:2 all have bearing on the status of women in the organization of the church. How shall we deal with the rather obvious differences in what they teach or imply?[38]

Using our criterion, we note that the Galatians passage is an immediate word about the meaning of God's self-disclosure in Jesus for the life of the community. It describes the new reality for those who were "baptized into Christ" and have "put on Christ." "In Christ" all Christians are children of God. They all have the same high standing which sons had in first-century culture. There are no rich or poor, male or female. It describes the fundamental relationship that should govern in the Christian community.

The other texts are cultural contextualizations which attempt to accommodate the new creation in Christ to the conditions current under the old creation (1 Cor. 11:7-10, 13-15). Notice that the adaptations are not the same even in the ancient cultural situations. They have authority as apostolic tradition (11:2), and as such are a helpful guide in cultural contextualization. But they do not have the authority of a revealed rule for regulating worship in the church universal.[39]

Third, our understanding of the Bible as *witness* to revelation implies that its record is not of the same nature or genre as modern scientific history. Secular historians attempt to reconstruct empirical happenings with precision and trace causality in the flow of the events themselves. Without apology, the biblical writers give an interpretative account of how God has disclosed himself through the events of history. While the Bible records trustworthy knowledge of historical events, it is not simply a knowledge of what happened at the empirical level. It is concerned with inner meaning and significance of the events as God's self-revelation. And it presents these events in such a way that this inner meaning will be clear to the reader.

Along with historical knowledge, Scripture writers also include what may be called *faith* or *spiritual* knowledge. They are convinced that history is God's story, and that God is working out his plan for the salvation of humankind in the events they recount. They explicitly give witness from the perspective of their own faith-insight, and appeal to a faith response from the reader. Only those who are "spiritual," wrote Paul, can comprehend this spiritual knowledge (1 Cor. 2:6-16).[40]

Fourth, when we interpret the "Bible" as "Scripture," the witness to revelation in Christ, we are making the body of faith (the church) the hermeneutical context for its understanding.[41] Hermeneutical authority lies in the ecclesial community, not the academic one. Scholarly genius is quite different from apostolic inspiration. It is the church which recognizes the Bible as Holy Spirit–inspired Scripture, and it is the church that must continue to authenticate its message as "gospel." Such authentic interpretation for life across the centuries and cultures is possible, to be sure, only by virtue of the Holy Spirit's continuing illumination.

We must clarify and qualify this assertion that the interpretative authority lies with the ecclesial and not the academic community. When we say ecclesial community, we mean in the first instance the original apostolic community. The authority remains with the original apostolic community and not the ongoing tradition of the "apostolic church." By the same token, the locus of authority does not shift to any contemporary church. The "inspired" witness to Jesus as the self-disclosure of God remains with the original apostolic community which participated in the historical revelation (1 John 1:1-5).

This means the authority remains with the original apostolic text and not with the contemporary scholarly historical and literary reconstructions. In this basic sense, the authoritative message remains located in the New Testament itself. The ecclesial function of "scientific scholarship" is to help the contemporary church more adequately understand the original witness, and to guard against misunderstandings. For example, the "quest for the historical Jesus" may help the church understand better what kind of Jesus the apostles recognized as the Christ. But this historical Jesus is simply a modern historical construct, and it cannot displace the original "Jesus of faith" and become the authority for contemporary theology and ethics. The work of scholarly research cannot substitute for the discernment of the body of faith as it gathers around the Word.

Finally, the authoritative hermeneutic remains one of faith, and the key to interpretation is the obedience of faith. This is the meaning of Hans Denk's oft-quoted words that no one can rightly understand Christ unless he or she is willing to follow him in life.[42]

Inspiration and Authority

As we noted at the beginning of the chapter, many sacred scriptures claim the allegiance of their followers on the basis of divine authority. Some of these claim to be the direct words of God and therefore to have ultimate authority for all humankind. How shall we view the authority claims of Christianity in this context? And how shall we authenticate those claims?

Traditionally, Christianity has not only claimed superiority for its Scriptures, but it has claimed exclusive authority for them as well. Shall we continue to defend this claim? Can we say that the Bible is the only "true" word of God, and that all other claims are "false" or "idolatrous"? Or shall we simply agree to the relative authority of each scripture for its own culture—Torah for Judaism, Koran for Islam, the Bible for Christianity, and the Bhagavad-Gita for Hinduism? If we maintain that the Christian Scriptures are unique, what gives them their unique character?

Inspiration as the Guarantee of Revelation

Conservative, or orthodox, Protestant theology has generally discussed the question of the Scripture's power to persuade our minds under the topic of "inspiration and authority" of the Bible. Especially since the seventeenth century, Scripture's authority has been grounded on its inspiration. The logic of the argument ran like this: The Holy Spirit inspired the Bible in such a way that its words convey an infallibly true message. It is a truly supernatural book by virtue of its supernatural origin and mode of transmission.

The doctrine of inspiration guaranteed the Bible to be revelation through the supernaturally transmitted messages of God to us. And so the defense and proof of its authority focused on the issue of its verbal inerrancy. Inerrancy is taken to be the mark of its supernatural inspiration. If the Bible is not inerrant, it loses its infallible authority.[43] The inner witness of the Spirit which gives the Scriptures an existential authority, should not be confused with this objective authority.

This rational approach was developed in the context of the philosophical debate about the natural or supernatural origin of reason itself. The medieval and post-Reformation position of the scholastic theologians was that reason had its origin in God. Therefore, the biblical revelation itself is the ground of reason. The new position, which emerged with the Deists and John Locke (1632-1704), was that reason is the product of human reasoning. According to the new position, the Bible must be squared with human reasoning and not vice versa. "Truth," which can be stated in words, was equated with rational ideas. And whatever its source, the test of truth must be human logic.

In answer to such humanistic rationalism, the orthodox Lutheran and Reformed theologians held that the truth of the Bible, that is, its theological ideas, were given in words by God himself. They must therefore be the test of what is reasonable. The inspired Scripture, not the human mind, is the test of truth. In this context, they defined the inspiration of Scripture as the modality of its transmission. The Holy Spirit, they held, so completely controlled the process of transmission that the words of the Bible can be called the words of God. And being the words of God, they cannot contain error.[44]

In the context of this rationalistic debate which defined truth as correct ideas and located the reality and meaning in the word itself, the elaborate arguments for inerrancy are understandable. But in prerationalist and mystical cultures, the theory and its rationale are at best irrelevant. Even in modern Western culture where empiricism has largely replaced rationalism as the dominant philosophical assumption, it has questionable value as an apologetic for biblical authority. If we begin with the extant biblical texts, there simply is no way to demonstrate their inerrancy.

From the empirical point of view, then, the rationalistic argument is circular in going from Holy Spirit inspiration, to inerrancy, to revelation from some divine source. And in those cultures where the words may have a mystical power but can hardly be locked into a logical chain of meaning, the argument seems unnecessary and slightly beside the point. From their perspective, the Bible, like other sacred books, either has its own obvious mystical power, or it is not worth defending. Given these contexts, how shall we speak of the persuasive power of the Bible? Why is it of such irreplaceable importance in Christianity? And how shall we give a reason for the Christian conviction that the Bible is God's authoritative word to us?

The Authentic Witness of Scripture

As we have repeatedly said, the fundamental importance of Scripture is its witness to Jesus as the Christ of God. In the beautiful metaphor of Martin Luther, it is the manger in which the Christ child lay and the swaddling clothes in which he was wrapped. This obviously refers to both the Old and New Testaments as witnesses to Christ. Since Scripture is virtually our only historical witness to Christ, we are vitally concerned with its accuracy and authenticity. And the Christian claim that Scripture is inspired by the Holy Spirit is the theological confession that we believe it to be a true and trustworthy witness. It is not a rational or empirical proof of this.

First, we are concerned that it is an accurate historical account of what Jesus did and taught. If Jesus was not essentially the kind of person he is represented to be, and if his ministry, death, and resurrection need serious historical reconstruction, then faith has little basis in fact. If, on the other hand, the story has a factual base, then it demands an evaluation and response.

The test for historical accuracy of a record is simply careful historical research. Such historical research can only establish a high degree of probability. However, after unprecedented research by thousands of scholars over the past two hundred years, we have the highest possible degree of certainty which critical historical examination can give, that the accounts are basically accurate. They are not "scientific" historical accounts such as modern historians would try to write. There is, nevertheless, ample evidence that the stories which were first remembered, told in the preaching of the early church, and then recorded for posterity, are historically based and trustworthy.

Second, we are concerned to know with surety that the apostolic understanding and presentation of Jesus is an authentic interpretation of Jesus' self-understanding and intention. This finally is a matter of faith which grasps the inner meaning of the cross and obediently follows in the Master's steps. But the agreement of the apostles who were eyewitnesses, and their participation in the power of the "name" of the resurrected Jesus in the midst of the church, are evidences to faith. Their demonstration of the Spirit of Jesus and power of his love to heal broken lives, authenticates their witness. Trust in the veracity and genuineness of the biblical witness can never be separated from the testimony of the Spirit in the life of the apostolic church. In this regard the indirect witness of the epistles to the dynamic of the kerygma is crucial.

Added to this is the ongoing witness of the Spirit in the life of the church and the individual. It is the reminding, renewing, confirming, and enabling Spirit of Christ who is the convincing witness to the authenticity of the biblical record. The veracity of the biblical witness is also closely connected with the authenticity of the contemporary church as it participates in the continuing mission of Christ.

One might say that the authority of Scripture still lies with the Spirit who originally inspired it and continues to enlighten and enable through its witness. The inspiration is not transferred to the pages of Scripture so that it becomes an autonomous authority. Instead, the Scripture—inspired, illuminated, authenticated, and verified through the enabling of the Holy Spirit—claims our allegiance for Christ.

The question of the nature and source of the Bible's authority, therefore, is not merely an academic one. Concern for the credibility of the Scripture's witness and its power to persuade is especially crucial in the cross-cultural mission of the church. One's view of Scripture affects one's strategy for missions and approach to other religious claims.

If one approaches mission in the theological stance of scholastic orthodoxy, with the assumption that Scripture's authority as the only true word of God is rationally defensible, several results follow. (We are speaking here of a theological stance, and not a personal attitude. However, the former almost inevitably influences the latter.)

First, such a stance sets up a confrontational situation, taking on the nature of a debate. The issues are of a true-false variety, and only a win-lose outcome is possible. The inappropriateness of this perspective becomes particularly obvious when one recalls that counter claims to *super*natural authority cannot be arbitrated by *natural* reason! On these terms the debate is bound to go on without resolution.

Further, the approach assumes that the rational system of the West provides the correct definitions and methodology for resolving the debate. Thus we have already begun with the assumption that the Bible is a Western book! Again, in Western style it implies that the biblical witness to Christ is a verbal statement calling for rational assent, rather than a call to trust and relationship. And finally, when the inerrancy position is strictly adhered to, it discourages—if not rejects—effective contextualization of the message.

We have argued that the Bible's power to convince lies in the intrinsic power of its message as a witness to Jesus Christ, not in the miraculous way it was inspired, or in the inerrant character of its text. If this is true, the way is opened to begin with a confessional witness. The message remains the *kerygma*—the simple story of Jesus. Its call is to faith in a person and commitment to a way of life. The persuasive evidence for its veracity and significance will be the authentic demonstration of the power of the gospel in the life of the church.

CHAPTER 3

God the Parent-Creator as Father of Jesus Christ

Introduction

It is not immediately obvious what or who we are going to investigate when the subject is God. After all, God does not have the specificity of a blueberry. He is not even as obvious as the more abstract, elusive concept of energy which physicists describe with algebraic formulas. Since God is not at all available to empirical investigation, philosophers traditionally have used rational speculation to arrive at some idea of his existence and nature. For them, God is a philosophical principle or rationally necessary presupposition—the "Unmoved Mover," "the Ground of Being," or the "dipolar Cosmic Reality" in process of becoming.

Philosophers and theologians like Thomas Aquinas had great confidence in the ability of human reason logically to demonstrate God's existence. Beginning with rational human experience, they were confident they could even discover at least the outline of God's nature by logical deduction. Such knowledge was referred to as "natural theology." Modern theologians give less credence to speculative reason and more to empirical methodology. For them, God is the problem. He is the boundary of our empirical existence, about which we can know very little—only the underside, as it were.

Biblical writers, strange as it may seem to some people, have more affinity with the modern empiricists than the traditional rationalists.

They are reverently agnostic about the inner workings of God. When Moses asked to see God, he was strictly warned that no one can see God's face and live (Exod. 33:20). He was allowed to see only God's back, and then only through a protective shield provided by God. When he asked for God's name, he was given only the cryptic statement, "I Am." This same reverence for the mystery of God's being is also present in the prophets and in the rabbinical tradition of Israel.

While the New Testament writers express a new intimacy and confidence in God's presence, there is still reverent respect for the mystery of God's being. Early in his Gospel, John cautions his readers that "no one has ever seen God" (1:18; cf. 1 John 4:12). Paul is confident that we have come to know God's will in Christ, and he never for a moment doubts God's existence or challenges his impartiality, love, and justice. However, he offers virtually no analysis of God's nature. He simply affirms that there is one God who is the ultimate source of life and Creator of everything. This one is the "Father of glory," who demonstrated his nature and will in Jesus Christ. Our destiny lies in his purposes for humankind. In all of this, the primary focus of his interest is Jesus Christ as the evidence of God at work in history.

In the text from John's Gospel, the uniquely Christian approach to knowledge of God is succinctly stated. "No one has ever seen God; *the only Son, who is in the bosom of the Father, he has made him known*" (1:18, RSV, emphasis added; cf. NRSV: "God the only Son, who is close to the Father's heart"). What we can most clearly and certainly know about God has been disclosed in Jesus. That is the fundamental meaning of Jesus' claim that God is his "Father," and that he knows God as only a Son could know him (John 5:37f.; 6:46; cf. Matthew 11:25-27).

According to both the apostles and the prophets, God is known by "signs." We can observe his "acts" and hear his "voice." The word we hear from him elucidates his acts which we have observed in the historical situation. This word is necessary because historical events are often ambiguous. We must ask what the act means and which of the multitude of contradictory "acts" in nature and history point to the true God. As Luther observed, God remains "hidden" even in his historical self-revelation. In the Bible, then, one comes to know God in and through the historical situation as the Mysterious Power at work moving history toward its destiny.

There is virtually no attempt to theorize, analyze, or speculate further on the nature of Deity. The biblical writers do not attempt to resolve the paradoxes or explain how God is related to his creation by metaphysical speculation. Rather, they "wait" for the mystery to be resolved in the outcome of the historical process. They are confident that God will fully make known who and what he is in the consummation of history—the *eschaton* (1 Cor. 13:12).

The writers of the New Testament understood Jesus Christ to be the eschatological revelation of the Mystery (Eph. 3:9). When we introduced the doctrine of Christ, we said, "Christology is a God-statement."[1] Therefore, we examined how Jesus may be understood as God's presence among us and what his role is as God's salvation. We concentrated on the question of how God is at work among us in and through Christ creating humankind in God's image.[2]

Now we will turn our attention in the opposite direction to ask how the self-disclosure in Christ affects our concept of God. We must first note that Jesus does not provide a completely novel disclosure. He stands in a historical tradition. He identified the "Father" as the God of Abraham, Moses, and David. He did not claim to present a newly discovered god. Instead, he claims to be the definitive revelation of this God of Israel. Specifically, then, we begin by asking how the normative disclosure of God in Christ modifies the general and prophetic revelation which God has given humankind apart from knowledge of the earthly Jesus. And, how does this new understanding affect our lives in the world?

The Idolization of God

Human ignorance of God presents us with a complicated picture. The problem is not a mere lack of awareness due simply to an elementary state of human social and intellectual development. All human knowledge is partial and flawed with misunderstanding, even at the highest levels! But ignorance of God is laced with denial, perversity, and willfulness. It is not innocent ignorance. Indeed, from the biblical perspective, the problem is not so much ignorance—a Greek diagnosis—as it is idolatry.

In Romans 1:18-25, Paul explains idolatry as an act of rational and psychological repression. He says the order of creation itself should make the mystery of God's "eternal power and divine nature" universally obvious to rational creatures. He claims that ignorance of God is really the result of the human ego's unwillingness to acknowledge its dependence upon God and God's rightful authority.

Paul's language suggests that there is an inner self-contradiction in the human denial of a supreme Being to whom everyone owes thanks and obedience. On one hand, he says that when humans deny their responsibility to an ultimate divine authority, they denigrate and debauch their own humanity. This is so because the highest expression of humanity lies in our *theonomous* relation—that is, in obedience to God's covenant mandate. And on the other hand, when humans assert their autonomy and reject the true God, they do not become "godless." In place of God, they create their own gods. As Luther so aptly put it, "Humans have either God or an idol (*Gott oder Abgott*)."

This is the origin of polytheism and "idolatry," the creation of false gods. The knowledge of the true God is repressed in favor of the wish projections of the human ego. Idols are the rationalizations of human desires. They are false gods—the manufactured masks of the human ego. They are the champions of self-centered values. And they are given their power by those who worship them.

Contemporary Pluralism

Today, much as in the biblical times, idolatry and pluralistic god claims remain the basic problem. Baal, which means *lord*, and his consort, Astarte, were the fertility gods of Canaan. They were the security for the good life, and they have their counterparts today.[3] Automated Industrialism and Advertising, which have given birth to a favorite daughter, Consumerism, still rule the so-called developed nations.

The polytheistic claims of our contemporary situation can be classified into at least three different categories. First, there is totalitarianism, whether of a collective or individualistic variety. It attempts an unqualified control and management of life, promising fulfillment and demanding allegiance. Such claims are supported by a variety of quasi-religious and secular ideologies, such as positivism, atheism, communism, scientism, fascism, and rationalism.

Religious cults present a second variety of god claims. In this case I refer to the non-Christian and post-Christian cults, such as astrology, Satanism, neopaganism or nature worship, and witchcraft and sorcery. These claims represent a revival of pre-Christian paganism, and they have burgeoned again in the midst of the secularism of the West. These two classes of god claims are clearly idolatrous rivals of the Christian God.

The third class presents us with a more complicated situation. These are the claims of competing world religions. As one Hindu scholar said to me, "Of course we know there is only one God. Our many divinities are merely the many aspects or faces of God."

The claims of these religious systems and their understanding of God overlap in significant ways. For example, there is the Amida Buddha,[4] the God of grace; Ushitora no Konjin, the high god of the Oomoto religion, the creator "who will reconstruct the world;"[5] Vishnu of Hinduism, who has come to the earth in a variety of incarnations to rescue it from destruction; and Allah, the God of the universe proclaimed by Islam. Are such names for God to be respected and approached in the manner of Abraham to *El Elyon*, the "God Most High" of Melchizedek, who is later identified with Yahweh? Shall we accommodate to a pluralism of religious concepts of God, recognizing that they are all views of the one and only God? Or should we consider them idols and rivals to "the God and Father of Jesus Christ"? This has become a crucial question in modern cross-cultural missions.

The question is greatly complicated by the pluralistic, conflicting claims within Christianity itself. Obviously, there is much idolatry associated with these religions, but unfortunately, that is also true in Christianity. Even among those who reverence the name of Jesus and cling tenaciously to a trinitarian theology, one finds the same kind of pluralism in beliefs and practices that are common in the third category of religions listed above. Hence we must distinguish between the true God and idols, within Christianity as well as in other religions (Matt. 7:21-23).

This analysis of the human situation provides the context for the biblical understanding of the God problem. The context is polytheism, not atheism. The problem is not whether deity exists, but which is the true God. The story of the Old Testament is the story of Israel's struggle with this problem. The New Testament proclaims a concept of God and his righteousness which requires a reorientation of even the "best" religious conceptions of God. Its writers call this reorientation *repentance*. In Christian theology we continue to wrestle with this problem and with the temptation to accommodate our vision of God to the "many gods and many lords" (1 Cor. 8:5).

Naming the True God
Identifying the Living God

The Bible's main concern is to identify, or name, the living God—the one who really exists as the ultimate authority and sustainer of all life. As we have seen, the Bible does not give us rational descriptions or proofs of God's existence. Instead, its concern in the context of competing polytheistic claims is to identify the authority which is truly ultimate and proper to full human existence.

This process of identification is basically historical rather than philosophical. God is identified by recognizing his action in and influence on human events. His name is not discovered by mystical contemplation or rational speculation, but by "hearing" (intuiting) his word and observing the historical events which confirm or reject the prophetic intuition (Deut. 18:21).

In the well-known passage of Exodus 3:13-17, where God names himself, the name is generally translated as "I AM WHO I AM." In traditional theological discussion, this has usually been interpreted as a philosophical statement. God is the self-existent mystery that at once transcends and surrounds us. However, taken in its context, the alternate possibility for translation is probably more correct. The God of Abraham, Isaac, and Jacob is the God who has guided Israel to the present moment. And he gives his name as "I WILL BE WHO I WILL BE." That is, his identity as the God of Abraham will be validated by his deliverance of Israel, according to his promise to the fathers.[6]

Christian theology identifies with this Abrahamic tradition. It further understands that "God, the Lord" has fulfilled his promises in the life, death, and resurrection of Jesus, the Christ. Thus, without rational elaboration, it begins from the self-evident prophetic intuition of Deity which is the counterpart of human self-definition. *God is that Ultimate personal authority and power of love which defines and creates the authentically human possibility.* It proceeds on the faith that this one will continue to reveal his true identity in human history, by fulfilling the promise to overcome the demonic powers of death and establishing the rule of God "on earth as it is in heaven."

The problem with which it struggles, therefore, is the *identity*, not the existence, of God. And that is essentially a historical rather than a philosophical problem.[7]

Naming God

To name an object is a distinctive way of identifying it. When we name it, we claim to have had some experience of it. However superficial our knowledge may be, it is the product of experience, not rational speculation. To "know God" in the biblical way of speaking, means to be aware of him concretely through historical experience. Therefore, when biblical writers speak of the God they have encountered, they name him. If further elaboration is necessary, they describe the encounter and report the "words" this God has spoken.

In the first instance, Israelites used the generic Semite word, *El*, or its plural, *Elohim*, to designate the God whom they worshiped. Somewhat like *Allah* in Islam, and *God* in English, *El* was used both as a name and a generic designation for the Supreme Being or Sovereign Power. Appellations like "Most High" and "Almighty" were added further to specify and describe this one. "God Most High" (*El Elyon*) was the name of the God of Melchizedek, whom Abraham honored (Gen. 14:18ff.). "God Almighty" (*El Shaddai*) was the special name revealed to Abraham himself (Gen. 17:1). It continued to be the name used by Isaac and Jacob (Gen. 28:3; 35:11, etc.). It is also the name by which God identified himself to Moses on Mt. Horeb (Exod. 6:3). These certainly were not different gods. In each case, they designate God, the Creator of heaven and earth—the Supreme Sovereign of the universe.

Through their own unique historical encounter with God, Israel was given a special name for him. This name, *Yah* or *Yahweh*, was the name of God in covenant relationship to Israel. Yahweh was none other than the God (*Elohim*) of their ancestors, who now made himself known to them in their deliverance from slavery in Egypt and in their formation into a nation. They are not naming a different God, but are identifying their new experience of the one true God.

In the same manner, Jesus is the new name given to designate the saving experience of God in Christ. *Jesus* is Greek for *Joshua*, which means "*Yah* is [our] Savior." As *Yahweh*, "Lord of the whole earth," was savior of Israel, so the church confesses that Jesus is Lord and Savior. Yahweh and Jesus are not two gods, but designations for two historical experiences of salvation by "the living God, who is the Savior of all people, especially of those who believe" (1 Tim. 4:10; cf. 2 Peter 1:1, 11).

The temptation implicit in this kind of approach to understanding God is to think of him as one's own personal or national god. In the rituals of ancient magic, knowledge of a name gave the magician control over the person named. In its modern version, knowledge—especially experiential knowledge—is power.

For this reason the prophets of Israel make clear that *Yahweh* was the name of the Almighty God, the Maker of heaven and earth. He had been the God of Abraham and had now revealed himself to Moses in the wilderness. This Creator of heaven and earth was also Israel's creator, not vice versa.[8] God introduced himself to them; they did not discover and adopt him.

The prophetic tradition uniformly insisted that Yahweh was not a tribal Israelite deity alongside others. God's identification of himself with Israel was an act of sovereign grace. He did not become Israel's possession. When he was identified as "the God of Israel" and contrasted to Baal, the contest was between the living God of heaven and a tribal idol, as the story of Elijah on Mt. Carmel dramatically makes clear (1 Kings 18:20-39).

But this point is already implicit in the Exodus narrative. The name

Yahweh was not chosen by Israel for their own tribal god. While in Egypt, the Israelites worshiped the gods of the nation that held them captive (Josh. 24:14ff.). Before the Exodus, Israel was not a cohesive "people" or nation. They were slaves who came out of Egypt a "mixed crowd" (Exod. 12:38). It was Yahweh's election and deliverance that formed them into a cohesive nation. Joshua challenged them, a nation in the birthing, to worship and serve this one who had revealed himself in their deliverance (Josh. 24:14ff.).

The point we have been trying to make is that we should not equate the sovereign God of the universe with our historical knowledge of him through a particular "name." This was a difficult lesson for Israel to learn. The prophets had to remind them constantly that Israel had not chosen Yahweh. Yahweh had chosen and created Israel. We must admit that this has also been the failing of the Christian church. Far too often the church has acted on the presumption that Christ is its own special possession and privilege! Accordingly, some present-day liberal analyses leave the impression that it was the faith of the church which created the Christ picture in the first place. We must learn what it means for the life and mission of the church to confess that God our Savior is the sovereign God of the whole universe.

God Known as "Lord"

The prophets of Israel were concerned with God's righteous character and authority rather than his metaphysical essence.[9] Their God is "the Lord," the personal God who confronts them as the Divine Subject and enters into covenant with them. This covenant comes to them as a "Word of the Lord," a word of promise and command they are to obey, not a datum of information to analyze and describe. The Lord is the one on whom they can depend, the one to whom they owe unqualified loyalty, the one whom they are to imitate and represent on earth.[10]

The prophets' primary concern was Israel's covenant relation to God as his people and the fulfillment of their destiny. The biblical concepts of God are fittingly expressed in metaphors of personal-moral relationship—parent and child, husband and wife, king and people.

Because there are no philosophical definitions of God's essence or discourses about his attributes, we must be careful not to read abstract philosophical meanings into such concepts as "One God," or creation *ex nihilo* (out of nothing). Such statements do have implications for philosophy, but they are not in themselves analytical rational statements such as one finds in Greek philosophy. Both Karl Barth and Emil Brunner have rightfully warned us against taking God's self-revelation as philosophical information to use for speculative analysis of the essential being of God.

In the Old Testament, then, God (*El*) is the Lord (*Yahweh*). Both the Septuagint (LXX) and the New Testament use the word *kurios* to translate *Yahweh*.[11] Actually, the two are not exact equivalents. *Yahweh* is a name and *kurios* is a title. But the name *Yahweh* designates God as the sovereign who gives the covenant. He is the one who has authority and power over Israel. *Kurios* means the one who has legitimate authority and power to control and command.

Lord (kurios) indicates one who has the moral right, as well as the power, to command. It emphasizes the legitimacy of his divine ownership and authority. This raises the question concerning the basis of God's authority. What warrants support God's claims of ownership and command?

In summary there are three. First, God is the only Creator. He is the rightful sovereign of the universe (Jer. 33:2ff.). His creation ex nihilo makes this same point. Since he did not use materials created by some other power, but simply spoke the original word of creation, no other power or authority can make a claim against his ownership. With humankind the analogy of God's ownership translates into the parental relation. We were created "in God's image," and his lordship is exercised as a family covenant authority.

Second, God is Savior. God is not simply a deistic creator who is detached and unconcerned for his creatures. Even when his children rebel and forget, he does not abandon them to destruction, but continues to sustain and save. God, the Almighty Creator, comes to Israel as Yahweh, the covenant God, to rescue them from Egypt and form them into a people under his authority. Throughout their history he is their "Redeemer" (Isa. 43:1-7). Nor is he content to be only *Israel's* redeemer. Under his authority Israel is to be a light to the nations so God's salvation "may reach to the end of the earth" (Isa. 49:6).

The saving grace of God is theologically prior to his creative power as the basis of his authority. As a consequence, human obligation is based upon grace, not upon coercive authority. The creation is viewed as an act of God's grace. He created order from chaos and formed light to push back the darkness (Isa. 45:18-21). In this same manner, Jesus, as the Word of creation, "full of grace and truth," is the Savior. He has been given all authority in heaven and on earth (Matt. 28:19; Col. 1:15-20).

Third, as the Creator-Savior, God is the only power who can fulfill the ultimate destiny of humanity and creation. Only God can establish equity and justice on the earth. Only he can bring in the eschatological *shalom*—"God's kingdom and justice." Thus God is the only legitimate ultimate authority. He only is the Lord.

Our knowledge of God, then, is an existential knowledge in which we know him as the ultimate authority in our lives. That is, we know him in the act of owning his lordship. As Lord, he claims our total loyalty and obedience as a response which is both his right and our own highest good. Only in submission to his covenant authority as expressed in Christ can we find ultimate "self-fulfillment" and achieve that personal meaning for which God created us. This is the corollary of humanity's creation "in God's image."

The Nature and Character of God
The Spirituality and Holiness of God

Although pre-Christian Jewish scholars did not develop a systematic metaphysical conception of God, Israel's experience with Yahweh as their God firmly established several basic conceptions about God's nature and character. These same convictions which come out of God's revelation to Israel, also furnish the presuppositional concepts of the New Testament writers. They are God's *spirituality, holiness, unity*, and *goodness*.

Spirituality. God's spirituality has three facets. First, he is *the living God.* (See Deut. 5:26 and Josh. 3:10 for examples.) As the divine living Spirit, God is the creative, life-giving power in the universe. We know many human and superhuman powers that can destroy life, but only God the Spirit can give life. At creation the life-giving wind (or Spirit) of God "swept over the face of the waters" as the creative dynamic (Gen. 1:2; Isa. 40:12-14). At the beginning of each human life, the Spirit is the agent of conception (Ps. 139:7, 13ff.; Luke 1:35). He is the sustaining breath of life within our bodies (Job 27:3; 33:4). And, in an exact reversal of the breath metaphor, the Wind, or Spirit, of God is the atmosphere in which and without which we cannot live. This atmospheric metaphor is the basis for Paul's concept of life "in the Spirit."

Again, it is the Spirit of God who raised Jesus from the dead and who will also "give life to [our] mortal bodies" (Rom. 8:11). Therefore, to speak of God as Spirit is to affirm that God is the life-creating and life-sustaining power who can even bring life out of our human death.

The spirituality of God as "the living God" asserts the reality of his power as Creator over against idols. The prophets asserted that idols are created by human hands. They have no breath (*ruakh*) in them (Jer. 10:14). The true and living God created the universe and gave breath to human beings. Idols are servants of their human creators. Indeed, the function of images is to control and manipulate the mysterious powers of nature through ritual. But God, the living Spirit, cannot be controlled or manipulated. He was not created by us to be our servant. We were created to serve him (Isa. 44:21; 45:9-12).[12]

Similarly, to affirm today that God is Spirit means to reject the idolatries of the modern age. The demonic powers of war and militarism are such false gods. All these idols are the creation of the sinful self for the purpose of controlling human destiny and satisfying our desires. Hence, the battle against what Paul calls "the flesh," as well as the "authorities and cosmic powers," is a battle against idolatry—those divinities that society and the self have created to satisfy our cravings and pacify our human fears.

Second, the spirituality of God indicates that he is a *self-conscious, personal being,* not an impersonal force of nature or supernature. In contrast to the mysterious, magical powers associated with animals, plants, and even inanimate objects, God is Spirit or Mind.

This understanding of spirit as personal being draws on the analogy of human self-consciousness as it was understood in the ancient world. In Greek culture the human spirit was conceived as the personal energy or soul (*psychē*), giving life to the body. It was especially associated with the mind (*nous*). Paul uses this metaphor explicitly in 1 Corinthians 2:10-11, saying that the Spirit of God knows the deep, hidden thoughts of God as the human spirit knows the heart.[13]

In this case we definitely should not try to make a psychological analysis of God's nature from the metaphor. As the passage clearly indicates, *Spirit* points to God in his self-revelation as a personal, self-conscious presence, making himself known in intimacy and depth to all those who are open to his influence. Indeed, the words *Spirit of God* most precisely and fully express the personal and rational divine influence.

In the Old Testament era, the highest expression of such influence was the prophetic word directly from God to the nation. In fact, the Spirit of God was nearly equated with the spirit of prophecy. In the writings of Paul and John in the New Testament, the Spirit's most definitive work is inspiring love in the hearts of Christ's disciples and leading them into truth (Rom. 8:16; 1 John 4:13).

Finally, the spirituality of God means that God in his transcendence of time and space is present among us in a manner that is not limited by physical or temporal obstacles. God is at work in, with, and through us to accomplish his purposes in the world (Hag. 2:5; Eph. 3:20). This is the Old Testament Hebrew meaning of God's transcendence rather than the Greek concept of distance and incommunicability.

In the many Old Testament passages where "Spirit of God" or "Spirit of the Lord" appear as parallels for God (or Yahweh), the focus is upon God's free presence in his world, especially among his people, carrying out his purposes. His presence is not enshrined in idols or temples. Neither is he present simply as a dynamic of nature. Instead, he is present as a transcendent divine influence, working to bring his will into effect. While the Spirit's presence may manifest itself in a variety of ways, the purpose of the manifestation is always to establish the righteous will of God.

Holiness. God is called "the Holy One of Israel" (Isa. 40:25; 43:3; Prov. 9:10). In the New Testament, Jesus is called "the Holy One of God" (Mark. 1:24; Luke 4:34). It is significant that it is demons who address Jesus as holy, because demons represent mysterious earthly powers of nature and death. These are the powers which also claim to be "holy" in the mystery of taboo and cult. Jesus as the true representative of God exposes their claims as false and ultimately powerless.

In the first instance, God's holiness meant his separation and transcendence. To say that God was holy meant that he existed in a sacred sphere of mystery and power apart from the everyday locus of activity. His mystery was associated with cultic consecration and taboos. God's separation was symbolized in the tabernacle and temple by the separation of the "holy of holies" as his dwelling. Only properly consecrated people dared enter that space.

Accordingly, theologians like Bishop Gustaf Aulén write, "To say that God is holy is in reality the same as saying that God is God. . . . That God is the Holy One means . . . that in relationship to the world he is exalted and sovereign."[14] Brunner writes,

> Holiness is the Nature of God, that which distinguishes Him from everything else, the Transcendence of God in His very Nature, as the 'Wholly Other.' Hence Holiness is not a quality which God possesses in common with other beings; on the contrary it is that which distinguishes Him clearly and absolutely from everything else.[15]

Holiness speaks of God's transcendent spirituality as mystery, glory, and purity—that which fills us with awe, wonder, and reverence. God's name is "holy and awesome" (Ps. 111:9). He is "majestic in holiness" (Exod. 15:11) and the object of reverent fear and worship (Ps. 96:9). God's glory and perfect purity separate him from the earthly realm of "uncleanness," weakness, and death. Consequently, the human reaction is to feel humiliation and shame in his presence (Isa. 6:1-5; Luke 5:8).

Understanding the nature of God's holiness developed in response to God's revelation in the history of Israel. The earliest concepts associated God's holiness with cultic taboo and mysterious power. As revelation progressed, righteousness and love became the distinctive characteristics of his holiness. Finally, as Paul says, we see the glory of God's holiness in the face of Jesus Christ (2 Cor. 4:6). He is the Holy One from God.

As Aulén warns us, we must be careful not to change God's holiness into righteousness or love understood from a human standpoint. God's love is *holy* love, a love which transcends and remains a mystery in its ways with us. And God's righteousness does not necessarily conform to human concepts of justice. Our temptation is to reduce God's love to indulgence and his righteousness to legal justice. When we do this, we lose the holy character of love, which causes it to suffer in the midst of sin and death. The final picture of God's holiness and glory is Jesus dying on the cross. And the mystery of holiness which no human eyes dare gaze upon, is the mystery of love's agony as it endures the shame, dying for our sin. This is the true measure of God's distance from us.

God's Attributes

What I have described as the meaning of God's spirituality is usually discussed under the heading of God's "attributes." Theologians often use the concept of attributes to describe God's relation to us in time and space. Since this is such standard procedure in evangelical Protestant theologies, perhaps we should explain their meaning further. They describe God as eternal, omnipotent (almighty), omnipresent, and omniscient (all-knowing).

Eternity. When we speak of God's spirituality as eternity, we do not mean to imply that God is in a realm totally other and separate from us and therefore incommunicable, as the neoplatonic concept of transcendence implies. It is important to note this correction, because neoplatonic philosophy has had a powerful and continuing impact on orthodox theology.

When the Bible says "God is spirit" (John 4:24), it means *God is a transcendent, creative, personal power manifesting himself in our dimension of existence, but not confined to it.* His transcendence is the exaltation of majesty and the freedom from existential limitation, not the ontological distancing of Absolute Being, as in Greek thought. As "spirit," God transcends the sphere of death and limitation, which characterizes mortal humanity (Isa. 31:3; 40:6; Jer. 17:5).

God's *eternity* indicates his transcendence above time and decay. This does not mean God is timeless or outside time, existing in perfect tranquility. It means rather that he is not confined to or limited by time like we are. We experience time as change—as opportunity for newness and growth, but also as deterioration, separation, and forgetting. Things get lost in time. In this sense we say God does not experience qualitative change. God does not become something new and different, or grow old and decay. God does not forget.

Because God created historical time, we believe he takes our temporal existence seriously. It is not a sphere of illusion from which we attempt to escape, as the Hindu concept of *maya* suggests. God comes to us in time. God relates to our temporal becoming. In this sense he changes with our change. But God is not limited by time, and God does not change in his inner character (1 Sam. 15:29; Mal. 3:6). As God manifests himself in Jesus Christ, he is "the same yesterday and today and forever" (Heb. 13:8).

Omnipotence. The term *omnipotent* literally means that God has all power and can do anything. But this is not its meaning for Christian faith. In fact, we must speak immediately of God's self-limitation as an essential aspect of his being for us. And we must note that he cannot act in a way contradictory to his own nature (2 Tim. 2:13).

The concept of God's "almightiness" is first an attempt to deny the dualistic idea of an eternal power of evil which prevents God from accomplishing his purpose. The "chaos" and "darkness" mentioned in Genesis 1:2, for examples, are understood to be creaturely powers which the Spirit of God overcame in creation.[16] They are not coeternal powers limiting his power. The "darkness" has never been able to overcome the light (John 1:5). Ultimately, God will defeat even the power of death (1 Cor. 15:25-26).

Second, God's almightiness means he is not locked into his created system. Thus, by implication it denies the determinism of fate and of cause and effect. God is not limited to the causality of the so-called natural process. Therefore, God's omnipotence is the ground for miracles.

When we confess that God is the "Almighty Father," we are affirming our faith that he has the power to fulfill his promises. It was in connection with his covenant promise to Abraham that God revealed his name as "God Almighty" (Gen. 17:1). The barrenness of Sarah's womb could not stymie God's purposes. In the New Testament, the resurrection and exaltation of Jesus Christ as Lord are the primary examples of God's power (Eph. 1:19-23).

Finally, God's almightiness is the personal power of love, not the explosive power of nature or the magical power of sorcery. He exercises this power through the self-limitation and defenselessness[17] of incarnation. God comes to us embodied in human weakness, laying aside power and prerogatives, and submitting even to death on a cross. He does not force his own way by overpowering our freedom of response, but instead grants us continuing freedom.

God in his own freedom chooses to accomplish his goals through our freedom of response to him. He joins with us in the struggle to overcome death and evil in such a way that his victory will also be our victory. His power is *for us*. It is not independent and exclusive of us, but inclusive of us. We are to be involved in God's powerful action, not merely as recipients, but as participants. Love chooses methods which are consistent with its own nature, and in this way accomplishes its purposes.

Omnipresence. Omnipresence is an analogy or metaphor of space. It means literally that God is present everywhere. In speaking of God's universal presence, the immediate concern of biblical writers was to assert that God is not confined to a sacred space, such as a temple or shrine. Neither is he the God of one nation, confined to the boundaries of that nation. No boundaries contain him.

By implication, then, God does not experience space as limitation and separation. Therefore, we can know his nearness to us always and in every place. There are no sacred places where one must go to properly worship him (John 4:20ff.). And there are no places where we are outside his protective care.

Perhaps our concepts of psychological or personal space provide a more adequate analogy. When persons seem uncommunicative, unconcerned, or personally unavailable, we speak of them as "distant." When we are disinterested in a subject, we might say, "I don't have the *remotest* interest in the subject." When someone is unaware of what is going on in his or her immediate presence, we say such a person's mind is a "million miles away." All these expressions refer not to quantitative spatial distance, but to a quality of personal relationship and awareness.

While there is an element of metaphor already in these psychological expressions, they nevertheless describe a real, empirical experience. This personal experience furnishes the analogy for our language about God. The psychological analogy of God's omnipresence speaks of his "nearness" to us in all of time and space. As the psalmist wrote, there is no place where we can escape his presence (139:7-12). And Jesus promised to be with us always, even to the end of the world (Matt. 28:20). There is no place where we are beyond his care.

This analogy of nearness, then, expresses or implies at least two related ideas. First, God has opened himself to us in a self-giving revelation. He has not withdrawn from us because of our offenses, as some African myths of the high god suggest. Rather, in all places and circumstances, he is present and available to us in our need. His omnipresence is his omni-availability.

Second, God is with us in an intimacy of relationship that defies spatial location and involves us in paradoxical language. He is not merely "with" or "alongside." In the language of both John and Paul, God is "in us" and "we are in him." This language of "he in us and we in him" might be interpreted as absorption, merging, or confluence on one hand, or of infusion of divine energy on the other. But the biblical categories of personal relationship suggest the immediacy of direct communication and of intimately shared life, attitudes, and purpose.

Omniscience. God's omniscience does not refer to his infinite store of technical knowledge of facts. The analogy is not a giant computer with its software! Much better, the metaphor is that of a loving parent who understands each of his or her children, anticipates their every need, and wisely plans for their future development. God has the kind of knowledge that enables him to envision and accomplish his purposes fully for the universe. Stated negatively, God is not limited by the kind of ignorance that often defeats our best intentions.

In more formal language, we might say that God's omniscience is relative to his purposes and the accomplishment of those purposes. To use a common expression, "God knows perfectly well what he is doing." That is, he knows not only what he intends to do, but how his intention and immediate action relate to the final accomplishment of that purpose.

In Protestant theology there has been a continuing debate about the relation of human free will and God's foreknowledge; that is, omniscience related to future events. The Calvinist tradition has held that God's knowledge must of necessity be equated with his decree, because God can know as certain only what he himself has destined to happen and will certainly accomplish. That is, he knows an event is certain to happen because he has decreed it to happen. If this is true, human freedom is limited by God's knowledge. In the Calvinist view, to say God foreknows means the same as that God foreordains.

The ramifications of this concept of omniscience are many and complex, and this is not the place to deal with them at length. Certainly the riddle has never been solved by either side of the argument. Indeed, this kind of rationalistic argument goes beyond the limits of the human analogy to describe God with definitive certainty. In any case, the Bible in no way uses the concept of God's knowledge to depreciate human freedom and responsibility. God has given us freedom to respond, and he knows us as free creatures. His purposes for humanity and his plan for their accomplishment are designed according to that knowledge.

The Unity of God

The words in Deuteronomy 6:4, "The Lord our God is one Lord" (RSV), or "The Lord is our God, the Lord alone" (NRSV), represent the highest point of revelation in Israel's experience (cf. Isa. 45:18c; Mark 12:29). They do not come as a mystical or philosophical insight, but as the word of command from the one Lord. They come as a call to focus and unify Israel's vision and to give unqualified loyalty to Yahweh. As Jesus himself was to say much later, "No one can serve two masters." And "the pure in heart . . . shall see God." In more technical language, we might say that although the text implies ontological monotheism— that no other gods exist except Yahweh—it speaks explicitly of ethical monotheism. Its asserts the ethical consistency and sole authority of God for Israel.

Isaiah addresses essentially the same point when he reports God saying, "Before me no god was formed, nor shall there be any after me. I, I am the Lord, and besides me there is no savior" (43:10-11). Here again, in the context of Israel's recognition of "strange gods," Yahweh asserts his originality and superiority over all other claims. Yahweh alone can be Israel's savior. He alone has a right to claim Israel's allegiance.

When we speak of the oneness of God, we are not speaking primarily in arithmetical terms. Instead, we are bearing witness to the unity, integration, and integrity of God's moral character and power. Yet in our finitude we cannot escape numerical associations with the idea of oneness. Only if we allow ourselves a certain amount of abstraction—for example, by thinking of God as spiritual "substance" which can manifest itself in different concrete forms— can we escape the numbers game. But this was not the concern of the biblical writers.

When we say God is one, or there is only one God, we do not mean to assert that God is a single individual unit (a monad) existing in transcendent solitude. The God of the Bible has a fully personal existence. Truly, God is the transcendent analogue for our concept of human personal existence, not vice versa. From the beginning, God is the "Word"—the expressive, communicating God (John 1:1-2). And we can say, after the analogy of our own personhood, that in himself he has full self-consciousness as person. This conviction about God's full personal existence is the philosophical ground of the Christian concept of *Trinity*, as we shall see later.

Therefore, when we refer to God as "one," we should more precisely speak of God's *unity* and *universality*. Jesus spoke of his own unity with the Father and prayed that his disciples "may all be one. As you, Father, are in me and I am in you, may they also be in us" (John 17:21). The mystery of such personal unity is also pictured in the sacrament of marriage where "the two shall be one."

So God is a unity of will and purpose. He is totally consistent in character and nature. He does not change like shifting shadows (James 1:17, NIV). God cannot lie or seduce us (Tit. 1:2). He cannot be tempted, nor does he tempt anyone to evil (James 1:13). It is in this unity of character that his justice or righteousness has its firm base.

Second, this one transcendent Personal Reality is the universal creator and ground of truth. As the "Creator of the ends of the earth" (Isa. 40:28), God has established the unity of the human race. There is one human family under one God. As the Covenant Maker, God's covenant law transcends the laws of the nations as the ultimate moral reality. God's righteousness is the basis for one universal concept of the right. In the biblical language that explicitly rejects human mythologies, there are not many gods and lords, each with their own national spheres of authority and cultural values. But we must note immediately that this does not establish any one human system of right as ultimate. Instead, it places all human systems under the judgment of God's righteousness.

Finally, the Christian concept of monotheism raises the question of the status of "other gods" and "other lords" (1 Cor. 8:4ff.). Do they exist in the sense that they have being independent of their worshipers? They undoubtedly have power and authority over those who acknowledge them, but what conclusions concerning the nature of this power are inferred by Paul's words? I suggest two. First, they exist as authorities and powers which have been created by humans and given their power by those who acknowledge them. They are "idols," which, as Paul says, have no independent existence (8:4). Second, we can identify such idolatrous power as the negative power of fear which is the projection of selfish ignorance and superstition.[18]

The Love of God

The story of Israel's experience with God and their developing understanding of God's character and relation to the nation, is most unusual in its ancient setting. They experienced God's love as a genuine

caring which took the initiative to create and then restore a relationship between himself and the nation. God was *for* Israel. He asked in
return only their exclusive recognition of his right to be Israel's God.
God's love was expressed in calling, delivering, and forming them into
his people (Hos. 2:21-13; 1 Pet. 2:9-10).

The distinctiveness of this pattern of relationship between Yahweh
and Israel becomes clear when we compare it with the religious and
political systems of other nations. In the religions surrounding Israel,
the people exist for the god, who is represented in the ruler. The divinity serves as a focus for national cohesion and loyalty to the political hierarchy. In this way the divinity, whether heavenly or earthly, provides
a surrogate self-worth for the subjects (not citizens) by allowing them
to identify themselves with royalty and the divinity which it represents.
In turn, the divinity uses the people for the defense and honor of his or
her name. The divinity may even "honor" subjects with "favors"—sexual and otherwise. (In this kind of situation, prayer is asking for a favor, in
contrast to the fully developed biblical concept of prayer as petition for
God's will to be done.)

But who had heard of a god or goddess that genuinely gave himself
or herself in sacrificial service to the subjects? What divinities truly
came to serve and not to be served? And where is the divinity that takes
a motley group of self-centered, complaining, recalcitrant "slaves" and
gives them a new self-image and self-worth by giving them his name?
What god finds an abandoned newborn child left exposed in its bloody
nakedness to die, and lovingly nurtures it through its temperamental
periods of self-doubt, rejection of its adoptive parent, and insistence on
returning to its "natural roots" to find its true identity (Ezek. 16:1ff.)?
What god rejects the imperial regalia of a kingly court and military
might to represent and defend his or her divinity?

The relation of devotees to pagan divinities takes various forms. It
may be fear of the divine mystery, mystical reverence, and worship. Or
it may be ascetic rejection of the self and absorption into deity. The divinity may require subjection, loyalty, trust, resignation, sacrifice, and
honor. The devotee may know, worship, honor, and obey. But where
else does one find the language of *loving and being loved* by God? Is not
this the language of human sentimentality and indulgence? Does one
relate to the transcendent deity in this way? Certainly the great religions of Asia would say no. This requires a definition of love. What is
there in the biblical concept of God's love to distinguish it from emotional sentimentality?[19]

First, we must recognize that the language of love and wrath in God is the language of human metaphor. We cannot determine what God's love is like by analyzing human love. Rather, we use human relationships as "parables" or picture images to describe aspects of God's relation to us. With this in mind, we can point to several characteristics of God's love which give it a distinct quality.

Second, God's love is "spontaneous." This is a word used by Anders Nygren and Gustaf Aulén to indicate that it stems from God's own nature and being. It does not derive from a desire for some external object.[20] When we say "God is love," we mean it is God's essential nature to love. God is the origin and source of love. It is God's love that creates value in all creaturely being, not creaturely value that excites God's love.[21]

Third, because God is the universal God—the God of all people on earth (Jer. 32:27)—his love is *without favoritism*. He called Israel for his special purpose, but that did not mean that he loved other people less (Amos 9:7; Jonah 1–4; Rom. 2:11).

Fourth, God is the "Holy One." Therefore, his love is holy. There is *no indulgence* in his love, as Israel found out. As the Holy One, God is radically opposed to evil. His righteousness will no more tolerate injustice in Israel than in other nations. Indeed, his righteousness is one dimension of his love. "It lies in the very nature of love that it must react against that which is incompatible with itself. If it is not to lose its own character, it *must* preserve its purity."[22]

Fifth, God's love is *sovereign* love. This love is not bound by law. There is no "natural law," no "law of justice," no "law of reason" that constrains God's love. This was one of Luther's great insights. God's love, he said, acts *contra legem;* that is, it cannot be constrained by legal systems, either in its means or its purposes.[23] This is a crucial consideration in the interpretation of the cross of Christ as atonement.

Finally, in our world of sin and moral offense, God's love is known as *grace*. It is the nature of God's love to take the initiative both in creating and in restoring relationship. As grace, God's love is *unconditional* and *unqualified*. That is, its offer is not dependent upon either our request or response. And it is *self-giving* love. God's gift of salvation is the gift of himself in loving, creative relationship.[24]

Israel experienced God's love as both "kindness" and "severity" (Rom. 11:22). The formal instrument of God's goodness is the covenant (Isa. 54:10). Under the covenant, sometimes spoken of as a parental covenant and sometimes as a marriage covenant, Israel knew the faithfulness (*khesed*), the beneficence, kindness, and mercy of God. Not only is God said to "do good" to Israel (Ps. 73:1), he is called "good"

(Exod. 33:19; 2 Chron. 5:13), and he "is good to all" (Ps. 145:9). In the dramatic language of Isaiah, God in his goodness is known to Israel as creating Father (63:16; 64:8), as Savior-Redeemer (60:16; 63:8-9), and as comforting Mother (66:13).

But Israel also knew the anguish and wrath of God's love. Such wrath was experienced as judgment when Israel was unfaithful to the covenant. Israel felt God's judgment as severe punishment, but because God's wrath is the wrath of love, Israel's repentance and restoration was always its goal. God's love is "an everlasting love" (Jer. 31:3).

God as Trinity

The doctrine of the Trinity is a distinctly Christian concept deriving from God's self-disclosure in Christ. The conviction that Jesus as Savior shared in the essential selfhood of God necessitated a reconceptualization of God. One sees the beginning of this reconceptualization already in the New Testament. The doctrine of Trinity has been so central to the Christian view of God that no serious theologian can ignore it, no matter what conclusions he or she may draw.[25] Writing at the turn of this century, William Adams Brown put its basic significance succinctly:

> In Jesus Christ . . . we have to do not simply with human ideals, however exalted, or human aspirations, however sincere, but with the great God himself as he is manifesting himself in gracious, fatherly love to his needy children. It is not man with whom we commune in Jesus, but very God of very God. When we take upon our lips the historic terms, consecrated by so many centuries of Christian usage, we confess with all the saints of the past that the God of all the earth is a self-disclosing God, one whose very nature it is to utter himself forth to men in some objective form of revelation; and so we dare to translate the nameless Absolute of philosophy into the God and Father of our Lord Jesus Christ.[26]

Difficulty of Formulation

Although the doctrine has been considered fundamental, theologians and biblical scholars of all schools agree there is no explicit doctrine of Trinity in the Bible. Conservative theologians like Charles Hodge spoke of a "biblical form" of the doctrine in distinction from its "ecclesiastical" and "philosophical" forms. B. B. Warfield, who followed in the tradition of Hodge, wrote a definitive article on "The Biblical Doctrine of the Trinity," insisting that the doctrine is more than "implicit" in the New Testament. Nevertheless, he began his article by saying that the doctrine has been constructed in "un-Biblical language." He quickly added, however, that it is thoroughly "Scriptural" and "purely a revealed doctrine."[27]

Other evangelical theologians like Otto Weber and Karl Barth speak of it as implicit in God's self-revelation. They agree that the doctrine is distinctively Christian and central for theology. Otto Weber, for example, says that for those who make Christ normative for a doctrine of God, "it is advisable to start with it [the Trinity] quite explicitly."[28]

The difficulty is to find language that will carry the freight of such God-talk. We simply do not have any adequate metaphorical analogies to use in describing this conception of God. Many have been tried. For example, from nature some have taken the analogy of "spring, stream, and lake," or "sun, ray of light, and lighted object." Some have suggested the analogy of human self-consciousness—the knower, the known, and the union of the two in self-knowledge.[29] Still others have used an analysis of religious knowledge and have suggested "faith, reason, contemplation"; or from the experience of loving, "the lover, the loved, and the love that binds the two in one." This latter has a long history, going back at least to Augustine.

The Hindu image of the *Trimurti*, which some have suggested as a parallel conception, presents another kind of difficulty. This is the image of the three faces of God skillfully carved into the one head, depicting the one divine Absolute (Brahman), known as creator, sustainer, and destroyer (Brahma, Vishnu, and Siva). But the Judeo-Christian tradition prefers to think of God as having only one face. The anthropomorphic language of emotions is used to describe the various expressions on that face, but it is always the face of the Parent-Creator.

The problem with more abstract, analytical language is that it either says too much or not enough. For example, to say that God is "three persons" leaves most people with the idea of three individuals. The Greek, Cappadocian Fathers of the fourth century even spoke freely of God as three centers of consciousness bound in unity of love, will, and purpose.[30] On the other hand, the "modalists" spoke of the one unitary God who appears to his creation in different modes. They thought of the "persons" as the different *persona* or masks that the single actor on the Greek theater stage used to portray different characters.

But the analogy of the Cappadocians leaves the impression of a divine triad, rather than a single center of consciousness existing in a trinitarian mode. For this reason, Menno Simons, who was clearly trinitarian in his thought, hesitated to use the technical word *person* when he wrote about the Trinity. When speaking of the Father, Son, and Holy Ghost, he preferred to speak of "names, activities and powers."[31] On the other hand, the modalist conception fails to depict the richness of God's manifold personal character. It pictures him as constantly changing roles and faces.

How and Why Formulated

What, then, is the significance of the doctrine of the Trinity and why has it held such a central place in theology?

In a word, the concept of Trinity is an attempt to recognize the manifoldness of God's being in relation to us without suggesting a triad of individual divinities. It places emphasis on God's essential unity in three-ness of manifestation (triunity). The German translation of Trinity as *Dreifaltigkeit* or threefoldness [of being] is particularly appropriate.[32]

The doctrine was formed in the first place as a corollary of the doctrine of Christ's essential deity. If the Christ was deity, theologians argued, he had existed as the "Son" with the "Father" from eternity. And since the essence of Deity cannot and does not change, they concluded that God had always existed as a multifold personal being. Nevertheless, their concern was to certify the essential divinity of Christ and his work, not to describe the inner being of the Godhead.

The experience of the Holy Spirit as the Spirit of Christ and God gave rise to a threefold rather than a twofold concept. In fact, emphasis on the Spirit as a full "person" in the Trinity came only after the christological decisions had been completed. The Spirit is not merely a messenger of God to us, but is the very presence of God as he is known to us in Christ.

We must hasten to point out that the doctrine was not an attempt to give a rational psychological or philosophical description of God's essence. While a few speculative theologians may have thought this possible, most now agree with Augustine, who gave the doctrine its classical shape in Western theology. He said, "We say 'Trinity' only in order not to be silent." Belief in the Trinity is a confession or testimony to the way in which Christians have come to know God through his self-revelation in Jesus Christ. They do not place their faith in the *doctrine* of the Trinity, but in the God who has revealed himself as a triune being.

Although philosophical theologians formulated the doctrine and the ecumenical councils ratified it, they did not use it simply as a doctrinal description of the Godhead. To be sure, it was used as a rational bulwark against heterodoxy and heresy, but the concept was also used widely in the spiritual disciplines and worship of the church. It lent itself to threefold liturgical expression in prayer. It was also used to express how human beings could have personal fellowship with God. These uses preceded its formulation as a dogma. As Mary Clark has suggested, the idea was first used symbolically, then conceptually; finally it became dogma.[33]

Both Catholic and Protestant Orthodoxy have postulated the doctrine of the Trinity to explain and defend the unity of God's work in creation and redemption. Emphasis on the substantial unity of the three persons is a metaphysical way of saying that God's creative, redemptive, and judging work all belong to his essential nature. Insistence on Christ's "substantial deity" was not intended to highlight his redemptive work in contrast to the Father's creative-sustaining work, but rather the opposite: to identify the two.

This was certainly the major interest of men like Melanchthon (Lutheran) and Calvin (Reformed) in the Reformation. And it is the emphasis of conservative modern theologians.[34] While they also distinguished between the *functions* of the persons, they maintained with Augustine that the work of each "person" was the work of all. As Melanchthon put it in his *Loci*, "every activity, be it creation or anything else, is an activity of all three divine persons."[35] This holistic principle of interpreting the work of God has been seriously neglected in some contemporary emphases on the distinct and separate work of Christ and the Spirit in the individual's life.

Anabaptist Concerns

Menno Simons was especially concerned about this last point. He emphasized the unity of God in his being and work. The three are "one incomprehensible, indescribable, Almighty, holy, only, eternal, and sovereign God." And if we "deny the deity of Christ, or the true existence of the Holy Ghost, then we fashion a counterfeit God unto ourselves, a God who is without wisdom, power, life, light, truth, Word, and without the Holy Spirit." This personal God who is a Trinity of "names, activities and powers" is one "in deity, will, power, and works." Although there are three, they "can no more be separated from each other than the sun, brightness, and warmth. For the one cannot exist without the other . . . or else the whole divinity is denied."[36]

Menno's concern for the unity of God's being and work is quite understandable in the Anabaptist context. The radical spiritualists were exalting a special work of the Spirit which in effect was independent of Christ. The Protestant Reformers theoretically held to the unity of the Trinity's work. However, in ethics and social analysis they distinguished between the justice and wrath of the Father on one hand,

and the *agapē* and grace of the Son on the other. For example, they interpreted Christ's work of atonement as the Son satisfying the wrath of the Father by paying the penalty for sin, rather than expressing the Father's love and anguish through solidarity with us in suffering for sin. Again, they understood justice as the outworking of God's wrath in the secular realm of creation. Love was the work of Christ, the Son, in the spiritual (church), and personal realm.

Consequently, Christians were called to exercise the justice and wrath of God as citizens of the state, while practicing the Christly virtue of forgiveness and love for enemies in the spiritual realm of the inner life. The church in its Christly function of judging heresy turned the heretics over to the state for execution. The work of the Holy Spirit as the expression of divine energy "proceeding from the Father and the Son," was caught in this ambiguity and contradiction.

Menno was right in sensing this contradiction between the unity of trinitarian theory and its practical ethical consequences in the life of the church and society. Anabaptism has continued to be sensitive to this problem. This may account for the persistent complaint by Protestant theologians that Anabaptism has a unitarian tendency.[37]

Trinity as God Revealed

On the contemporary scene, neoorthodoxy has shifted our attention to revelation—rather than metaphysical substance—as the context for understanding trinitarian language. In part this is in response to the modern understanding of God's essential being as personal. That is, God should be understood as "Subject," after the analogy of human personal subjects in relationship, rather than after the analogy of a unitary being.

Barth discusses the Trinity under the larger topic of "the Word of God." He speaks of "the trinitarian repetitions of the knowledge of the lordship of God."[38] Or again,

> The name of Father, Son, and Spirit means that God is the one God in a threefold repetition; and that in such a way, that this repetition itself is grounded in His Godhead; hence in such a way that it signifies no alteration in His Godhead; but also in such a way that only in this repetition is He the one God.[39]

This leads Barth to speak of the "persons" as "modes of being." That is, the one God both exists and reveals himself to us in three modes: as Father, Son, and Spirit.[40] He does not split existence from revelation, but speaks from the perspective of self-revelation. With Barth we not only confess that we cannot know God's inner being; we also do not attempt to go beyond the immediate implications of self-revelation for our life as Christians in the world.

When we understand revelation as primarily God's self-revelation in Christ, the significance of Barth's emphasis on "repetition" in the modalities of revelation becomes clear. We have the revelation of the Father through the Spirit in the modality of the "Word" in creation. This is repeated in history in the embodiment of the Word in Jesus Christ through the Holy Spirit. The revelation of the Father through the Holy Spirit in creation and the Son is the revelation of the one self-consistent God.

Within such a conceptual context, we do not reduce God to Jesus when we focus on the Son as the revelational norm. Nor, on the other hand, do we introduce another individual person alongside the Father. This was also Menno Simons' concern. On the practical level, amid the ambiguities of the historical situation, we are concerned to have a consistent normative guide for our life as Christian disciples *in the world*. In the Anabaptist tradition this guide has been located in Jesus Christ.

Finally, when we confess that God exists as Trinity, we are concerned to affirm that God as he has been revealed in Christ is fully personal within his own mode of existence, and that he wills to give himself to his creatures in loving relationship. Our contemporary understanding of person as a *being-in-relation* with other persons implies a necessary plurality in God. But just how to define that plurality involves us in an inevitable paradox.

If God is love as Jesus taught, we know love finds its fulfillment in the loving relationship. And if all we have said about God's transcendence of temporal and spatial limitations applies also to his personal being, we can also say that his being fully personal, and the paradigm for our personhood, is not dependent upon his relation to creatures. That is already implicit in the eternal deity of the Godhead.

God is "beyond personality," as C. S. Lewis put it. Or as C. F. D. Moule wrote in his article on "God" in the New Testament, "his unity is not a simple 'dead,' and undifferentiated unity."[41] Nor is God simply the unified philosophical first principle. It is not surprising that the monadic deity of Islam tends to recede in transcendent austerity to be known only through the written words of the Koran.

"The Glory of God in the Face of Christ"

Our understanding of God's self-revelation in Christ has strongly colored what we have called "a biblical perspective." We have in fact interpreted the prophetic revelation through the lens of christological revelation. That is, we have assumed that revelation before Christ is the product of the Logos in preparation for its embodiment in Jesus Christ (John 1:14). Now we focus our attention on Jesus as the Son and self-disclosure of God. How does that personal disclosure affect our understanding of God's nature and character?

Jesus as the Representation of God

When we confess faith in Jesus as God's Son, we draw attention to him as the *normative disclosure* of God. The Law revealed to Moses is *not* the normative disclosure of God; nor are the prophets and prophetic writings of Israel; nor is David, although the Christ is "Son of David"; nor is Caesar or any other political divinities. And certainly no one from the pantheon of the world's religious systems supplies the normative understanding of God. That is why we call Jesus *the* Son, and God the Father of Jesus Christ.

We do not mean to divert attention from God to the Jesus of history or to substitute Jesus for God when we focus our attention on Jesus as the normative revelation of God. Today some piety with its almost exclusive reference to Jesus, implies this kind of shift. Instead, we are saying that the God of the universe is the kind of God which is most clearly *present* and *represented* in the life, death, and resurrection of Jesus of Nazareth.

When we say God was "present" in Christ, we mean that Jesus' ministry of identification and suffering with us and for us is truly God at work among us and on our behalf. For example, God is not the aloof, even though "All-Merciful," God of Islam. He is the *com*-passionate one—the one who suffers with us, bearing our sin. This is why the creeds have always insisted that Jesus is truly God in the flesh. He is not merely a prophet of God (the representative in God's place), but the presence of God among us, suffering the limitations of our human weakness.

But to understand the full significance of this presence of God in a human life, we must also speak of Jesus as a *representation*. The full impact of his life among us speaks to us of the nature of God's being and work. If this is true, then we must change our ideas about the nature of God and his way of working with the human race. To have faith in Jesus means we must repent (change our minds) of our old rationalistic and legalistic misconceptions of God and the nature of his righteousness. This was the concern of Paul in 1 Corinthians 1:18-25, where he speaks of the cross as the weakness and foolishness of God, a scandal to

Greeks and Jews alike. What changes, then, may be called for in light of Jesus?

Jesus as "the Son" is definitive and therefore normative for the Christian view of God as the heavenly Father.[42] We turn our attention, then, to the alterations which his self-revelation of God has made. First, we will consider briefly some feminist concerns about the use of such exclusively masculine terms as *Son* and *Father* in our talk about God.

God and Masculine Imagery

Patricia Wilson-Kastner points out that some feminist theologians have rejected the male figure of God and have repudiated Jesus Christ as a "male embodiment of the divinity,"[43] though most Christian feminists have not. Kastner herself is far more sympathetic with the traditional Christology of the church than many. Nevertheless, she is understandably concerned about the way some have used christological interpretations of God to justify the suppression of women in the church as well as in society at large.

If we take the historical character of revelation seriously, we must recognize that it would have been unthinkable in first-century Judaism for the Messiah to appear as a "Daughter of God," calling God her "Mother." The more significant question therefore is what kind of a male Messiah Jesus was and what kind of an image of God he projected. Did he insist on his masculine prerogatives? Did he in fact reinforce an exclusively masculine image of God? The answer to these questions is clearly no, as many feminists also freely recognize. In fact, the concept of God which he accentuated with the image of God as *Abba* (Papa) highlights characteristics that would have been considered distinctively feminine. He himself exemplified and endorsed so-called feminine virtues, such as meekness, forgiveness, patience, and tenderheartedness. As a result, the significant theological issue lies in the christological interpretation of God.

We cannot deny that in the centuries immediately following the New Testament, christological interpretation was formulated in exclusive male categories. In his exalted form, Christ was pictured as the universal Ruler, represented in the male pope and emperor. God the Father receded into ever more imperial transcendence. The suffering Christ remained as a male human figure hanging on the cross. The "Virgin Mother" Mary was given a divine but subordinate place in the heavenly oligarchy. In this way the more radical implications of the self-revelation in Christ were subverted. The "Father of Jesus Christ" became increasingly a transcendent, universal male Monarch.

Certainly one must agree with Sallie McFague that "God is she and he and neither."[44] To think of God exclusively in masculine gender turns him into an idol.[45] Ontologically, we must define God as "beyond gender," just as we recognize him as personal but "beyond personality." Obviously, those personal qualities and relationships which we know as masculine and feminine in the human analogy exist in the God whom Jesus revealed. Jesus' own relationships to both women and men not only transcended the historical cultural limits placed on the male-female relationship. They also achieved a dimension of loving inclusiveness in which there was "neither male nor female."

The question of appropriate metaphor adds yet another dimension to the problem. Metaphors are conditioned both by cultural context and religious tradition. The metaphor implied in "Lord," for example, is so firmly fixed in the Judeo-Christian tradition that although it is no longer used in everyday parlance, it retains its religious usage. It designates an authority that *boss, foreman, leader,* or the like cannot approximate. And the use of *Father* in prayer is so firmly fixed through its use in Scripture and liturgy that the substitution of the generic *God* can only diminish the intimacy and respect implied in the parental image of *Father.*[46]

From culture to culture, metaphors must be contextualized. Literal repetition of biblical metaphors will not resolve the problem, since the meanings of metaphors change. But we need to grasp the import of biblical metaphors both in their historical and literary contexts, before attempting to contextualize them. "Critical contextualization" does not mean simply adapting to different cultural norms.[47] Instead, it means finding appropriate metaphors to carry the full message of the biblical witness to God.

God as "Abba": Redefining God's Character

In his book, *The Human Face of God,* John A. T. Robinson has said that, for Christians, Christ is the definitive revelation of God

> because it is inconceivable to [them] that there could be any higher revelation of God *in human terms* than "pure, unbounded love." And [they] judge that empirically it is true that no one comes—or has come—to the *Father,* that is, to God conceived in the intimacy of *"abba,"* but by Jesus Christ. . . . Certainly it is not true of Moses or Mohammed, Buddha or Vishna [*sic*], Confucius or Lao Tsu.[48]

There is both continuity and discontinuity with the prophetic view of God's lordship in the *Son's* self-revelation of the *Father.* We have already seen how it added a threefoldness to the concept of God's one-ness, thus accentuating and enriching the personal nature of God's be-ing for us. This same kind of correction, reaccentuation, and enrich-ment significantly modifies the entire configuration of God's authority, holiness, and love.

These modifications all pivot on Jesus' distinctive relation to God as his Father. It was not simply a matter of Jesus' teaching on these sub-jects. The disciples' new understanding stems from his mission and destiny as "Son of the Father." They viewed his life as the fruition and expression of his relation as a son to a father. They understood that Je-sus had come to "show [them] the Father" (John 14:8-11). The apostol-ic revisions of the concept of God are implied in that relationship and clearly are developed from it.

First, the nature of God's *authority* is clarified in Christ. As the Son, Jesus exercised God's authority. The nature of God's authority becomes clear in Jesus' exercise of authority. According to John's Gospel, the Fa-ther gave the Son both his own empowering life and authority to exe-cute judgment (5:26-27). This authority was given to him as the embod-iment of the "Word" of creation (1:1ff.) and as the Savior of humankind (3:16-18). According to the Synoptics, he has authority over the de-monic and "authority on earth to forgive sins" (Mark 2:10). Matthew says God has invested him with "all authority" (28:18).

According to this portrayal, God's authority grows out of his will and power to save humankind. God has legitimate authority because he wills life, and he alone has the power to give life and to save humanity from destruction. Authority is not based upon coercive power, but upon God's intrinsic goodness as the Parent-Creator. The powers of death and the fear of death are false authorities which exercise their rights by force.

In Christ, the authority of God is not canceled in favor of human au-tonomy and relativity, but it is stripped of all heteronomous, externally imposed sanctions. As John says, "If the Son makes you free, you will be free indeed" (John 8:36). Authentic authority fosters freedom and the fulfillment of human life. That is the nature of God's authority.

Christ's revelation accentuates the theme of covenant authority. God offers a covenant of life and peace (Isa. 54:10; Mal. 2:5) which defines the nature of his authority. God says, "I will be your father, and you shall be my sons and daughters" (2 Cor. 6:18). The "King" is "Father," not a political hierarch. The authority is familial and must be freely ac-cepted to be authentic.

In Christ the lordship of God as Creator is defined not as supernatural power from outside the universe, but as incarnate example in service of humankind. Again, John tells us that Jesus, "knowing that the Father had given all things into his hands," took a towel and washed the disciples' feet (John 13:3-5). In that position as servant king, he gave them the commandment to do as he had done for them. Further, in that chapter we are told that God is "glorified" in the suffering of this servant (13:31; cf. Mark 10:45). The authority of the Creator is the authority of a *servant*. As Creator still at work among us joined with us in the completion of our creation in Christ's image, God claims the right to our obedience (John 5:17).

In addition, the authority of God is exercised as "Savior of the world" (John 4:42). It is not an extraneous legal authority of Judge or Lawgiver. The Lord is the Redeemer, the one whose power is exercised in giving eternal life, not in condemning but in saving from destruction (John 3:16-18). To be sure, there is judgment (*krisis*), but the judgment is manifested as self-condemnation in the rejection of light and truth. God's authority comes to us as the intrinsic power of "truth and light." It defines the authentic nature of our own existence and offers true fulfillment in our recognition and submission to it.

In our modern Western culture there has been an explosive rebellion against false claims to authority, whether political, religious, or psychological. Because the true and false claims are often intermixed in the institutions of society, the tendency has been to reject all authority in favor of self-determination (autonomy) and relativity. Anti-authoritarianism often identifies all authority with autocracy and totalitarianism. And the Christian claim that God rightfully has total authority in our lives is often equated with such totalitarianism.

Paul Tillich wrestled with this problem. He made an important and valid distinction between two kinds of authority, which he labeled "theonomous" and "heteronomous." The latter is an authority imposed upon us—not by reason, but by superior power. Theonomous authority—God's lawful authority—corresponds and appeals to our deepest human rationality and good. In his words, God's authority corresponds to "the depth of reason."[49] We find our true, self-fulfilling freedom in submission to this theonomous relationship of self to God.

Second, the *holiness* of God is redefined in Christ. Western culture, which has been deeply influenced by Greek philosophy, tends to relate God's holiness as impassibility and immutability. These terms suggest that God in his transcendent holiness cannot suffer the effects of evil or in any sense change in response to it. God is perfect and entirely separate from evil, and then by definition impassive and distant. But we must revise such an understanding of God's holiness when we view it in the context of the incarnation, if we are to speak of one "who knew no sin" being "made . . . to be sin for us" (2 Cor. 5:21, KJV). Holiness as revealed in the Son is seen as "sinlessness" and "purity" in the midst of existential evil.

Jesus was called "the Holy One of God" in the context of impurity (Mark 1:23-24). According to John, his disciples also recognized him as "the Holy One of God," in contrast to those who demanded strict observance of the Mosaic holiness code (6:67). His purity was not the ceremonial purity of the Mosaic Law. It was not the result of cultic avoidance of the taboos, such as touching people who were unclean. Jesus made no attempt to avoid contact with sinners. Instead, his holiness is "purity of heart," steadfast dedication and obedience to the Father's will in the midst of evil. Here in the midst of sinfulness and uncleanness, he is sinless.

All this suggests a dynamic rather than a static view of holiness. The Holy One is involved in the battle against evil. His holiness is expressed in determined, uncompromising opposition to and noncooperation with evil. In the midst of conflict with demonic and cultic uncleanness, it is uncontaminated. Indeed, it becomes the source of cleansing and healing. Its power is its purity; that is, its adamant refusal to compromise or cooperate with evil even for good ends. The crucifixion is the outcome and therefore symbol of this holiness. Such is the new picture of God's holiness.

The meaning of God's holiness and righteousness tends to coalesce. God's righteousness, like his holiness, is not defined by taboo, custom, legal standards, or natural law. Righteousness is not justice (*dikē*) which can be given legal codification. It is the power of God at work righting what is wrong. This righteousness of God (*dikaiosunē*) was pointed to in "the law and the prophets," and supremely manifested in the self-sacrifice of Christ on the cross, where God demonstrated his unyielding opposition to and noncooperation with evil (Rom. 3:26).[50] Its normative ethical character as justice is vindicated in the effective power of the resurrection. The gospel of the cross is the "power of God for salvation" (Rom. 1:16).

This holiness or righteousness of God will be fully revealed in the *eschaton*, when the Lamb is victorious over evil. Death, the ultimate desecration, will be overcome. Darkness, fear, frustration, and every shameful thing will be banished. In glorious light God will be declared the "Sovereign Lord, holy and true" (Rev. 6:10; 15:4).

Such a dynamic view of God's holiness has implications for both the context and style of discipleship, inasmuch as God's people are called to be holy as God himself is holy (1 Pet. 1:15-16). No longer are they called to be a "holy nation" in cultural and political separation. They are now to "shine like stars in the world," in the midst of a "crooked and perverse generation" (Phil. 2:15).

This change already becomes evident in the life of the New Testament church. The church was first gathered in Jerusalem as a messianic community set apart in holiness to wait for Jesus' return as victorious king. The legalistic element in the church attempted to maintain the holiness codes and preserve this cultural separation, but the new dynamic could not be contained. The call to imitate God was a call to a quality of life in the world (Eph. 4:30–5:2; John 17:15-19).

The dynamic Enabler for such a life is the Holy Spirit of God, present in the church. The Spirit's work is the spiritual consecration and ethical purification of disciples (John 17:17; 2 Thess. 2:13; 1 Pet. 1:20; Gal. 5:16ff.) and the prosecution of evil and unbelief in the world (John 16:16). So today the church is called to maintain holiness after the pattern of God's holiness in its struggle against evil.

Third, the meaning of God's love as *agapē* is specifically manifested in the life of Christ. It has become commonplace to say that the sovereignty of God's love is the central christological disclosure, especially in the cross of Christ. John can say, "God is love," and that the highest manifestation of that love is the sending of the Son for our salvation (1 John 4:8-9). Because of this, a great deal hangs on the critical understanding of love. It must never be confused with indulgence. Love's patience and kindness must not be mistaken for tolerance and approval of evil (Rom. 2:4). Its optimism should not be confused with naïveté, or its quiet submission with weakness or lack of resolve.

God's love, which we refer to as *agapē*, is his unconditional and unqualified good will toward his creation. It is unconditional in the sense that it is not contingent on human initiative or response. Paul can say, "While we were still weak, at the right time Christ died for the ungodly" (Rom. 5:6-8). It is unqualified in the sense that it cannot change into its opposite, apathy.[51] This is precisely the meaning implicit in Christ's submission to crucifixion in a spirit of forgiveness. As we should not think of Christ's sacrifice as changing an angry God into a loving one, so we do not expect a God of love to become a God of vengeance at the end of history. "Love never ends" (1 Cor. 13:8).

For this reason we must speak of God's wrath as an aspect of his love, not as a separate characteristic in paradoxical contrast to his love. God's love is holy. It is inexorably opposed to sin and evil. As strange as it may sound, we must say that God's wrath is the anguish and indignation of God's love confronting evil and its consequences. Wrath is the determined opposition of God to all that opposes his love. It was this kind of love-wrath that was manifested in the cross. As two sides of the same coin, both wrath and love are revealed in Christ's crucifixion.

Wrath, like jealousy or desire, is a human emotion metaphorically attributed to God. While we may properly speak of God's "reaction" to sin, we should not attribute to him such emotions as vengeance which are generally associated with human wrath. Wrath as a theological term describes the historical consequences of God's unalterable antagonism to evil. It is "God's real and effective No to sin" and all that opposes his love.[52]

In the apocalyptic literature of the Bible, the consequences of sin—such as anger, hostility, war, pollution, and vengeful punishment—are described as the hostility and vengeance of God against evil. These consequences of human rebellion are spoken of as the "eschatological wrath" and judgment of God. We need to understand, however, that these *events* of wrath should not be projected onto God as punitive, vengeful attitudes (see chapter 7).

Thus, while the consequences of sin may properly be viewed as the *judgment* of the Creator who said No to chaos and darkness, we should not attribute punitive and vengeful motivation and attitudes to God. God's No to evil is not a vengeful punishment inflicted by superior force. It is rather the intrinsic result of attitudes and actions which contradict God's love. Where love is genuine, it cannot tolerate self-contradiction. It may choose to suffer hostility from sinners (Heb. 12:3), but it cannot ignore it.

In conclusion, the "glory of God in the face of Jesus Christ" (2 Cor. 4:6) is the glory of holy love. The *agapē* of God is totally involved with us. As only love can, it confronts and overcomes the consequences of sin in anguish, indignation, and hope. The "human face of God" in its glorious holiness is a face wrenched in pain and agony too intimate and personal to be gazed upon.

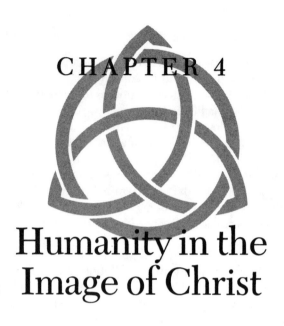

CHAPTER 4

Humanity in the Image of Christ

Introduction

A Crucial Current Issue

Defining the essence of humanity has become a serious ethical and political issue today. The human rights revolutions around the world, as well as the abortion controversy, have thrust the issue center stage. Are the blacks and coloreds of South Africa, and the aborigines of Australia and the Americas, fully human and deserving of the same social and political rights as the whites? Do women and children have the same political and economic rights as adult males? Do human fetuses have the same legal rights of a child already born? If we define humanity in such a way that all these groups are equally human, then, of course, they have full human rights. But what does it mean to be human?

And what about balancing individual and group rights? Can we define an individual's humanity apart from his or her personal relation to the group? Is there some inherent private characteristic such as rationality that makes an individual human? In a theological analysis it is not our task to weigh the pros and cons in each of these ethical and political decisions, but we need to establish the basic meaning of the adjective/noun *human*.

In Christian theology we often speak of humankind as created in God's image and likeness (Gen. 1:27). But as our discussion of Christology has shown,[1] the New Testament materials add another perspective to this. Jesus Christ is called the "image of God" and we are to be re-created in his image. In this chapter we want to explore what this kind of language means. What is the "image of God"? What does it mean to be "human"? And how is our self-knowledge as sinful creatures related to "the image," or essential selfhood? We have already examined at length the concept of Christ as the fulfillment of the image of God, and his work in restoring that image in us.[2] Now we need to look at the implications of calling Jesus the true fulfillment of the divine image for our understanding and definition of humanity itself.

The Anthropological Context for a Definition

To understand the significance of the Christian view of humankind, it is necessary to see it against the backdrop of other cultural views. We need to recognize what Christian thought has borrowed from other cultural systems in forming its own theological synthesis. We also need to understand what is distinctive in the Christian view if we are to enter into missionary dialogue with other cultures. Every culture has its own self-understanding and self-definition. A missionary theology must work in the context of these cultural systems. As the apostle Paul contextualized the message of Jesus Christ across the Graeco-Roman and tribal cultures of ancient Asia Minor, so our theology today should be in missionary dialogue.

We may take brief note of three widely scattered worldviews into which the gospel message has penetrated. The primal or *tribal* view underlies most views of humanity and lingers on in many of them. *Human* is defined as belonging to the social group (tribe). Outsiders are considered less than human. We see allusion to this idea in the word *barbarian*, which indicated beings less than fully human, making nonsense sounds, *bar bar* (Col. 3:11).

The rationale for this view is usually associated with the concept of humanity as an ongoing social phenomenon which incorporates the ancestors. For example, some African tribal systems view the distinctly human characteristic as a participation in the spirit-soul of the group. Immortality is understood as an ancestral existence in the memory and ongoing vital force of the descendants.

In Asia, especially China and Japan, Confucianism elaborated this view and built a complex ethical and social system upon it. It holds that human beings are a combination of a material body and a "vital force." They are body, spirit, intelligence, and breath in a living harmony. When the body dies, the vital force disperses back into the elements—

not as an individual spirit, but as a force still present in the descendants. Sincere filial piety of children can call the vital force [spirit] of the dead ancestor back into being. But one should not think there are individual spirits which continue their self-conscious existence after death of the body. Concern and attention must continue to focus on the continuing life of the human family in this world.

A second widely held view is the *monistic*, which links the human soul to the soul of the universe. Although there are many philosophical schools of thought in Hinduism, the dominant motif is monistic. The essential soul of the universe—that which truly exists—is Brahman. This ultimate spirit which pervades all things emerges at its highest level in the phenomenal world as the self-conscious *atman* or soul in humans. Brahman-atman is one (monistic) reality. Thus the saying, "Thou art this [one eternal reality]," is central to the Hindu definition of humanity. The greeting *namasti* with the hands held in the attitude of prayer, a greeting now accepted as a secular greeting, originally indicated the recognition of this spark of divinity in each human being.

This basic idea is overlaid with the concept of *karma* (destiny, justice, retribution) and reincarnation, which accounts for the inequalities within human society. The temporarily individuated Brahman is reembodied generation after generation, according to its previous achievements. A person of high caste who squanders his or her spiritual inheritance, may be reborn in a low caste. The final resolution of this process is *moksha*, when the individual atman is released into the greater reality of Brahman.

In the modern West, so-called *scientific* methodology has developed yet another definition. According to secular science, one must define the human phenomenon according to observable characteristics. Physical features like skeletal formation, size and shape of the cranium, bone structure of the hand, and other unique biological characteristics, are used to describe Homo sapiens. Psychological features like the possibility for self-transcendence, planning for the future, rational control, and intellectual achievement serve as parameters. The cultural anthropologist's interest centers in the nature of group activity, belief and interest in an afterlife, tool-making, and how food and shelter are provided.

In none of these areas is a transcendent aspect and relationship considered. Humans are "psychosomatic" creatures who have developed by a process of evolution to the point where the creature can begin to alter and control his or her environment. Desmond Morris reminded us in his book, *The Naked Ape*, that humans are only highly sophisticated animals. We should not presume that they have an infinite capacity.

In sharp contrast to this latter view, Christian theology teaches a transcendental definition of humanity. Philosophically, it teaches a modified dualism in contrast to monistic views. And it teaches there is one human family under God in contrast to the various tribalisms.

The Traditional Christian Synthesis

Traditional Christian definitions of what it means to be a human are an amalgam of Greek philosophical analysis and Hebrew-biblical descriptions. The teachings of men like Plato and Aristotle have left a significant impact on the way we in the Western world think about being human. In theology, their philosophy has so thoroughly blended with biblical concepts that we need to begin by distinguishing the significant differences in the two viewpoints. Therefore, we must look briefly at both approaches and the concepts which emerge from them. Then we will be ready to look at our contemporary thought and terminology to determine how to convey the concepts in our present cultural contexts.

Plato taught that the soul (spirit, mind) is the essence of a human being. It is the rational part which distinguishes humans from other animals. The body, the irrational seat of the passions, is accidental, and the spirit is freed from it at death. Aristotle also defined the distinctly human aspect of humankind as rationality. Humans, he said, are "rational animals." He thought the male philosopher was the ideal human specimen. Both men viewed women generally as inferior human types.

Both philosophers held that the essential meaning of a human life resides in one's social, economic, and political status and accomplishment. As Aristotle put it, humans are also "political animals." Thus society or the state defines one's identity and human value by the way it classifies the individual—as slave, artisan, soldier, businessperson, politician, and the like.

For Plato and Aristotle, the social order was the Greek republic or city state. Those outside the body politic were "barbarians" and considered less than human. Later philosophers like Epictetus (59-135 C.E.) and Mark Aurelius (121-180 C.E.) expanded the concept of society to include the whole world and made rational intellect the essential determinant. Wherever they found the evidences of rationality, they recognized the people as sharers in universal reason and therefore in humanity.

In the following centuries this concept of universal reason and the biblical concept of the image of God often were blended in theological definitions of humanness. The *imago dei* was equated with humankind's superior spiritual and rational capacities. We need to re-examine the difference between these two ideas and explore further the implications of the biblical concept for our contemporary theological definitions.

In modern Western culture, psychological rather than philosophical patterns and vocabulary dominate the descriptive analysis of the human psyche. In this context the "image" language of the Bible is translated into the language of self-identity and personhood. What kind of beings are we? What does it mean to be a "person"?

Put in these terms, the question is how we achieve self-identity and personal fulfillment. Is it through intellectual achievement? Is it through gratifying our desires? Is it through the manipulation of power—especially power over others—to achieve our own ends? Or do we find authentic *human* fulfillment in a responsible, mutual relationship with God and other human beings?

The Bible elaborates this last alternative. Human self-identity is the concomitant of responsible personal relationships. *We achieve our authentic potential for human selfhood in a covenant relationship with God, the Ultimate Person, when we live in mutual interdependence and personal respect for others under that covenant.* This order of relationship which puts God first is implicit in the phrase, "the image of God." Humans are not merely in the image of their family, society, or culture.

To be made in the "image of God" means that humans have the capacity for a relationship which demands an ultimate commitment. The attainment of authenticity as a personal being is directly connected with the quality of our commitments. Where the confidence and resolve to commit is lacking, a vital dimension of personal reality is lacking, and our self-identity as creatures in God's image is impossible.

This ability and need to make an ultimate commitment is integral to personhood. Therefore, the question of a responding subject who can bear such a commitment is fundamental to our definition of the human person. Put another way, the god to which we make an ultimate commitment—whether nation-state, self, family, or Creator of heaven and earth—becomes the source of our self-image. The biblical language of humans in the image of God implies that we can fully attain authentic human self-identity only in an ultimate commitment to the transcendent Creator. For this reason, social and individual views of God are important for the formation of the human self-image. It determines what kind of person the individual will become. (On "image of God" in the Bible, also see pp. 113-119.)

Creation as the Context for Humankind

Creation as Prophetic Insight

From the biblical perspective, humankind is the climax of the creation process. The Genesis accounts clearly establish a hierarchy of interdependent creatures, with Adam and Eve at the pinnacle and placed in charge of the other creatures. Hence we must examine our understanding of humanity's nature and significance in the context of creation.

The Genesis account of creation is the work of a prophet concerned primarily to identify the theological origins of Israel. From his perspective, Israel belongs to God both by creation in Adam and by her special calling in Abraham. This understanding of the creation account is underscored by the genealogy of the Messiah in Luke 3:23-38. Luke traces his ancestry through David and Abraham to "Adam, the son of God," thus establishing his human identity as an Israelite.

In the words of John C. Wenger, the account is written from a "geocentric" perspective based firmly on a "theocentric" assumption.[3] Its descriptive language is that of a layperson, not a scientist. And its focus is not on the creative process, but on the relation of humankind to the world around them. They were created as the crown of God's work to function as his counterpart and co-workers within the created order. The story of creation therefore runs in a reverse hierarchical order, from the formation of earth and sky through the various species of animals which inhabit sky, water, and earth. Finally, human animals are created "in God's image" and are given responsibility for the care of other created beings.

Therefore, the prophetic witness makes it clear that the Yahweh who covenanted with Moses is the same God as El Shaddai, who called Abraham out of Ur and covenanted with him, and as the Elohim, who covenanted with all humankind through Noah and Adam in creation.

The story sets up the context within which Israel was to understand her covenant calling to be the people of God. On the one hand, Yahweh is not simply the tribal God of Israel, but the creator of the universe. On the other hand, Israelites are not defined as uniquely human through their national covenant as God's people.[4] All persons by virtue of the covenant of creation are God's people (Ps. 24:1b; Acts 17:26).

Creation by God's Word

The causative agent of creation is God, and the instrumental agent is "God's Word." The theological import of telling the story this way is significant. First, we learn that the created universe is the *expression* of

God and not an *extension* or emanation of God. Thus creation—and humankind as part of creation—is not divine. God is the transcendent Creator, "the Maker of heaven and earth," as the Apostles' Creed puts it. The universe is creaturely, both limited and dependent. We must look beyond it for the purpose and goal of life (Heb. 11:10).

Second, the universe is understood as an intentional act of creation, not a spontaneous materialization of emergent evolution. As such, the creation belongs to and is the responsibility of God (Ps. 24:1). For this reason creatures, especially human beings, are responsible to God, upon whom they are totally dependent. The universe is not *autonomous* but *theonomous*. That is, it is not a law to itself, but is under God's covenant law.

The account does not speak to the question of the further development of varieties and species, which is the concern of scientific evolutionary theories. It merely states that various plants and animals were created "of every kind."[5] And so the account clearly rejects secular humanistic theories of the universe's origin. But it does not give scientific answers to questions such as the age of the universe, the emergence of our solar system, or further evolutionary developments of plant and animal species on the earth.[6]

The christological implications for a doctrinal interpretation of the creation account are most explicit in John 1:1-14 and Colossians 1:15-20. These passages are generally read only as exalted descriptions of the cosmic significance of Christ. But obviously more than that is involved. They also speak of the significance of the revelation in Christ for understanding the nature of the cosmos. In both passages concepts of creation and incarnation are interrelated in such a way that the creation is fulfilled in the incarnation.

John identifies the Christ with the creative "Word," which is the agent of creation. He goes on to identify him with the light which struggles against and overcomes the darkness in creation. These concepts speak of the rationale and dynamic which inform and form the created order. John equates them with the Word embodied in Jesus Christ.

When the creation account is read as a preface to the formation and history of Israel, as the rabbis did, the informing principle of creation is the Torah (Wisdom and Law), and the goal of creation is the Sabbath. When the Christ is identified with the divine Word of creation, then not "the law of Moses" but the "grace and truth" embodied in Jesus become the dynamic and goal of creation (John 1:14, 17). And the Sabbath is not the conclusion of God's creative work, but God's gift to his creatures. It is to remind them of his gracious right as Creator (Mark

2:27), and of the goal of creation. Jesus said God is still at work and that his own miraculous ministry of healing was an example of that continuing work (John 5:17).

In Colossians 1:15-20, Paul speaks both of the cosmic significance of Christ as the one who has the preeminence, and of the significance of Christ for understanding the cosmos. For purposes of theological analysis, I have arranged Paul's cluster of images into a developing order.

He speaks first of Christ as the archetype (*prototokos*) of creation, as though the whole idea of creation was *pre*-formed in him (1:17a). Second, he calls him the "image of the invisible God," in whom all "the fullness of God" dwells (1:15, 19). This indicates that he is the consummation and fullness of creation as God intended it. Third, he says he is the agent "in whom" and "through" whom all things visible and invisible were created. And he emphasizes that he is the one prior to and preeminent to all things (*autos estin pro pantōn*, 1:17). Fourth, he calls him the sustainer of all things—the one in whom everything coheres (1:17b). Fifth, he is the reason and goal of creation, the one *for whom* everything exists. And last, he is the reconciler-redeemer of all things in heaven and on earth (1:20; cf. Eph. 1:9-10). Thus he is described as both the divine agency and the creaturely fulfillment and goal, or in the words of the Revelator, the *Alpha and the Omega* of creation.

In this divine-human role, he is then named "head . . . for the church, which is his body" (1:22-23). As such he is "the beginning" of the new creation by virtue of the resurrection from the dead. This means that the Messiah and his body, the church, are made the illuminating clue for the meaning of creation as God intends it.[7]

This is clearly the fundamental meaning of creation by the word of God when viewed from the New Testament perspective. When we attempt to contextualize the message, we must exercise caution to avoid fruitless arguments with peripheral aspects of other worldviews. Especially we in the West must avoid reading modern "scientific" meaning into the biblical data, obscuring its witness to Christ. On the face of it there is no particular reason to think that the biblical concept of creation should be understood in the categories and terminology of modern secular science. Our hermeneutical focus should be upon the crucified Christ (the Word) as God's method and purpose in creation.

Creation "Ex Nihilo"

The nearest thing to a biblical statement that the universe was created out of nothing is in Hebrews 11:3.[8] In this passage the writer is praising the virtue of faith which sees past the transient realities to the eternal. He affirms that by faith we grasp the truth of creation "by the word of God." Faith, which he calls "the conviction of things not seen," is the ground of our assurance that God who made the world out of "things not seen" exists for us. The phrase "things not seen" indicates eternal realities in contrast to the transient (2 Cor. 4:18b). Faith penetrates to and is grounded in eternal reality. It understands that a transient and dependent world is sustained by the eternal word of God, which called it into existence in the first place. And in that faith it dares to hope.

In a similar vein, Paul indirectly refers to God as the creator when he speaks of him as the one who said, "Let light shine out of darkness" (2 Cor. 4:6). This one who is the ultimate and sole source of light has "shone in our hearts to give the light of the knowledge of the glory of God in the face of Jesus Christ" (4:6). Certainly Paul's purpose is not to explain creation, but to identify the light of Christ with the light of creation. He identifies faith in Christ as faith in God himself.

Neither of these statements is in any sense a philosophical explanation of the mode of creation. We should not use them as a major premise for a syllogistic speculation about creation ex nihilo (out of nothing). They do illustrate the biblical affirmation of God as the ultimate reality upon which our faith and hope rest. They are clearly written in the spirit and tradition of Isaiah 40.

The more philosophical statement of creation de novo and ex nihilo makes the philosophical point that no ultimate reality exists outside of God. There is no eternally limiting factor—no chaos, darkness, or evil power—which can challenge God's power and love. The older systems of eternal dualism, such as Zoroastrianism, taught that the struggle between light and darkness, good and evil, is eternal. Christianity, on the other hand, has always taught that God's purpose for creation will not be frustrated in the end either by the defective quality of the material he had to work with (Platonic) or by some opposing power (Zoroastrian, Manichaean). The doctrine of creation out of nothing is intended to assure us, therefore, that God is ultimately in control and that final responsibility lies with him.

The Genesis story of creation actually speaks of a chaos and darkness which God overcame with his word, "Let there be light." By an act of self-communication, God reconstituted life and order out of the formless chaos and darkness. This is so clearly stated in Genesis 1:1-2 that it has led some commentators to interpret the following account as a recreation of a primal universe destroyed by powers of evil (Satan or Lucifer).

Whether or not we posit a primal creation, it is obvious that in the

Genesis account creation is already understood both as a beginning and as a new beginning. The story is not simply a logical accounting of the origin of the universe in the perfection of God, such as we wish for in a philosophical or scientific account. Instead, the origin is posited in verse 1:1 and the new beginning is described from 1:2 onward. It is told as the beginning of known history. Thus the *eschaton* (completion) of history is realized in the formation of humanity in God's image (Gen. 1:26-27) and in the coming of the rule of God. This formation is described as God's ongoing creative work. The words of Jesus, "My Father is still working, and I also am working," highlight this double reference of the biblical texts (John 5:17).[9]

Here also is the implicit concept of creation through a self-communication ("the Word") which culminates in a creature *in* God's image. What is most significant for our present purposes is that God creates and commissions human beings as his covenant creatures to join him in the ongoing process. *The meaning and fulfillment of our humanity is attained in being partners with God in the continuing formation of the universe.* This partnership is represented in the participation of Mary in the creation-birth of Jesus, the Messiah, who is the fulfillment of God's image (Luke 1:35). Then Jesus as "the second Adam" fulfills the intended participation of humanity in the completion of creation. As the writer to the Hebrews says, we do not yet see the completion of the process with all things under human control, but we do see Jesus, who has been given the priority of place (2:8b-9).

Humans as Creatures

Psychosomatic Creatures

The biblical writers describe human beings as creatures—part of the creation. *Adam*, male and female, was made out of the dust of the ground, thus linking them explicitly to the earth system. Into these earth creatures God breathed life—a unique life, to be sure, but still a creaturely one. In Hebrew psychology the soul (*nephesh*) is the life which has been breathed into the human body. In some instances it is the life which resides in the blood. In either case human beings are psychosomatic *creatures*. They are a holistic unity of body and soul, both of which are creaturely.[10]

When we speak of the human soul (*psuchē*) as "immortal," we must remember that such a soul came into being at a time and place. It is created. The biblical concept of immortality does not include preexistence in the spirit realm (the Platonic concept; cf. Wisd. Sol. 8:19-20; 2 Enoch 23:5). The soul's future immortality is totally dependent on

God's continuing sustenance and creative action. Immortality is not an endowment or characteristic of the soul. Nor is it the essential self, which gives it an independent spiritual existence and exempts it from death.[11]

This view is in contrast to concepts of humans as the descendants of the gods, or the equation of the human spirit or soul with the infinite Soul of the universe—Brahman-Atman. The Bible does not teach that the soul is a spark of divinity or that it has independent immortality. Rather, humans were created as spiritual animals—strange as this combination may sound to our ears. By God's eternal grace they were enlivened and enabled to share in communication and fellowship with himself. Their life is and eternally remains God's prerogative.

Creaturely Limitations

To speak of humankind as creaturely, or created beings, implies limitation, conditioning, and dependence. Such limitation is immediately obvious in the physical realm. We are limited by time and space. Death is the ultimate symbol of this temporal-spacial limit. We are conditioned by the geographical and ecological context into which we are born. We are becoming increasingly aware of our symbiotic dependence upon the ecosystem. The very "laws of nature" which provide the regularity and dependability that make a purposeful life possible, also define the limits of our lives.

As creatures we are definitely a link in the chain of biological life. We are not exempt from the limitations implicit in that creaturely relationship. We do not have "infinite possibilities" as independent rational spiritual beings who can transcend their creaturely status. We can manipulate nature, but we cannot escape or fully control the consequences of our manipulation. Pretension to such independence is *hubris*, or pride. It leads us to repeat the primal mistake of Adam and Eve, when they reached for the forbidden fruit.

This same limitation applies also to the social and rational dimensions of our existence. The society and culture into which we are born, limits and conditions our self-definition and understanding. Even our knowledge is sociologically conditioned. We work largely within the framework and assumptions of the culture we have inherited. Furthermore, in our most precise pursuits of scientific knowledge, we have learned that our very instruments and methods of acquiring knowledge condition and limit our results.

In yet another essential element of our human nature, we are limited. Humankind was created with freedom to respond to God. This is implied in the command which God gave to Adam and Eve. But here again it is a creaturely freedom. We are not free to change the command. We are free only to obey or disobey.[12]

Our freedom is limited by our ignorance and relative powerlessness as creatures. And each choice fixes the limits for the next. But even more seriously, our freedom is limited by what one scholar has called a "congenital disposition" to make self-centered and self-serving decisions. One sees this tendency constantly at work in political decisions which so often defeat desirable long-term goals. One sees it also in the commercial greed for short-term "profits" at the expense of environmental pollution and the welfare of others. We will examine the results of the human choice to disobey the command more thoroughly in the discussion of humanity's sinfulness.

Creaturely Dependence

The inescapable character of our creatureliness implies that above and beyond the dependent creature stands a dependable Creator. This is clearly the fundamental meaning of the biblical story of creation and it is at the heart of Christian faith. Such faith leads to the recognition of what Schleiermacher called "absolute dependence." The whole creation, including humankind, depends upon the Creator for its continuing existence. Such existential dependence clearly implies the everlasting power and deity of the Creator, as Paul argues in Romans 1:19-21.

As "the Father, Creator of heaven and earth," God has set the conditions for the fulfillment of human destiny in his covenant with humankind.[13] The confession of our creatureliness involves our free submission to this covenant in the recognition that the command is not arbitrary; that it is for the good of humanity. It defines the lines of our responsibility and freedom to achieve our human destiny.

The proper human virtues, then, begin with a recognition of our dependence and an attitude of submission to the ground rules (covenant mandate) which the Creator has established. Such dependence is a corporate action which includes our mutual interdependence upon our environing ecosystem as well as upon each other. Such a stance is quite at odds with the virtues of Western modernity, which emphasizes independence, self-assertiveness, competition, and the exploitation of nature for self-serving purposes.

Humans in God's Image

Meaning of the Image

In biblical terminology the unique potential of the human animal and the human species for a free, self-conscious, and responsible relationship to God is referred to as being "made in God's image." According to the Genesis story, God made humans to be his representatives and co-workers on earth. Therefore, they were made according to God's own image and likeness (Gen. 1:26-27).[14] Claus Westermann speaks of the image as a correspondence of humans to God. He points out that in contrast to other ancient creation stories, Adam and Eve were not created to "bear the yoke of the gods" as their slaves. They were not created to do the gods' dirty work, but to be God's vice-regents on earth, to manage the world for the benefit of all life on earth. While humans share the "breath of life" with other living creatures (Gen. 1:24, 30; 2:7), it is the *image* which defines their unique spiritual endowment.[15]

The "image of God" is not a separate spiritual part that God joined to a physical body. Instead, it defines the capacity of the whole personal-physical being for a special kind of personal communication with God in covenant relationship.[16] The image is especially seen in the capacity to understand and feel a covenant obligation and to respond to God's mandate in responsible freedom. In contrast to Aristotle's definition of humankind as "rational animals," it marks humans out as *covenant animals*. The image is a unique potential realized in the crucible of responsible relationships with fellow humans and with God. It was fulfilled best in Jesus Christ, who is "the image of the invisible God" (Col. 1:15; cf. 2 Cor. 4:4).

Christ as the True Image

When we approach a theological definition of humanity in this way, it becomes obvious that we must do more than analyze the ancient creation stories for their original historical and theological import. It is not merely a matter of reading the Genesis account for the light it might throw on our modern philosophical and psychological understandings. We must read the creation stories in light of their fulfillment in Christ. And we must understand the original intention of the Creator in light of the incarnation.[17]

If we do not use Jesus as the biblical paradigm, we are left with an imaginary Adam and Eve as they must have existed before the Fall. Classical orthodoxy, both Roman Catholic and Protestant, has followed this hermeneutic. It uses a Greek conceptual model to describe the original human male as a perfectly rational moral being. He is pictured as a spiritually superior individual possessed of "original righteousness" and sophisticated rational and moral acumen. In the words of the famous English orator and churchman, Robert South, "An Aristotle was but the rubbish of an Adam, and Athens but the rudiments of Paradise [Eden]."[18] There is, obviously, no biblical grounds for such speculation, although one can find such ideas in rabbinic literature.

If we approach the concept of humanity in God's image from a christological perspective, the hermeneutical pattern shifts. First, creation is understood as the primal, anticipatory act of incarnation. Creation is the first expression of the "Word" in the beginning and incarnation is its climactic expression. Incarnation is not merely the conditioned response of God to human sin. It is the conclusive act of creating a being fully in God's own image. The goal of creation—the formation of personal beings in communion with God—is accomplished in Christ, the "second Adam." Thus Christ, and not Adam "before the Fall," becomes the paradigm for the image of God.

Second, creation and salvation are integrally related. Creation is understood as the overcoming of chaos and darkness. It is an act of salvation. And the soteriological work of Jesus is understood as a continuation of the creative work of the *logos* (Word). Salvation is essential to the completeness of creation. In the Gospel of John, the *logos* which was both the pattern and dynamic of creation is embodied in Jesus, who is continuing the work of the Creator (John 5:17). And that work is *the consummation of the image of God in humanity.*

Third, the hermeneutical shift will affect the way we understand the formation of human beings into the image of God. There are at least two ways to understand the biblical data concerning the relation of creation and human history in the formation of humanity in the image of God. As we have noted, one way is to think of the original creation including humans as instantly perfected in every respect, and the consequent sinfulness as the result of a "fall" from that perfection.

The other possibility is to interpret the original "goodness" of creation as innocence, rather than perfection. The words, "it was good," which sum up each day's creative activity, would then be understood as an expression of God's satisfaction with his work, rather than a pronouncement upon its glorious perfection.[19] Sin then is failed potential, when creatures attempt an autonomous achievement of the image. The failure is blameworthy, to be sure, since it is a deliberate act against covenant.

From this perspective history is a continuation of God's creative redemptive work. History is consummated in the final realization of God's image in humanity. The incarnation—already implied in creation —is the anticipatory fulfillment and revelation of this eschatological goal. Jesus is understood as the first authentic fulfillment of the "image," the one through whom we also can attain the image (1 John 3:2b).

This latter view actually fits the metaphor of God's children being formed in his image better than the former. It is certainly in keeping with the unfolding biblical picture. It is clearly the psychological and spiritual pattern alluded to in Ephesians 4:15-16.

Changing the hermeneutical grid does not imply a rejection of "original sin." It merely changes our perspective on the nature of that sin. When we think of creation as issuing in a fully developed rational and moral perfection, sin is understood as a "fall" from such perfection. The purpose of the incarnation, then, is interpreted as the redemption and restoration of the image through atonement on the cross. Theologians have debated endlessly whether such a fall totally destroyed or only seriously marred the image, and consequently how to understand the effects of the atonement.

When we think of the creation as issuing in a stage of immature innocence which was satisfactory to the Creator, we view the "image" as a potential to be fulfilled in relationship to God, fellow humans, and creation. Sin is failed potential through unwillingness to submit to God's covenant. Such autonomous action thwarts the maturity of the promised image.

In the incarnation of the Word, God's image was finally fulfilled in Jesus Christ. Through his submission to the way of God in crucifixion and resurrection, he manifested the fullness of the image and became the "firstborn within a large family" (Rom. 8:29). Through Christ, the true and living way (John 14:6), we find renewal and the possibility of attaining the authentic image of God as his true children.

The nature of human potential and the meaning of human failure to realize the image, become starkly clear when we understand that Jesus, the "heavenly man," is the divine prototype of the image of God (1 Cor. 15:45-48). The image was not realized in the freedom of Adam to disobey, but in the obedience of Christ. Adam represents potential failed. Jesus Christ becomes the paradigm for authentic human personhood through his free submission and obedience to the divine mandate (Phil. 2:5-11). We should therefore interpret the image concept in Genesis in christological terms to understand its full eschatological meaning for human destiny.[20]

Characteristics of the Image

When we view the image as that unique potential fulfilled in Jesus Christ, two characteristics stand out: the capacity for responsibility and for love. These two are grounded on the capacity for self-knowledge and self-transcendence implicit in the command to "have dominion over and subdue" the rest of creation. We may refer to this ground as human rationality in the broadest sense. We see it demonstrated in Jesus' power to heal, to cast out evil, and to control nature. Such rationality is everywhere taken for granted in the Hebrew tradition, but it is not the decisive parameter as in the Greek tradition.

H. E. Brunner has stressed the first of these elements. The essence of the image, he says, is *Ansprechbarkeit*, the capacity to perceive and respond in freedom to an absolute responsibility. He wrote, "The kernel of man's being is responsibility, and responsibility is the essence of humanity."[21]

In the Genesis story this capacity for responsibility is implied both in the commission to take care of the garden and subdue the earth, *and* in the command not to eat of the tree of knowledge of good and evil. We should note here that the latter command does not come as a threat, but as a warning for their own good to stay within the bounds of the covenant relationship. The command, as Westermann points out, is an appeal to Adam to exercise his freedom in responsible obedience to his Lord.[22] Humankind's primal responsibility under the covenant is to care for the created world which belongs to God, and to do so under the guidelines of the covenant. In fulfilling this covenant responsibility, the image will be realized and we will truly know creaturely "goods and evils."

This is certainly a proper interpretation of the implications of the Genesis account. However, it is in Jesus' obedience "even unto death" that we understand the full meaning of responsibility under God's covenant. There is an ancient tradition in theology that contrasts the tree which was the nexus of Adam's failure to attain to the image, and the tree upon which the true sonship and image of God were revealed in Jesus. The full submission of Jesus to the authority of the Father (John 5:19) is the primary characteristic and sign of his "sonship" and likeness to God.

Second, the image is demonstrated in the human capacity to love. This is implied in the so-called social mandate to "multiply" and to "fill the earth and subdue it" (Gen. 1:28). However, the full meaning of love is exemplified in the incarnation of the Word in Jesus. The covenant with Moses spelled it out as neighbor love and compassion for the strangers who lived among the Israelites (Lev. 19:18; Exod. 23:9; Job 31:13ff.). The new covenant as enunciated by Jesus in Matthew 5 goes beyond this and describes love of enemies as that which makes us like the Father in heaven (Matt. 5:45).

Humans are able to transcend the reflexes of animal instincts and even the dictates of rational self-interest in acts of genuine self-giving (*agape̅*). In the self-disclosure of God in Christ, we learn that this self-transcendence of love is the essential "form" (*morphe̅*) or image of God. The cross is the symbol of Jesus' ultimate self-giving. He "emptied" himself of the kingly prerogatives that are generally associated with the image of deity and took the human form of a servant. It is this servant "in human likeness" who is exalted above every other name as the paradigmatic image of God (Phil. 2:6-11).[23] That is, Jesus demonstrates the ultimate glory of God's image in this act of self-transcending love. In this act it becomes the paradigm of that image for all humanity.

Male and Female in the Image

The image of God in which humanity is created applies to "male and female" in relation to each other (Gen. 1:26-27). The phrase *male and female* does not indicate that individuals of each gender independent of the other are in God's image. Rather, it indicates that man and woman are in God's likeness when they in intimate social discourse are "fruitful . . . subdue the earth . . . and have dominion over" it. The passage clearly implies a social dimension to the image as it is primely represented in the relation of male and female.

This "male-female" relationship is not strictly limited to the sexual union, as much of traditional theology has assumed, but it surely includes the sexual union.[24] How else were they to "fill the earth" with their own kind? It is in procreation and the nurture of the family that one most explicitly sees the interdependence of the two genders. However, the male-female relationship which manifests the image is not equated simply with the marriage relationship. Instead, the image is reflected in mutual recognition of interdependence and respect for the broader complementary roles each gender plays in society.[25]

We may draw this conclusion from New Testament insights into the interrelatedness of men and women in the kingdom of God. Jesus himself models a new dimension of male-female intimacy and interdependence. Although he apparently was unmarried, his sensitive recognition of women as full partners in the kingdom of God and in his own mission surely is one element in the fulfillment of this dimension of the image. Paul's recognition that "in Christ" there is "neither male nor female" indicates a radical change in the traditional understanding of the human relationship. "In Christ" is realized the true meaning of the image as mutual submission and respect for the complementary roles and gifts of each gender and person (Gal. 3:28; Eph. 5:21).

Surely the healing of this most generic and primal human relationship is included in Christ's reconciliation of fractured humanity to itself and to God. Surely as "our peace" he is the creator of male and female into "one new humanity" in the image of God (Eph. 2:14-15).

The Nature of Sin

We have spoken of creation as good in God's sight. Humanity is formed "in the image of God" and is highly satisfactory to the Creator. However, when we look around us, we see much human suffering from disease and natural catastrophes—what we usually call *natural* evil. We also see the animals attacking and killing each other for food. How do these things fit with a "good" creation?

Even more troubling is the evil in the human heart, *moral* evil. It is appalling how human beings treat each other! Discrimination, extortion, cheating, oppression, torture, massacres, and war are the order of history. What has happened? Is God responsible? Was there a flaw in his creation? Is he unable to control what he has created?

Are these evils simply the result of our limitations as creatures? We *are* limited in knowledge and power. Is the problem, then, basically one of ignorance? The ancient Greek philosophers as well as most Asian religious teachers have thought so. Other religious and philosophical analyses use different words and concepts such as *fate, pollution,* and *illusion* to diagnose the human problem. If one takes the evolutionary view, these behavior patterns can be understood as the result of characteristics inherited from earlier animal stages of development.

Christian theology speaks of this calamitous situation as *human sin* and its consequences. The word *sin* itself suggests that the problem has theological dimensions since the term specifically relates the wrongdoing to God. Sin by definition is an act against God, just as crime is an act against the law. The Genesis story of humankind's first disobedience to God pictures natural evil and grief as the consequence of human sin.

These various ways of analyzing the problem have been classified into four general patterns. First, the *animistic* view understands sin as transgression of a taboo. Second, the *monistic* view equates sin with creatureliness. Third, the *legalistic* view defines sin as a deviation from an externally imposed law. Finally, the Judeo-Christian *personalistic* view sees it as a rejection of and revolt against a personal God.[26] Each definition of sin has its corresponding conception of human responsibility and fault. Each diagnosis suggests a cure. For example, if the problem is basically ignorance, the solution is education.

Since the Christian view is a self-conscious alternative to the first three, its full significance can only be understood against the background of these religious views. It will be helpful, therefore, to look at these briefly before elaborating the Christian analysis.

Sin as Transgression of the Taboo

Primal animistic cultures think of the world as a network of interwoven beings and powers. There is a mysterious power that connects and flows from one creature to another. The relationship is closer to the mystery of magic than to modern scientific cause and effect, or personal influence.[27] Both animate and inanimate beings have this elemental power. It is a power for good or evil. It may bring good or bad fortune. There is no clear distinction between moral and natural.

Since the mysterious power can bring both good and evil on the whole community, one must treat it with caution and respect. Like atomic radiation it is the source of both beneficial power and pollution and death. Since this power is dangerous as well as beneficial, it must be separated and properly contained for the safety of the community. The area of separation and containment is the realm of the sacred, or holy.

The taboo or prohibition defines the limits of contact with the sacred power. Sin, loosely defined, is any action which breaks the taboo and thus endangers the social group. It has little or nothing to do with what we call the moral. When an individual sins, he or she becomes polluted (unclean) and must be separated from the group. In ancient cultures such people were exiled or even executed, but in the latter case we should understand that the execution was a means of cleansing and protecting the group by getting rid of the defiled person. (Compare Joshua 7:1, 15, 25.) It was not a matter of punitive justice. When sin contaminated the whole tribe or nation, rituals of purification were performed to rid the land of defilement.[28]

Sin as Creatureliness

The monistic systems which dominate the Asian cultures are really sophisticated philosophical rationalizations of the animistic web or chain of existence. In a monistic system the modes of being and goodness are arranged on a parallel vertical scale from perfection to nothingness. Everything that has being has some goodness. But as one approaches the lower end of the scale of being (nothingness), evil increases coincidentally with the inferiority of the creatures. In these terms, then, sin is not a moral fault for which we are responsible, but the error and ignorance of inferior beings. Sinfulness is creaturely inferiority. One cannot fully escape it since one is caught in the limitations of material existence.

In this system, *sin* is an act against the harmony of the universe (*dharma*). But the harmony of the universe must be seen as a pattern in which light and darkness, good and evil, superior and inferior are necessarily interwoven. The darkness is not thought of in moral terms of personal responsibility, but in terms of superior and inferior being. Right action maintains the order and harmony defined by dharma. Sinful conduct is that which threatens the social order.[29]

This concept is generally associated with a system of social class or caste in which those at the top are considered more holy or superior in status and privilege, while those at the bottom are objects of contempt (unclean). This holiness has little or nothing to do with moral character, although the high classes are usually expected to live by carefully prescribed rules that keep them properly separated from the inferior classes. Likewise, the rules for those without caste status are for the purpose of preventing them from contaminating the superior classes with their own inferiority.

Such a system is related to human actions by the law of *karma* and the idea of the transmigration of souls. Manu, a medieval Hindu philosopher, explained, "If a man performs only good actions, he will be born a god; if he performs mixed actions, he will be born a man; and if he performs only evil actions, he will be born a bird or an animal."[30] Those condemned to inferior existence in this life may be presumed to have lived unworthy lives in a previous existence.

Sin as Offense Against Law

One of the clearest expressions of sin as deviation from an external norm is found in the Old Testament, which equates it with transgressing the law of Moses. The Mosaic Law contained elements of taboo as well as genuinely ethical precepts and social legislation. Obedience to it was open to different levels of understanding. One sees in the Old Testament writings a variety of legalistic and moralistic concepts of sin. In its highest and most spiritual expression, however, the Law was understood as God's covenant with Israel, and obedience meant faithfulness to the Lord himself. During the prophetic period before the exile, one sees a growing awareness of sin as idolatry and unfaithfulness to Yahweh (the adultery metaphor).

Following Israel's return from the Babylonian captivity, there was a development of literalism and legalism. This period saw increasing emphasis on the observance of the Law as the means by which righteousness could be achieved.[31] Toward the end of this period, Jesus criticized the Jewish leaders for exalting the letter of the Law over its original intention and for defining sin in legalistic rather than covenantal terms. This, of course, is a perennial human temptation.

A legalistic definition of sin does not include the effects of the conduct and the character of the sinner in the definition. Sin is simply an act against the law of God. The advantage of such a view is that people are judged by what they do, not by their status in society. (Paul enunciated this principle in his ad hominem argument with his Judaizing opponents [Rom. 2:6, 12-14]. Not the one who receives the law, he writes, but the one who keeps it will be justified by it.)

But the phenomenon of human sinfulness is much more systemic and pervasive than a legal definition of sin might indicate. Paul recognized this when he wrote that even before the law was given to Moses, sin was in the world and death reigned (Rom. 5:13-14). A legal definition does not by itself adequately account for the selfishness and irresponsibility that human deeds of violence, deception, and greed reflect. It does not account for the stubborn and pervasive nature of sinful disobedience. Therefore, in failing to diagnose adequately the profundity of human sinfulness, legalism also fails to prescribe an adequately radical cure.

Sin as Rejection of a Personal God

Christianity accentuates the personal character of the sinful offense. The writings of both the apostles Paul and John emphasize this. Paul's understanding of sin clearly reflects his reaction against an earlier legalistic background. He sought to be freed from the letter of the law (Gal. 5:1). In place of the literal precept, he put love as the fulfillment of the law (Rom. 13:10). In contrast to the precisionist obedience to the law demanded by his fellow Pharisees, he said a living relationship to Christ requires keeping the true intent of the law (Rom. 8:3-4).

In his Gospel John contrasted the "Word" (*logos*) which came in Jesus with the law (*nomos*, or Torah) of Moses (1:17-18). He calls Jesus himself "the Way" rather than a new law (14:6). Sin is "not believing in Jesus," not recognizing that God's true will is disclosed in his character, life, and teachings (16:9). John emphasizes that the rejection of Jesus as the one who shows God's true glory is in fact a morally self-contradictory act of human volition (5:39-40; 7:16-17; 10:37-38).

We will examine this tradition in more detail, so we need not develop the contrast further here. Rather, we should point out that both Paul and John present their insights as interpretations of Jesus, not as new revelations of their own. It was Jesus, "the image of God," the one "who knew no sin," the "last Adam," who provided the paradigm of righteousness against which the true nature of sin and sinfulness might be defined. Stated formally, sin and sinfulness is what Jesus was not.

Both the conviction that the man Jesus was the disclosure of God in human existence, and the teachings of Jesus themselves, called for a new understanding of sin. First, if Jesus, the sinless one, is the "Word made *flesh*," we cannot equate sin with being in the flesh. Nor can we regard sin as being "born under the law" (Gal. 4:4) or being "in the likeness of sinful flesh" (Rom. 8:3). Neither in the Platonic sense of inferior being nor in the Augustinian sense of "fallen" beings can one call physical existence itself sinful. Further, we cannot equate sin with the mistakes made because of limited knowledge. Even Jesus "learned obedience through what he suffered" (Heb. 5:7-8). Nor can we equate sin with temptation, for Jesus was tempted to the extreme.

Second, according to Jesus' teaching and action, sin cannot be defined as breaking taboos of clean and unclean, or sacred and profane. He taught it is not what goes into the stomach, but what comes out of the heart that makes one sinful (Mark 7:2-5; cf. Col. 2:20ff.). The connection between sin and taboo was radically broken in the life and ministry of Jesus.

Further, sin as breaking the Mosaic prohibitions was challenged (Mark 2:27; Matt. 12:1-12). According to the Gospel of John, one of the two main accusations against Jesus was that he broke the Mosaic Law and therefore was a "sinner" (John 9:16, 24). Instead, sin is rebellion against the "Father" (Luke 15:18, 21). If it is thought of as breaking a command, it is breaking the command to love God and one's neighbor (Mark 12:29-31).

We see the sinlessness of Jesus in his steadfast desire to do the Father's will and to honor him (John 5:30; 7:8; 8:50). Unlike Adam, the model of sinful humanity, he did not grasp at the image of God in a selfish attempt to gain knowledge and power. He humbled himself (Phil. 2:6-7; Matt. 4:1-11). Even in the face of bitter disappointment and seeming defeat, he prayed, "Not what I want but what you want" (Matt. 26:36-46). According to this model, sin and sinfulness are understood as a lack of trust and loyalty to God, and as unfaithfulness to his covenant.

Sin and Human Potential

The "Original Sin"

Both the Jewish rabbis and the New Testament writers used the Adam story to describe and account for the sinful human condition. However, there is a fundamental difference in the way the two interpret and use the figure of Adam to diagnose the present human situation. The rabbis pictured Adam as a paragon of virtue and wisdom who in a moment of weakness fell into sin. Adam, both in his original goodness and original sin, was the archetype or model for humanity. But in Paul's writings, Adam is "the man of dust" who provides the typological backdrop to contrast Christ as the "last" (*eschatos*) and normative Adam. Therefore, the Christian paradigm for righteousness over against which sin is defined is Christ, not Adam.[32] Thus we take our clues for understanding sin from Jesus. Theologically, we interpret the Genesis story in light of the new understanding he brought.

According to the biblical account, the origin of sin and evil is strictly historical. This is in contrast to typical mythological accounts of the time. For example, according to the Babylonian cosmogony (*Enuma Elish*), evil antedates the creation of the world. The primordial gods plan evil and experience anger, spite, loathing, and the like, even before Marduk, the god of Babylon, was created. Indeed, part of Marduk's greatness lay in the fact that he conquered evil and brought order in heaven. After he had subdued the primordial rebellion and secured order, he executed the god who had planned the rebellion and created human beings from his blood. These servile human creatures were created to do the onerous manual labor the gods did not want to do. Hence, according to this account, humankind was enmeshed in the web of evil, treachery, and violence from the moment of creation.

By way of contrast, we have two stories in the Bible—the story of creation followed by the story of the human creatures' deviation from God's intention for them. Creation is an act of bringing light and order to the chaotic emptiness. Accordingly, there is an incidental reference to a precreation chaos and watery darkness which the Creator Spirit overcame by his word of command.[33] There is no violent struggle; only the word of authority. And the results of the Creator's efforts, including his human creatures, are pronounced "very good." The Bible does not explain the presence of evil in the creation story itself. The account of sin's entrance into the experience of the human family is left for a second story.

Evil is not coincidental with creaturehood. It is a perversion of authentic human existence.[34] Sin is not equated with creaturely limitation or with the reflexes and desires of the physical body. It is not the kind of desire one can overcome by ascetic disciplines, such as yogic breath control, fasting, and muscular contortions. It is not an ignorance from which more knowledge will free us. In short, it is not a creaturely flaw or immaturity that evolutionary development and education will eventually overcome.

Sin is an existential and relational concept, not an essential and ontic one. It is not inherent in our being, either as a result of creation or as the inherited consequence of the original sin. Humans were not, as in the Babylonian myth, created as treacherous, servile animals to serve the whims of the gods. Neither were they turned into such savage creatures by eating a magic apple. The biblical phrase "in the image of God" is probably the closest approximation to an ontological description of human beings. There is no suggestion that this image was destroyed and replaced with an evil image—"the very image of the devil,"as one post-Reformation Lutheran theologian held. Instead, in sinful humanity the image is misapprehended, misrepresented, and misused in idolatrous, self-serving ways. Therein lies the evil (Rom. 1:20b-23).[35]

If sin is existential and relational, then its origin must be sought in the historical and psychological context where humans are related to God. We cannot appeal to a supernatural metaphysical agent or to an ontological flaw as its cause. The possibility of sin grows out of human freedom in the context of covenant responsibility. According to the Genesis story, the original covenant was to care for the garden as God's delegated custodians. And the serpent was one of the creatures of the garden. Although the serpent was later associated with the devil, there is no suggestion in the story itself of intrusion by a supernatural agent. The temptation, which we will examine more closely, arises in and comes out of the historical situation itself. Insofar as there is freedom to respond to God's covenant command, the rejection of that command—sin—is also possible. Sin always lies at the threshold of human existence (Gen. 4:7).

Satan and the Origin of Sin

The biblical writers do not speculate further about the origin of sin. In this respect James 1:13-15 is typical. When Satan is brought into the picture as the adversary of God, he too is represented as a creature who misused his freedom, not as a primordial anti-god.[36]

Whether Satan is an individual evil spirit or the personification of the power of evil manifest in superhuman guise ("the ruler of the power of the air") is not always clear. Indeed, Paul himself used the terms in different ways (cf. 1 Cor. 8:4-7; 10:19-20). We see something of the same phenomenon in the tendency to personalize sin as a slave master while treating it as a human behavior and characteristic.

How we decide this question makes little practical difference for our understanding of the source and nature of evil. In either case, several things need to be kept clearly in view. First, evil in the biblical view is not a black magic performed by a master shaman completely outside human will. We are not protected against it by the charms of white magic, such as incantations or the sign of the cross. The New Testament does mention fear of evil spirits or demons causing all kinds of mishaps, illness, and unpleasant things current at the time. However, it is remarkably free from the fascination with imps and spirits that characterizes later Christian piety.

Second, Satan as the ultimate personification of evil is not beyond the control of God, as shown in the Lord's Prayer: "Rescue us from the evil one" (Matt. 6:13). He is not the eternal enemy, as in fully developed dualistic systems. Hence, he is not the ultimate source of evil. He too is a creature gone wrong, the personification of creation gone wrong through the selfish misappropriation of knowledge and power. As such he is the instrument of temptation (Matt. 4:3; 1 Thess. 3:5) and the vindictive accuser of those who yield to temptation (Rev. 12:10).

Third, he has no power over humans except that which they themselves give him. In making this point we should note, however, that Satan's power is not simply the power of an individual tempter. He has all the force of institutionalized evil and its power of death. Christ's resurrection wrested this power from the adversary and gives us the power to live beyond the fear of death and ultimately beyond the power of death. Paul assures us that no power on earth or in heaven can separate us from God's love (Rom. 8:37-39).

When the law is related to sin, it is not as a cause of sin. The law enlightens. Such enlightenment "increases the sinfulness of sin." But Paul is careful to say that sin and death reigned over humanity before the law was given (Rom. 5:13-14; 1 Cor. 15:22). The source of sin lies at the beginning of the human race "in Adam." The mystery of the human heart holds the secret of sin's origin.

The Primal Temptation

Selfish desire is the matrix of temptation and spawns sin (James 1:14). An analysis of the source and the inner disposition of temptation can help us to understand the nature of human sinfulness. Was the primal temptation a sexual enticement? Was it an illicit curiosity for esoteric knowledge? Was it a subconscious resentment gradually breaking into consciousness? Or was it greed, the will to power, or some other urge that gave birth to sin?

The biblical accounts of primal temptation are given in the stories of Adam and Eve and of Jesus' temptation in the wilderness (Gen. 3 and Matt. 3). While there is no contrived parallelism in these stories, they do sound the same theme. Jesus, the second Adam, also faces the original temptation of the typical person. In both cases a "child of God" is wrestling with self-identity and destiny as a creature "in God's image" and under his covenant.

In both accounts the human creatures are tempted to distrust God's wisdom and love. In both cases they are tempted to exceed the limits of creaturely dependence and demonstrate their status as God's children through the exercise of divine prerogatives. Specifically, Jesus is tempted to disregard his dependence upon God's word and world by turning stones into bread. He is tempted to abuse the limits of love by the violent political control of others. And to put God to trial in a self-gratifying, gratuitous public display of piety at the temple (Luke 4:1-12). In each case Jesus is tempted to overstep the boundaries of the original covenant in an act of self-assertion and independence. These temptations are amplified in the Genesis story.[37]

The setting of the story is the garden of Eden, the fruitful earth which was created with a wealth of resources to sustain human life. The immediate occasion of the temptation is the cryptic command not to eat the fruit of one tree, and a warning that disobedience will mean death. The agent of temptation is the serpent, who calls special attention to the prohibition and points out that God has offered no rationale for it. The serpent further suggests that this seemingly arbitrary prohibition stems from God's jealousy. He does not want them to have the "knowledge of good and evil." (One has only to read a few of the creation myths of the nations around Israel to understand why such a suggestion might have a powerful effect!) The subject of the temptation is Eve and Adam, humankind at its source.

Eve in this case does not represent the female tempting the male sexually or in weakness deluding him, as medieval theologians suggested.[38] Instead, she represents that element within each of us which is intuitively and sympathetically in touch with the productive fertility of nature. As Paul Ricoeur puts it, "Every woman and every man are Adam; every man and every woman are Eve; every woman sins 'in' Adam; every man is seduced 'in' Eve."[39] It is good to remember that we are reading the account after the birth of the Christ and to note that it was also the "woman" who gave birth to the Savior and presented him to man. In any case we are clearly dealing here with humankind as covenant creatures "in the image of God."

The serpent was an animal associated with magic and taboo. It had power for both good and evil. It is the symbol for fertility and healing as well as for craft and deceit. The serpent was thought to be especially wise and was worshiped by many of the nations around Israel. Here it comes as one of the familiar "wild animals" (3:1) that was respected and feared for its esoteric powers. It is in itself the symbol of the mysterious powers and intelligence of nature which humankind has sought to manipulate and control through magic and science.

What is at stake in the story itself is the nature of the command. Is it the taboo of a jealous god, or a covenant command made for the good of humanity? The association of the serpent with the temptation strongly suggests that it is a temptation to take the command as an animistic taboo. If it is such a taboo, then a Promethean revolt would be the mark of human achievement. If it is a loving, rational command that marks out the proper creaturely limits—"a covenant of life and well-being" (Mal. 2:5)—then obedience to the prohibition and a daily walk with God is the way to achieve knowledge of life's goods and evils.

The tree, as the text says, is a symbol of the "knowledge of good and evil." The good and evil in this case are not restricted to moral awareness. The tree does not bear magic apples which will give moral insight if eaten. The goods and evils are those experienced in the lives of human beings. So we may paraphrase, "the tree of the knowledge of how to achieve the good and avoid the evils of life."

It is important to note there is no indication from the Creator that the knowledge of good and evil is possible only through eating the fruit. There is only the prohibition not to eat because eating will cause death. The sin is in the "taking and eating"—appropriating the fruit of the tree for one's own selfish enjoyment and advantage. Nor is it suggested that humankind should not acquire the knowledge of good and evil. Indeed, the command to "subdue the earth" implies the need of such knowledge. It is the tempter who implied that the only way to realize the full potential of the image was to grasp for the knowledge which would enable them to control their own destiny. And he hinted that it was precisely that power that was being denied them. Then he suggested that the only way to achieve the image was by disobeying the command and assuming the prerogatives which belong to God alone.

The tree with the prohibition represents the creaturely limits for humankind. The prohibition defines those limits. Transgression of creaturely limits means death. The question is not whether humanity should grow in moral and scientific knowledge but rather: How should they acquire and use such knowledge? Autonomously, for selfish gratification? Or in fellowship with God, for his broader purposes? The man and the woman must choose between keeping the command not to eat, and experiencing the pain, frustration, and death that follow disobedience and overstepping the limits. Everything depended upon trusting God and living within the boundaries of his covenant. We see the real nature of the test in another garden and under another tree where Jesus prayed, "Yet not what I want but what you want."

The story of the original temptation, then, underscores the personalistic nature of sin and evil. The source and nature of temptation is not some mythical, magical power or metaphysical contamination to be exorcised through cultic magic. While the occasion and agent of temptation are from outside the human psyche, nevertheless the source of vulnerability and the motivation are in the human heart. "One is tempted by one's own desire, being lured and enticed by it," wrote James (1:14). Creaturely limitation is in no sense evil. Nevertheless, it triggers the existential anxiety and provides the setting for temptation.

The lure of evil is in its deceptive promise to give us peace and freedom through our own aggressive self-serving efforts. We can see, for example, the economic oppression perpetrated in the name of free trade and the sacred right of private property. We see the political torture engaged in by upright human beings fighting "terrorism" with terror. We see the domination of a demonic military complex in the name of peace and freedom with justice. On the individual level, we justify the pollution, waste, and prostitution of personal relationships to satisfy our insatiable desire and bring human fulfillment.

The power of evil is the power of its devotees—those who through weakness and self-deception accept its rationalizations. Whether evil poses in the guise of an ideology, a fanatical political leader, a destructive or lascivious urge, or a superhuman power, its power resides in the response and support of those who yield to its blandishments.

Finally, the primal temptation is the temptation to assert self above God—to become our own god. The test is whether we will respect the limits implied in our creaturely interdependence. This interdependence is manifested in three types of relationships: to nature, to other persons, and to God. Will we respect the limits implied in our ecological relation to nature? Will we respect our responsibility under God for the cultivation and enhancement of the natural order? Will we respect the limits of love in our interdependence in human community? And

will we confess our total dependence upon God for life and sustenance? We demonstrate human sinfulness in our unwillingness to
acknowledge God's authority and in our selfish and irresponsible disregard for our ecological environment and our fellow creatures, both animal and human.

Grace and Human Potential

We must not end our discussion of humanity with a description of
human failure and sinfulness. The final word about humanity has been
spoken in Christ, not Adam. That word is that the potential for full realization of the image of God still remains. Potential failed is not potential
obliterated. However, when failure to achieve one's potential flows
from disobedient and even rebellious self-assertion, it creates a distinct
problem and disability. Such failure (sin) results in shame, self-
negation, self-isolation, resentment, projection of blame, and finally,
exclusion and alienation.[40] All these traits are skillfully represented in
the story of the "original sin" (Gen. 3–4).

The image of God, as we have seen, involves us in personal and social
relationship. Such relationship must be restored before our human potential can be reached. Self-fulfillment is a social accomplishment, not
merely an individual achievement. Therefore, we cannot attain it by
stoic self-assertion or by stumbling bravely ahead in the face of culpa-
ble failure. The offending person must receive (and give) acceptance
in renewed relationship through forgiveness before he or she can attain the promised image. This is what is meant by the Christian assertion that the fulfillment of human destiny can be achieved only by
grace as a gift of God, not through human effort and manipulation. Jesus Christ is God's gracious offer of renewed relationship. And this
offer is the key to humanity's destiny as children of God.

CHAPTER 5

The Holy Spirit as the Spirit of Christ

Introduction

The decisive new understanding of the Spirit of God in the New Testament is linked closely to the new disclosure that came in and through Christ. However, the older Hebrew understanding of God's Spirit is presupposed and influences the Christian concepts. As Jesus' messiahship can be understood only in light of Hebrew history, so also the Christian concept of the Holy Spirit must be understood in the context of the Hebrew Bible. Therefore, we begin with contextual concepts and definitions and follow with a discussion of the Holy Spirit as the Spirit of Christ. What are the experiential and theological implications of this change?

Before the time of the historical Jesus, the Spirit was known simply as the "Spirit of God" or the "Spirit of the Lord" (*Yahweh*). After the resurrection, when Jesus was recognized as *Lord* of the church, it was an easy transition to substitute *Christ* for *Lord* in the title *Spirit of the Lord*. As we shall see, the two descriptive titles were used side by side in a most casual way without any hint of a problem.

When we discuss the Spirit as though it were one part of the Godhead, we must keep in mind that we are speaking of the way in which God has made himself present and known to us. While our time and space metaphors point to transcendent reality, we dare not assume that our finite perceptions can capture fully the mystery of the Eternal. We are not analyzing the ontological nature of God. We must of necessity limit ourselves to a far more humble task than that! We are speaking of the way in which God, the eternal Spirit, has manifested himself historically in this postresurrection era signalled at Pentecost.

When we say God reveals himself as Father, Son, and Spirit, we are actually speaking of *our perception or experience of God's presence*. We are aware of him as creative source and sustainer (Parent-Creator). We have come to know him as the Savior in the historical Jesus Christ (the Son sent from the Father). And since the resurrection of Jesus, we have continued to experience him as the divine presence and power of the living Christ. We refer to this divine presence and power as the Holy Spirit.

We experience God as Spirit in a way that does not cancel out or supersede his self-revelation as Father and Son, but enhances it, instead. Accordingly, we speak of the Spirit both as "the Spirit of God, the Father," and "the Spirit of Christ, the Son." In a clause added to ancient Western creeds, the Spirit is said to proceed not only from the Father but also from the Son.

The Personification of the Spirit

When we speak of the Spirit of God, we are speaking of God as he is actively and creatively present with us.[1] As Berkhof put it, "The Spirit is the name for God himself in his activity among us."[2] But in the history of the church, the matter is not so simple as this. The definition of the Spirit of God and his role has been a major cause of controversy and schism in the church. This may be due in part to the many different ways Scripture itself refers to the Spirit.

Grammatically, there are two ways of relating the word *spirit* to God. We may speak of "God *as* Spirit," and of "the Spirit *of* God." The first phrase indicates that God's mode of being is spirit, not material or physical existence, as we noted in chapter 3. In effect it says the same as the sentence, "God is spirit" (John 4:24; cf. 2 Cor. 3:17-18). The phrase *Spirit of God*, however, suggests that *Holy Spirit* is not simply synonymous with *God*, but represents a particular aspect of God's self-disclosure to us. With this name, the Holy Spirit is distinguished from the Father and the Son.

We have spoken of God as Spirit ("the spirituality of God") to establish the unity of God's being as one universal spiritual presence. This is especially important where the cultural assumptions are basically polytheistic. Where there are many gods and lords, we must first point out that the Spirit is none other than God himself in his completeness. The Spirit is not one individual deity in a triad of deities—a concept called tritheism. Such a tritheistic concept merely limits polytheism to three rather than 3,000 or 33,000,000 deities, as in the Hindu pantheon. Neither is the Spirit one part of God. God does not have parts. Indeed, *parts* is a descriptive category that belongs to the physical realm. We have already noted that God is Spirit.

Already in the biblical literature itself one notices some tendency toward the personification of the Spirit as a special manifestation of God's presence. But in the Old Testament the spirit of Yahweh—like his voice, mouth, and wisdom—identifies an activity or effect of God's presence, rather than a personal aspect of God's being.[3]

When the effects of God's presence are indicated, the term *spirit of God* may merely indicate the special skill, wisdom, or character which God has given. In these cases—and there are many of them—the *spirit* of God equals *godly* wisdom, character, or power as it is observed in the life of the individual. Where it indicates God himself, *spirit* points more specifically to God's presence as a holy, purifying presence (Ps. 51:10-12), or as a special enabling presence and power.

New Testament Conceptions

The New Testament continues to use the terms *Spirit of God* and *Spirit of the Lord*. To them it adds *Spirit of Jesus* (Acts 16:6-7), *Spirit of Jesus Christ* (Phil. 1:19), or simply *Spirit of Christ* (1 Pet. 1:11). However, *the Holy Spirit* or *the Spirit* are more indicative of the developing personification that eventually led to the idea of the Trinity.

Sometimes in the Old Testament the Spirit of God is characterized by the adjective *holy* in the same manner as God himself is said to be holy (Ps. 51:11). But in the designation *Holy Spirit*, the word *holy* is no longer merely an adjective. It has become part of the name. The Holy Spirit appears to be a fully personal divine center of activity, and is spoken of in liturgical formulas as one of the Godhead along with the Father and the Son (Matt. 28:19-20; 2 Cor. 13:14). This Holy Spirit is "sent" (1 Pet. 1:12; John 14:26), "teaches" (1 Cor. 2:13), and "testifies" (John 15:26; Heb. 10:15). All of these imply a fully personal agency.[4]

In the New Testament itself the language about the Spirit continues to be experiential and functional rather than philosophical and analytical. The Spirit is identified with God and Christ's presence and activity. He is God (or Christ) at work in and through the new messianic community and the world at large, furthering the mission of Christ. On the one hand, Spirit is identified with the personal God. On the other, it is always God in a special activity or function. The Spirit is characteristically associated with God's influence, power, wisdom, and holiness as the community experiences them in prophecy, witness, healing, giving assurance of God's parental presence, and producing unity.

The Spirit of God or of Christ (Rom. 8:9) is designated by his role of *Paraclete* (John 14:16, 26). He is the "Spirit of our God" (1 Cor. 6:11), with us to counsel, encourage, and strengthen. Without attempting a complete list of the distinguishing designations, the more familiar ones describe the Spirit's character and functions. The "Spirit of the Lord" is the "spirit of wisdom and understanding, the spirit of counsel and might, the spirit of knowledge and the fear of the Lord" (Isa. 11:2). Peter refers to this Spirit as a "spirit of glory" that rests upon martyr-disciples (1 Pet. 4:14). John's most distinctive characterization is "Spirit of truth" (14:17; 15:26; 16:13). Paul's is "spirit [or Spirit] of adoption" (Rom. 8:15-16).

Beside these there are the designations "spirit of holiness" (Rom. 1:4), "Spirit of life in Christ Jesus" (Rom. 8:2; cf. Rev. 11:11), "spirit [or Spirit] of faith" (2 Cor. 4:13), "of promise" (Eph. 1:13), "of grace" (Heb. 10:29). We are reminded that "God did not give us a spirit of cowardice, but rather a spirit of power and of love and of self-discipline" (2 Tim. 1:7).

In each of the above cases, we must note again that the designations are of such a nature that the word *spirit* may and likely does indicate both God's effective presence and the attitude or spirit which it effects in us. So closely are these two dimensions of spirit related that the New Testament texts often have both meanings at the same time. To be precise, we should probably translate *pneuma* with "Spirit/spirit." For example, Paul wrote, "Anyone who does not have the Spirit[/spirit] of Christ does not belong to him" (Rom. 8:9). And John says our relationship to God is assured because "he has given us of his Spirit[/spirit]" (1 John 4:13).

We therefore come again to the recognition that when we speak of the Holy Spirit of God, we are speaking of God's enlivening, purifying, encouraging presence in and through the lives of Christ's followers. And while we should avoid language that suggests pantheistic identity of God's Spirit and the human spirit, we must also recognize the intentional blurring of functional lines in the biblical language.

Trinitarian Developments

In the confessional language of the church, the threefold appellation became the formula for referring to God. He is the thrice Holy One of the prophets (Isa. 6:3) or "the Father . . . Son and . . . Holy Spirit" of the baptismal formula (Matt. 28:19) and the doxology (2 Cor. 13:13). From the baptismal formula the threefold designation became the framework for the Apostles' Creed. In its ultimate formulation, the distinction developed into a full doctrine of the Trinity in which the Son was said to be "born" of the Father, and the Spirit to "proceed from" the Father from all eternity.

To explain the Spirit's individual relation to Deity, the theologians followed the same general philosophical formulae and rationale they had used to relate Jesus to God. According to this formula the Spirit was of one substance with the Father and the Son, but was also a distinct *persona* in the Deity.

To mark the distinction between the Spirit and the Son, the theologians spoke of Jesus as being "born" of the Father, whereas the Spirit "proceeded from" the Father. They pointed out that if the language of generation were used of the Spirit as well as of Jesus, it would imply that they were brothers! In this manner trinitarian language developed to maintain both the Spirit's full identity with God, while recognizing the distinctive role attributed to the Spirit in the Bible. Indeed, Athanasius argued that because the work of the Spirit is a fully divine work, he must be identical to God in divine being.

The church councils insisted on the full deity of the Spirit in opposition to some teachers who said the Spirit is an angelic being or a created personification like the Platonic Logos, Wisdom, or the Law of God.[5] By contrast, the trinitarian formula emphasized the fully personal and divine identity of the Holy Spirit.

How the Spirit's individuation should be conceptualized was hotly debated between the Eastern and Western churches. By the fifth century—after the time of Augustine—the language of *one substance and three personae* generally became standardized. *Persona* was a technical Latin term which indicated more than the Greek *prosōpon* (face), but not as much as *hupostasis* (personification). Thus the church attempted to give individual identity to the Spirit while avoiding tritheism.

In Western society today, however, this way of identifying the Spirit as one of the "persons" of the Trinity has become problematic theologically because a person is a separate individual with distinct personality. Hence, to speak of the Spirit as "a person" seems to indicate he is a separate center of consciousness in a social personality of God. The so-called social theory of the Trinity actually encourages this concept. But this is more than what the language of the Bible itself indicates. And it is certainly more than human reason can affirm with any certainty.[6] The

Greek Fathers attempted to analyze and give substantial definition to what the Bible does not separate.

The Spirit as Personal Power

Perhaps we should look more carefully at the implications of the fact that Scripture does not analyze and individualize the "persons" of the Godhead. Certainly this fact leaves us the freedom to adapt the traditional language of orthodoxy in those cultures which are not dominated by the Greek rationalist tradition. What we want to affirm is the full divinity of the Spirit's presence and work among us (Phil. 2:13; Rom. 8:9-11; 1 Cor. 6:19) without adopting all the philosophical shibboleths of the Greek tradition.

Nor is this a purely theoretical issue. Improper concepts of the Spirit's separate being and work have led to unwarranted distinctions in the Christian's experience of God and have become the cause of endless disunity in the church. What was intended simply as an analytical description of a unified experience of God's gracious reconciling presence, gets divided into a series of religious and emotional experiences attributed to the separate "persons" of the Trinity.

In this regard it is important to note again that according to the technical meaning of Trinity, God does not have three parts or three distinct centers of personality. The Spirit is not one part or personality in this tripersonal God. Consequently, one should not parcel out the different aspects of the Christian's experience of God's salvation between the different members of the Trinity! On the contrary, the Spirit should be fully identified with God himself as he is present and active among us in Christ.

Accordingly, modern theologians have suggested a number of formulas to describe the relationship. George S. Hendry has suggested "dynamic identification" of Christ's presence and the Spirit.[7] C. A. Anderson Scott spoke of a "practical equating" or of "equivalence," but not "identity."[8] What we want to say is that the Spirit's character, power, and work are God's power, character, and work as manifested in Jesus Christ. The Spirit of God at work among us is the Spirit of Christ. And his work in us is Christ's work.

This emphasis on the personal character of the Holy Spirit raises a further important consideration. Personal presence and power are expressed in and through persons. That is, the Spirit's work is not primarily in the powers of nature or in quasi-personal effects on the human mind. The emotional frenzy of the inspired seers of early Israel is a distinctly *Old* Testament effect of the Spirit's presence (1 Sam. 19:20-24).

While the Spirit is by no means equated with the human spirit, the Spirit accomplishes his most characteristic work in and through humans who are open to his influence. And the greatest work or fruit of the Spirit is love (1 Cor. 13:13; Gal. 5:22-23).

Here the paradigm is the incarnation itself. The incarnation was by the influence and power of the Spirit. By that same power Jesus was declared to be the Son of God (Rom. 1:4). So also the work of Jesus was the work of the Spirit of God. This was true to such a degree that to attribute Jesus' work to Satan was to blaspheme the Spirit (Mark 3:28-29). And this same Spirit/spirit continues to work in and through the human spirit.[9]

Jesus and the Spirit

In the New Testament the Spirit comes to be identified directly with the work of Jesus Christ to such an extent that the postresurrection/ascension spiritual presence of Jesus with his community is virtually equated with the Holy Spirit. The work of the Holy Spirit is the work of Christ. His authority is the authority of Christ. His power and character are those of Christ.

From the time of the New Testament church, there has been a tendency to divorce the Spirit and his work from Christ and his mission. Already at Corinth some understood the new religion to be a "spiritual" religion introduced by the Jewish Messiah. Invariably, such spirituality led to ecstatic and mystical excesses in which the true spirit and concern of the historical Christ were overlooked. At the opposite pole, rationalistic religion has tended to equate the Spirit with universal reason and associate it with human rationality. The Spirit's character and role in history were defined accordingly.

In the New Testament, however, the Christian understanding of the Holy Spirit is uniquely tied to the Messiah and his universal mission in a relation one might call a dynamic equivalence.

In this section we will examine the nature and significance of this relation for the life of the church. We want also to try to understand how this came about historically. How did the work of the Spirit and that of Jesus Christ come to be virtually equated?

From Israel to Church

Israel knew God's Spirit as God's comforting, enabling, and self-disclosing presence with his people. He revealed himself primarily through the visions and words of the prophets. In time prophecy came to be accepted as the main manifestation of the Spirit in Israel's life.

God communicated directly with his people through the prophets.

Prophecy in this case does not refer simply to individual predictions or oracles, but to the recognized word of God to the nation, beginning with the words spoken through Moses. The lines of prophetic leadership continued through the judges, of whom the prophet Samuel was the last. Then prophecy increasingly became a distinct office or function in the community.

The prophets spoke to the people in God's name about national issues. They were an integral part of the theocratic authority in Israel. Their word was primarily a spoken word given in and to the immediate situation. However, some of the prophetic utterances were preserved in written form. These became the authoritative word of the Spirit for future generations when living prophecies were no longer part of the theocratic pattern.

Prophecy as a national function died out following the return of the Jews from the Babylonian exile. Ezra, the *scribe*, began the process of gathering the writings of former prophets. These came to be recognized as the authoritative guide for God's people, the Jews. These writings were their *Bible*. Scribes, lawyers, and rabbis became the important authorities who interpreted and applied the word of God written in an earlier age when the Spirit of prophecy had been active.

These rabbis and scribes taught that the Spirit of God still enabled men like Judas Maccabaeus to bring military victory to Israel so the law of Moses could be obeyed. They also taught that God gave his Spirit to individuals who were especially pious as a reward for their faithfulness to the Law.[10] But they believed God had withdrawn the Spirit of prophecy as a public charismatic office. They held that the will of God was now known through the law of Moses, not through prophetic visions and words given directly by the Spirit.

Further, it was taught that the Spirit would not return to Israel until the nation had proved itself worthy of the Messiah. Although the picture of the Messiah and of the messianic age was not precisely and clearly drawn, the association of the Spirit's return to Israel with Messiah's coming was clear. Before that time the prophet Elijah would appear (Mal. 4:5), and then with the Messiah the prophecies of Joel 2:28-29 and Jeremiah 31:31-34 would be fulfilled. The Spirit of the Lord would rest on the Messiah and upon all God's people as the prophets had predicted.

It is against this historical background that we can begin to see the significance of the New Testament's witness to Jesus as the Messiah and the bearer of the Spirit. All the Gospels, and especially Luke, present the life and work of Christ as the revival of the Spirit's presence with God's people. They picture this revival as beginning with the ministry of Jesus among his Jewish people and continuing through the church to become a universal reality.

The Spirit in the Life and Ministry of Jesus

Surprisingly, there is little direct reference to the Spirit at work in the ministry of Jesus. In Luke there is virtually no mention of the Spirit in Jesus' ministry after chapter 4:18.[11] This also is true of the other synoptic Gospels, although Matthew says Jesus cast out demons "by the Spirit of God" (12:28). John's Gospel, while different in its approach, makes the same kind of distinction between the Spirit in the ministry of Jesus and that of his followers after the resurrection. He even notes explicitly that the Spirit had not yet been given to the disciples during the earthly ministry of Jesus (7:39; cf. Luke 11:13).

The focus of the synoptic Gospels remains upon Jesus himself. This singular focus is epitomized in the account of the transfiguration of Jesus (Mark 9:2-9 and parallels) when the voice from heaven says, "This is my Son, the Beloved; listen to him!" The power and authority in Jesus' ministry are attributed to himself as the Christ, albeit anointed by the Spirit. Jesus himself gave the disciples authority to cast out demons as an extension of his ministry (Matt. 10:1), and so thereby they also work in the Spirit's power while doing the deeds of the Messiah (10:20; 12:28). They healed and preached the kingdom "in Jesus' name" (Mark 9:38). It is Jesus, "the Son," who reveals the Father, while in Paul's letters the Spirit is assigned this role. Jesus promises that he himself will be in the midst of his disciples as they gather in his name (Matt. 18:20).

Except for the scene just after Jesus' baptism (see below), there are only a few clues in the Gospels that Jesus' relationship to God as his Father is mediated by the Spirit. Compare this with Paul's accent on the Spirit assuring us that we are in God's family (Rom. 8:15-17; Gal. 4:6). When John emphasizes God's intimate presence in and with Jesus, he calls such presence "the Father," rather than naming the Spirit. The Father, not the Spirit, is said to be the source of Jesus' authority. It is the Father who draws men and women to himself (John 6:37, 44). There is little reference to the Spirit as the divine agent in Jesus' ministry, such as we find in the Acts and Epistles.

This sparsity of references to the Spirit is significant. The Gospels were written in the context of the church's life long after the resurrection and Pentecost experiences, when the experience of the Holy Spirit's activity was well-known and attested. We may rightly conclude that this is not a mere difference in the theological perception and understanding between the writers of the Synoptics and Paul, as some have suggested. The negative half of the picture serves to highlight the distinctive new aspect of the Gospels' witness to Jesus as the bearer and dispenser of the Spirit.[12] In the Gospels the relation of Jesus and the Spirit of God is represented as qualitatively different from that of a prophet inspired and empowered by the Spirit.

Luke depicts this new relationship between Jesus and the Spirit by beginning his account with the revival of the Spirit's activity in the births of both John the Baptist and Jesus. While the Spirit's activity is prominent in both births, it is soon evident that there is a significant contrast in the relation of the Holy Spirit to John, the *prophet*, and Jesus, the *Messiah*. (Compare 1:14, 35, 41, 67; 2:25f.) His description of the Spirit's relation to John follows traditional patterns of thought. John is filled with the Spirit while still in the womb. However, with Jesus, the Spirit is the special divine creative influence in his conception and birth. By virtue of this special generative relationship, he is called "Son of God" (messianic title).

The contrast continues when Luke tells us the crowds were considering whether the Baptist was the Messiah. John demurred, saying that Jesus is greater than he and will "baptize . . . with the Holy Spirit" (3:13-16).

Luke makes the baptism the occasion for the public presentation of Jesus as the messianic Son, the "Servant," who has God's full approval.[13] The announcement is made by the descent of the Holy Spirit "in bodily form, like a dove," and by the voice from heaven. Then this Son, "full of the Holy Spirit," (4:1) was led into the wilderness, where he resisted satanic temptation. He then returned "with the power of the Spirit" to begin his ministry (4:14). As a programmatic climax, he read the biblical text of Isaiah 61:1-2, "The Spirit of the Lord is upon me," in the synagogue of Nazareth and announced that this word was fulfilled in himself (4:18ff.).

After this introduction, Luke is strangely quiet about the Spirit's influence in Jesus' ministry. Without further statement Jesus' power and authority are assumed to be that of God and of the Spirit. The Spirit is not a divine prophetic influence coming on occasion to empower him for ministry. Instead, the Spirit is the immediate, abiding, identifying presence of God himself making Jesus the messianic Son and giving power to overthrow Satan and demons (4:1-13; 10:17-22; 11:14-22).

The other Gospels also affirm this special relationship between Jesus and the Holy Spirit. Matthew's birth account concurs that the Spirit was the divine agent active in Jesus' conception and birth (1:18-21). All accounts, including John's, associate his baptism with a special anointing of the Spirit by which he is designated messianic Son (Matt. 3:13-17, Mark 1:10). Although Mark does not explicitly attribute Jesus' power and identity to the Spirit, his account surely suggests that the authority and power of this "Holy One of God" were qualitatively different from that of all others (1:21-27). Both Mark and Matthew call the accusations that Jesus is a diabolic sorcerer a "blasphemy against the Holy Spirit" (Mark 3:28-30; Matt. 12:24-31). Finally, all agree that this one upon whom the Spirit came and "remained" is the one who gives the Holy Spirit "without measure" to his followers and "baptizes" them with the Holy Spirit (Matt. 3:11 and parallels; John 1:32-33; 3:34; 15:26; 20:22).[14] *The Spirit of God, both in identity and function, is the Spirit of the Messiah.*

The Spirit as the Presence of the Risen Christ

The disciples had fully expected that Jesus' death would mean the end of the movement. His presence as an effective leader was removed from them. The Spirit, so evident in his life and ministry, had stirred new life and hope in them. But now the Spirit was gone with him. Nothing could be the same again. His death meant disruption, discontinuity, and cessation of the Spirit's activity. But they soon discovered that although they could not see and talk with Jesus as a historical human being, he had not left them "orphans" (John 14:18). His real and powerful presence was with them, and his mission would continue. Resurrection meant transformation and continuity.

Written in the 1940s, Donald Baillie's description of the disciples' surprising discovery still remains unrivaled for clarity and beauty.

> But what happened through Him did not come to an end when "the days of His flesh" ended, though His disciples thought it would and were appalled at the prospect of His being taken from them. Very soon afterwards they made two great discoveries. They discovered, first, that the divine Presence of which they had become aware while their Master was with them in the flesh had come back to them and was going to continue, in a far deeper and more marvelous way, in a way that was independent of His actual presence in the flesh, though not independent of His having lived on earth in the flesh. It was the same, and yet different, for it was as though their Master had now drawn them into something of that union with God which had been His secret, and now they know God for themselves and he has taken possession of them. And their second discovery was that this experience, which depended entirely on Jesus, need not be confined to those who had known Jesus in the flesh. It could come to any-

body anywhere through the story of Jesus and their witness to its meaning.[15]

This "divine Presence" of which Baillie speaks is none other than the Holy Spirit, the Spirit of Christ. But the disciples' understanding of the meaning of this new development advanced slowly.

The "Coming" of the Spirit

The report of developments up to the Pentecost experience is perhaps the most graphic account of the disciples' expanding awareness. First, they experienced Jesus as the risen Lord who had now been given ultimate authority (Matt. 28:19; Acts 1:8-11). This is the theological meaning of the ascension and enthronement of Jesus at God's right hand.

But the recognition of Jesus' lordship did not immediately bring with it the clarity and resolve needed to take the next steps. There was a period of "waiting"—a period of study and prayer without knowing what would happen next (Acts 1:12-26). Would Jesus return shortly as "Son of Man"—the heavenly warrior—on the clouds of heaven? The message of the "men in white robes" (Moses and Elijah?) implied this (1:10-11). And certainly the promise that they would receive "power" when the Holy Spirit was poured out also suggested a return of the heavenly Messiah in power as well as their own anointing to be his emissaries. Only later would they know the true meaning of this power. The meaning of the promised baptism (Luke 24:49) with the Spirit was still unclear.

What happened next began to change the picture. During the Jewish festival of Pentecost, while they were together in the temple precincts, they experienced an explosive, overwhelming group ecstasy and urge to witness. They were seized by the power of God and emboldened to announce publicly that Jesus of Nazareth was the true Messiah. As a result the new messianic movement was inaugurated. Those who joined experienced the promised blessing of the Spirit of God.

The apostles recognized this as the awaited "baptism of the Spirit" which Jesus had promised (Acts 1:5). Jesus himself in his new role as "Lord" had taken the next step in the formation of the new Israel. Even at this point, however, the freshly formed movement did not clearly understand the identity and role of the Spirit. They still awaited the return of Jesus to continue and fulfill the mission which the earthly Jesus had begun.

In the apostolic churches there were two ways to describe the relation of the risen Christ to the Spirit. The one tradition spoke of a baptism with the Spirit by Jesus. The other described it as Jesus breathing his Spirit upon the disciples following the resurrection. The first, namely baptism, provides the imagery and language for the Lucan account of Pentecost and what followed. According to this tradition, the ascended Jesus himself sends the promised Spirit or baptizes the new converts with the Spirit, thereby attesting that they are members of the messianic community.[16]

This baptism is especially associated with the transmission of power and boldness for witness. The Spirit is the authority and convincing power vitalizing the apostles' message. While one may infer that the healings and exorcisms were also done in the power of the Spirit, Luke consistently associates them with the name or authority of Jesus. They are accomplished by "faith in his name." The Holy Spirit's power is most explicitly associated with prophecy, ecstatic speech, and convincing words of witness.

As the narrative of Acts unfolds, the mission of the new movement is defined and the Holy Spirit takes an authoritative role to direct the mission (Acts 13:2, 4). However, in Luke's writings there is no clear indication of just how the Spirit came to be accepted as the authority of Christ himself directing the mission. The one clue is the early equation of the risen Christ with the "Lord" (Yahweh) of Israel. The Spirit in Israel was known as the "Spirit of the Lord." When the resurrected Jesus was recognized as Lord, it became most natural to associate the Spirit with him—the Spirit of the Lord Jesus.

Paul also recognizes this interrelationship of the lordship of Christ and the authority of the Spirit in the church. The Lord has given his Spirit to the new community of followers. The Spirit in turn prompts faith and loyalty to his lordship (1 Cor. 12:3). Paul can even say, "The Lord is the Spirit, and where the Spirit of the Lord is, there is freedom" (2 Cor. 3:17-18; cf. Gal. 5:1). Thus he points to their functional identity in the life of the church.

The second tradition, namely, the Spirit as the "breath" of the risen Lord himself, appears in the Johannine writings. It provides imagery that more immediately identifies the presence and authority of Christ with the Spirit in the church. According to John, the resurrected Jesus breathed on his disciples and said, "Receive the Holy Spirit" (20:22). Hence, the Spirit (*pneuma*) of God is identified with the breath (*pneuma*) of the risen Lord, and this Spirit becomes their life breath. Christ is alive and they share his life.

This enlivening breath is received in the context of their commissioning. They are sent as Christ was sent by the Father. However, they do not go forth to take the place of a fallen leader. Instead, the leader whom they followed before the crucifixion continues to be leader. The Spirit of wisdom and authority which they perceived in Jesus, continues as the Spirit of Christ to be their leader. The disciples move forward "in his name" under his authoritative command. They participate in his life, and they share his ongoing mission.[17]

In the immediate context of John 20:22, the breath of Jesus is the breath of authority—the same authority Christ had to release people from their sins. If we consider the larger context, we may add that the mission for which they received Jesus' life (breath or Spirit) is to give others life in his name.

This tradition gives a wider scope to the Spirit's work in the extension of Christ's mission. It suggests an intimacy and a personal dimension not included in the metaphor of baptism with the Spirit. And yet John is by no means bound to his metaphor of breath. The Spirit as the personal presence of the living Christ, the Paraclete, gives encouragement and counsel. Through the Spirit the disciples share Jesus' joy and participate in his truth. His life within them gives peace and confidence in God. His Spirit draws them into the unity which he himself has with the Father (John 17:21).

The Identity of the Spirit

The Gospel of John makes it clear that the Holy Spirit which will come to the disciples is none other than the presence of the risen Jesus. On the one hand, he will be another (*allos*), but not different one (*heteros*).[18] George S. Hendry suggests the term "dynamic identification" to describe this functional equivalence. Whatever terminology we use, we must take careful note of the New Testament's virtual identification of the Spirit and the presence of the risen Christ in the church.

Some interpreters separate the character and function of the Spirit from that of the Son and teach that a new and different "dispensation of the Spirit" was begun on the day of Pentecost (dispensationalism). Such interpreters have not done justice to the continuity between the two. On the other hand, those who fully identify the Spirit's coming with the promised return of the Messiah ("realized eschatology"), minimize the eschatological distinctions.

The genuinely new thing that happened in historical experience was the coming of Jesus as the Messiah. The disciples' new understanding of the Spirit of God developed directly from this new disclosure of God in Christ. "So completely has the New Testament writers' understanding of Spirit been shaped by their beliefs about the person of Christ," writes C. F. D. Moule, "that the Spirit of God can become the Spirit of Christ."[19]

As we have seen, the disciples had expected the eschatological outpouring of the Spirit and the return of the prophetic gift under the reign of the Messiah. Israel expected the Spirit as the consummation of messianic blessing after a repentant nation had been reestablished under the victorious Messiah. Once again the Law would be respected and observed. The Spirit of the Messiah would also be the Spirit of the Law of national Israel.

But the messianic mission of Jesus was quite different from what the disciples expected. A "suffering servant" Messiah was the farthest from their thought. John the Baptist had introduced Jesus as the judge who would "baptize with fire" and with the Holy Spirit. They expected a military empire like that of Judas Maccabaeus, with a reigning Messiah ready to punish sinners. They would be his ministers of state with honored positions in his court (Mark 10:37ff.).

At first it was beyond their comprehension that Jesus' mission would be one of reconciling the nations rather than conquering enemies, of love and forgiveness instead of judgment. Certainly they did not expect the Messiah's mission to follow a pattern of death and resurrection. Even late in Jesus' ministry, Peter rebuked him for talking about a cross and death.

Finally, they expected "the day of the Lord" to usher in an *immediate* restoration of the kingdom to Israel. Even after Jesus' death and resurrection, they were still asking questions about the restoration of the kingdom to Israel with the obvious expectations that it would be soon (Acts 1:6). They eventually perceived that the *Paraclete* was representing the suffering Messiah and continuing his mission of witness to the salvation of God. This completely changed their agendas and their concept of the Spirit's work.

More explicitly, they learned that this Paraclete was not a substitute for a victorious Messiah who would return in his own good time with a rod of iron to rule the nations (dispensationalism). Not an interim comforter who consoles believers with a spiritual salvation as they wait for the Messiah to return and reinstate his earthly kingdom by violent revolution. No, the Paraclete was the Spirit of the Messiah who had already inaugurated the truly revolutionary "rule of God" *as we have come to recognize the nature of revolution in Jesus' life and teachings.*

Thus we also see that the Paraclete is the Spirit of the crucified Lord whose glory it was to be lifted up on a cross. He is the Spirit of the Sermon on the Mount, which depicts the nature of the revolution. It is through participation in this Spirit that we are enabled to share in the "sufferings of Christ" and participate in his continuing mission to bring life and light to the world. As the one who makes this participation possible, he is the Spirit of the church which is the "body of Christ."

The writings of John and Paul provide the most fully developed examples of the functional equation of the Spirit with the risen Christ in the church. Although John never refers to the Spirit as the "Spirit of Christ," it is he who most explicitly speaks of the Spirit as the continuation of Christ's presence. The Johannine Spirit is *allos paraklētos.* He is another enabling, guiding presence of the same identity and fulfilling the same role Jesus himself exercised among them while he was on earth. As one commentator has put it, the Spirit is the continuing divine presence so closely related to Jesus as to be his "alter ego."[20]

In yet another way not immediately obvious to the casual reader, John bears witness to this "dynamic identification" of the Spirit and the risen Christ. John, writing many years after the events, can present the fuller meaning which the Spirit has revealed as though it were a verbatim report of what Jesus himself said. It is a simple equation of two things: (1) what the Spirit reminds them of Jesus' words (14:26), and (2) the further understanding of Jesus' meaning ("all the truth," 16:13) which the Spirit teaches. This freedom of John simply to identify the truth of the Spirit with the intention of the historical Jesus is itself a most interesting commentary on his view of their dynamic relationship.

Paul makes the identification explicit in the designation "Spirit of Christ."[21] But here again our understanding of the relation of Jesus and the Spirit does not depend upon the use of the literal phrase alone. Paul's usual designation is simply "the Spirit" or "Holy Spirit." However, he clearly equates the Spirit's presence and work with that of Jesus throughout his letters. And he freely uses phrases like *in Christ, in the Spirit, Christ in you,* and *the Spirit in you,* to refer to the same realities in the Christian's experience.[22]

Perhaps the best example of this virtual identification of the Spirit and Christ in Paul's writings appears in Romans 8:9-11. Here in brief compass he uses *the Spirit, Spirit of God, Spirit of Christ,* and simply *Christ* where he is obviously speaking of the same divine presence. Clearly, as Barth has written, "We are not concerned in the Holy Spirit with something different from Him [Christ] and new. . . . The Holy Spirit is the Spirit of Jesus Christ."[23]

Finally, we can characterize this functional identity with three words: *character, work,* and *power.*

First, the Spirit has the *character* of Jesus. As C. A. A. Scott put it,

> This Being has character—and character which is known. It is in fact the character of Jesus of Nazareth. Whatever is known as to the purpose of His life, the relation into which He entered with men, the direction which His influence took may equally be predicated of the Holy Spirit.[24]

We see this most clearly in those passages where the Spirit of Christ is at work in the lives of Christians, producing in them the spirit of Christ. The "fruit of the Spirit" (Gal. 5:22-23) is the character of Jesus. To participate in the Spirit is to have the "mind of Christ" (1 Cor. 2:14-16).

Second, the *work* of the Spirit is the work of Christ. In brief we can say that the work of the Spirit is salvation, the same salvation which Jesus came to bring.[25] By the Spirit's prompting we call Jesus "Lord." By the Spirit at work in us we are reconciled to God and to each other. By the Spirit's consecration we are called and set apart to the work of Christ. The Spirit's "gifts" are for the welfare of the church as it carries out the mission of Christ. "Through him [Christ] . . . in one Spirit," we are being built into a "holy temple in the Lord" (Eph. 2:18-22). And so one could continue. The work of the Spirit is simply the fulfillment of the mission of Christ.

Third, the Spirit's *power* is the same power that we see at work in Jesus' ministry. In the words of Eduard Schweizer, "This power was not anonymous or unknown. It was identical with the exalted Lord in his work forming the community."[26]

As the "Spirit of him who raised Jesus from the dead," he has the power to give life to our spirit and bodies (Rom. 8:11). His power frees us from self-centeredness ("the flesh") and directs our concern to the purposes of Christ and his mission. Above all, the Spirit's power is the power of love. And his work in and through us is the work of love. (See Rom. 5:5; 15:30; Col. 1:8; and 1 Cor. 13 in its setting.) By his power the gospel is demonstrated in the life of the church and effectively preached to the world.

The immediate practical implication of this should be evident. This functional identity provides the test by which the "spirits [of the teachers]" can be discerned (1 John 4:2). The test for "prophets" who claim to speak by the Spirit is whether they recognize and take with full seriousness the significance of Jesus' humanity. The test for "spiritual gifts" is their value in the service of the continuing mission of Jesus (1 Cor. 12). And for "tongues" in particular, the test is the confession that "Jesus is Lord" (12:3). Above all, the test is whether faith produces in us the love of Christ.

The Mode of Christ's Presence and God's

If the identity of presence is the same, the mode of presence is different. As George Hendry has said, "The presence of the Holy Spirit was known, not as an alternative to, but as a mode of the presence of the living Christ."[27] Emil Brunner noted that "when we say 'Holy Spirit' we mean that mode of God's being by which He is present within us, and operates in our spirit and heart."[28]

Both of these observations are based upon the Johannine portrayal of the transition from the historical Jesus to his presence as spirit. Christ is no longer present among his disciples as an exterior example and authoritative teacher. Now he is with them as an inner authority, an influence prompting, enabling, guiding, and strengthening them for service in the kingdom of God. The Spirit gives words of witness and defense of the gospel (Matt. 10:20). The Spirit and the "name," that is, the authority of Jesus, provide the *power* to heal, the *authority* to forgive, and the *boldness* and *wisdom* for the transcultural preaching of the message.

The Holy Spirit makes Christ our contemporary.[29] He is Christ to us—not in the sense that he displaces the historical Christ, but rather that through his mediation we know Christ and participate in his work (1 John 3:24b). This presence is sometimes called an "indwelling of the Spirit," or "Christ in us." It invites an intimacy of relationship also described as a "communion of the Holy Spirit" (2 Cor. 13:13). Such a participation is not described so much in ecstatic or mystical terms, as in moral and personal categories. Through the Spirit, we share the "mind of Christ" and are being changed into Christ's likeness (1 Cor. 2:16; 2 Cor. 3:18). It is this sharing in the mind of Christ that enables us to share in his sufferings (Phil. 3:10), that is, in his mission.

This mode of presence has the advantage of freeing Christ's followers from literalism and legalism. They are no longer restricted to an external, historically or culturally defined authority, however exalted it might be. They are also assured of the active presence of the "Spirit of Jesus," who will continue to relate them to the historical Messiah. This Spirit will certify the meaning of his life to them and authenticate the ongoing contextualization of his message (John 16:12-14). Surely, this is what Jesus meant when he told the disciples it was to their advantage that he go away so the Spirit could come.

We should also note in this connection that it is the Spirit—and not simply a written corpus of his teachings—that has taken the authoritative place of the historical Christ in the church (see chapter 2, above). It is the work of the Spirit to set us free from literalism and legalism, much as Jesus himself was free from the legalisms of the scribes and the rabbis of his day (2 Cor. 3:4-6, 17; Gal. 4:28—5:1). This is possible insofar as the Spirit produces the "mind of Christ" in us (1 Cor. 2:15-16; Phil. 2:1, 5).

The Spirit of the Church

Where in the World?

We come now to a crucial question. Where and how is God's Spirit at work in the world today? Where and how do we see most clearly the signs of the Spirit's activity? Unless we can "hear the sound" of the Wind or Spirit of God blowing (John 3:8), our theological descriptions remain abstract.

We confess that God is at work in all phases of historical development. Our problem is to identify the influence and effects of the Spirit of Christ in the ambiguous historical situation. Surely the Spirit is at work in all movements for the humanization of society and for peace in the world. But do we identify that presence and work primarily with scientific developments that have improved human life? With political and economic revolutions that have liberated oppressed peoples? With peace movements that are attempting to avert war and bloodshed? The Christian's answer to this question is that the Holy Spirit, the Spirit of Christ, is identified primarily as the Spirit of the church, which is "the body of Christ."

We are now ready for a provisional definition of the Christian doctrine of the Holy Spirit. *The Spirit is God's living presence among his people, carrying out the mission of Christ, which is the creation of a new humanity. The Spirit is the motivation, power, and guide of the "God Movement," enabling it to transcend human institutional possibilities in the formation of the open, vicarious, sharing community of salvation, the church.*

Our definition gathers up aspects of the discussion we have already noted. The Spirit is God's living presence with us and the purpose of his ministry is the furtherance of the mission of Christ. Now we must explore further how the Spirit as the Spirit of Christ is at work in the world, especially through the church.

Undoubtedly this focus upon the church as the primary sphere of the Holy Spirit's activity will raise the question whether the Spirit of Christ is restricted to the activity of the institutional church.[30] The answer to this question is most certainly no, but the answer requires further elaboration. In the New Testament the church is clearly the focus of the Spirit's activity in the world. Almost nothing is said about a cosmic activity of the Spirit.[31]

When we speak of the Spirit as the Spirit of the church, we must be extremely careful not to imply that the institutional church possesses the Spirit or in any way controls his activities. We must not assume that the institution called church, whether Catholic or Protestant, has a monopoly on the Spirit's activity. On the contrary, the various ecclesiastical organizations of Christendom are provisionally related to the movement of the Spirit as they open themselves in repentance and "waiting" for the Spirit's power and guidance. Only in this way can they become the instruments of the Spirit under his control. Only as such can they correctly be equated with the church of Christ.

Further, we must not limit the Spirit's activity to special religious effects in the church. The Catholic tradition has emphasized the Spirit's authority in the definition of doctrine and has associated his dynamic with sacramental effectiveness. The Protestant tradition has associated it with inspiration of Scripture and illumination for preaching. Calvin, and especially John Wesley, added to this the work of sanctification. The Pentecostal-charismatic tradition has emphasized a unique "spiritual" experience. While all of these may be considered manifestations of the Spirit, his work is not thus restricted to the religious activity of the churches.

The Sphere of the Spirit as Church

We quoted Barth earlier to the effect that the Spirit is the Spirit of Jesus Christ. Now we are ready to continue the quotation. He wrote:

> The Holy Spirit is nothing else than a certain relation of the Word to humans. In the outpouring at Pentecost there is a movement—*pneuma* means wind—from Christ to humans. . . . What is involved is the participation of humans in the word and work of Christ.[32]

These words bring us directly to the church as the sphere of the Spirit's manifestation in the world.

To speak of the Spirit as the Spirit of the church is not in any way to restrict the sphere or goal of his activity. Instead, it identifies the Spirit as the Spirit of the body of Jesus Christ in distinction from the many "false prophets [that] have gone out into the world" (1 John 4:1). It does that by identifying the authentically *Christly* community and activity.[33] The freedom of the Spirit to work where and when he will is not the freedom to be any other (*heteros*) than the Spirit of Christ. As the Spirit of Christ, he consistently manifests himself as the Spirit of the crucified Lord.

The activity of the Spirit marks the sphere of the church. That sphere is identified by the authentic witness to the crucified Christ as the victorious Son of God. Both Paul and John write in these terms (1 John 4:1-6; 1 Cor. 2). The perversion of this dynamic relationship between Spirit and church arises when the identifying sign is translated into a verbal norm used to identify the orthodox ecclesiastical institution; and when that institution's boundaries in turn are used to define the nature and limits of the Spirit's activity.

The signs of the Spirit's activity, then, are present where we discover the spirit and power of the resurrected Christ in the world creating the "church." This in turn connects us with the apostolic witness to Jesus of Nazareth as the Christ. The Spirit of the church of Jesus Christ is the Spirit of the New Testament Messiah as depicted in the Gospels.

For the church, then, the Spirit is the "Paraclete"—the Spirit of encouragement, truth, love, wisdom, and power. Only as he bears primary witness can the witness of the church be effective (John 15:26-27). He empowers and gives the words for effective witness. He is the power of conviction behind the witness (John 16:8-11; 1 Cor. 2:3-4). By the same token, only as the church participates in the power and gifts of this Christly Advocate can the convicting witness of the Spirit convince the world.

In this manner the Spirit of Christ becomes the Spirit of the church, the new *ekklēsia* of Christ. He is the formative, enabling presence which authenticates the new *ekklēsia* as the body of Christ in the world. We might note in passing that the word *ekklēsia* clearly has political overtones the word *church* does not convey. This new bodily organ of the Spirit is no new religious institution. It is a social movement empowered by God's Spirit (Acts 2:43-47; 4:32-37).[34]

The trinitarian baptismal formula of Matthew 28:19-20 clearly indicates a recognition of this relation of Spirit and *ekklēsia*. The striking and unexpected addition in this formula is the words "in the name of . . . *the Holy Spirit*." (Note that in the Acts the general formula is simply "in the name of Jesus.") The discipled "nations" were not only a special people of God the Father, called out in the name of Jesus the Son, as a messianic community. They were to be a movement characterized by the eschatological Spirit. The church is that Christian *ekklēsia* in the world that has been baptized "in the name of" or "by" or "with" the Spirit of Christ.

When we call the Holy Spirit "the Spirit of the church," therefore, we must not equate the church with ecclesiastical organizations. The affirmation that the Spirit of Christ is the Spirit of the church involves a redefinition of *church* rather than a relocation of the Spirit's sphere and role. The "church in the power of the Spirit," to borrow a phrase from Moltmann, is the expression of a qualitatively new character of human community—a new order of creation—which becomes possible through participation in the Spirit. The Spirit's sphere of action is no more restricted today than before the incarnation. The Spirit is still the active presence of God in the whole universe, and involved in the birthing of the new creation.

Participation in the Spirit

The Nicene Creed—as it was adopted by the Western churches—calls the Spirit "the Holy One, the Lord and Giver of life who proceeds from the Father and the Son." The Constantinopolitan Creed (381 C.E.) calls the Spirit "the Lord and life-giver who proceeds from the Father."

The words *Life-giver of the church* are not found in the Scriptures, but the function is depicted both as an act of birthing (John 1:12-13; 3:5) and as the divine immanence animating and energizing the church. Finally, as we shall see in the next section, the Spirit is the pledge or guarantee (*arrabōn*) of everlasting life.

Various metaphors speak of this formative function of the Spirit: indwelling (1 Cor. 3:16), baptism into, and drinking of (1 Cor. 12:13), for examples. Paul also speaks of our living "by [or in] the Spirit" (Gal. 5:25). But the dynamic relationship is more generally spoken of as participation or sharing. The church is a sharing in, or *koinōnia*, of the Spirit.

This concept of participation in the Spirit is not easily understood in cultures that have individualized and subjectivized the concept of spirit. The phrase *koinōnia pneumatos* is generally translated "fellowship of [or with] the Spirit," but the NRSV correctly uses "sharing in the Spirit" in Philippians 2:1. "Fellowship *with* the Spirit" individualizes the Spirit as a personal participant with us. "Fellowship *of* the Spirit" leaves open its possible interpretation as the fellowship of individuals created by the Spirit. "Sharing *in* the Spirit," on the other hand, suggests a shared reality which we experience together in community.[35]

Societies in which individualism has shaped the governing concepts, more easily comprehend the phrase "the Spirit in you" (1 Cor. 6:19; Rom. 8:9-11). From classical ancient culture on, the Spirit's influence has been understood as an infusion of energy, skill, wisdom, or the like.[36] And so the Spirit has tended to be associated with the mystical and elusive, the strange or unusual, in the experience of the church.

The New Testament concept of the Spirit's relation to the church is more intricately and reciprocally involved with both the individual and the group than this would suggest. The Spirit is the bond of unity between individuals and the group. It is the energy that empowers the group. It is the personal influence and motivation which marks the group's identity and goals. The phrase *sharing in the Spirit* is inclusive of all of these. *The Spirit of the community is that "objective" corporate personal unity and dynamic of the group which constitutes its character and purpose.*[37]

To say that the Spirit is an objective reality means in this case that spirit is not the subjective creation of the group. It means rather that the social reality (the church) is created by the Spirit. In this sense the Spirit is not to be equated with the "group spirit." It is not the product of group psychology—the collective of individual spiritual experience, gifts, and manifestations. Instead, as Paul puts it in 1 Corinthians 12:12-13, the various members with their Hellenistic and Jewish backgrounds and identities were formed into "one body" by having been baptized "into one Spirit (*en heni pneumati*). The individual received a fresh family identity by participating in "a spirit of adoption" (Rom. 8:14-16) upon entering the new group. Those who truly belong to the group participate in the spirit of the group. Thus Peter in his Pentecost sermon promised the Holy Spirit to those who joined the group (Acts 2:38).[38]

It follows that "the unity of the Spirit" (Eph. 4:3-4) of which Paul speaks is not a unity produced by uniformity of law and doctrine. It is the unity created by the Spirit. Such unity is maintained by "sharing in the Spirit." In a similar manner, Paul was concerned to preserve the unity of the Spirit in the Corinthian church. The schismatic individualism of its members who claimed special individual gifts and manifestations of the Spirit was threatening its harmony (1 Cor. 12—14). The concern of the Spirit, Paul wrote, is for the "common good" of the body and of each individual as a "member" of that body (12:4-7).

When we understand the Spirit in this way, we begin to see the close and inseparable relation of the Spirit of Christ and the Spirit of the church. Christ's Spirit is the Spirit/spirit of *agapē*—of forgiveness, joy, and peace (Gal. 5:22-23); the spirit of boldness in testimony to the crucified and risen Christ; the spirit of faith and wisdom. And above all, Christ's Spirit is the spirit of that love manifested supremely in Jesus.

This is the Spirit who enables the church to transcend cultural differences and find fellowship across language, economic, political, and racial barriers. It was precisely this Spirit of *agapē* that produced the "*koinōnia* of the apostles" (Acts 2:42-45). The "*koinōnia* of the Spirit" and the apostolic *koinōnia* were viewed as virtually identical. Peter could even say that Ananias lied to the Holy Spirit when he falsely represented the spirit/Spirit of the group (Acts 5:3). A falsification of the authentic nature of the church is a falsification of the Spirit of Christ.[39]

For this reason Paul severely reprimanded the Corinthian Christians for their cavalier attitude and unbrotherly behavior at the Lord's Supper (1 Cor. 11:28-29). Their attitudes and actions contradicted the essential meaning of the Supper, which is the central symbol of participation in the body and Spirit of Christ.

Finally, in our definition of the Spirit as Spirit of the church, we spoke of his enabling the church to transcend the possibilities of human institutions and form an open, vicarious, sharing community of salvation. This is the evangelical task of the Spirit in and through the church. He is the Spirit of the continuing messianic mission to extend the rule of God. Therefore, participation in the Spirit means sharing in the mission of Christ.

Human communities have their own collective egos, which, like individual egos, easily become self-centered, self-protective, and closed to those outside their self-imposed perimeters. When this happens, the Spirit of the gospel and evangelism is lost. Sometimes in its place a crusading spirit makes the advancement of the church itself the goal of missionary activity and masquerades as the Spirit of Christ. At other times in history, the church has simply become a defensive religious institution, "grieving" the Spirit of the gospel (Eph. 4:30).

The Role of the Spirit

Therefore, the Spirit is associated with the activity of God among us. His presence and nature is defined largely by his role in the life of the community of the Spirit. His work is identified and he is named as the Worker of the work. The Spirit is the Spirit of life, of wisdom, power, love, and peace.

The Spirit of Life. God's gift of the Spirit is the gift of new life—a spiritual life which frees us from excessive attachment to this earthly ("fleshly") life. The prophets of Israel already anticipated this new life. Ezekiel's vision of the spirit breathing new life into the dry bones of Israel symbolizes it (37:1-14). Joel (2:28-29) and Jeremiah (31:33) predict it. The gift is a spiritual birth or a resurrection to new life. In either case this life is the "new life in Christ."

Life in the Spirit makes possible life in a different dimension of relationships to God and to each other. It does not cancel or demean life in the body. It enables us to transcend those aspects of our lives that must end at death. For example, the love we know as physical beings is enriched and given a depth dimension which death of the body cannot destroy. It awakens new sensitivities to spiritual reality as it was portrayed in the life and death of Jesus Christ.

Already in our historical existence, this new spiritual life has been given to us as a renewing energy. Paul speaks of the life in the Spirit as contrasted to life in the flesh. Or he may refer to it as God's gift of the Spirit. In the latter case, the Spirit is seen as the author of the new life, and the "guarantee" of its completion even beyond the grave. Because this new life is only partially known in our earthly existence, the gift of the Spirit is referred to as a "marking" or "seal" (Eph. 1:13-14; 2 Cor. 1:22), a "down payment" (*arrabōn*) or pledge of life to come (2 Cor. 5:5).

The gift of the Spirit as the beginning of spiritual life is also called a "consecration" or "sanctification," a setting apart for God's holy purposes. It is associated with—but not equated with—baptism. Baptism marks the entrance into the life of the Spirit through entrance into the spiritual body of Christ. But this is not something different or separate from participation in that social community—the congregation of saints—where the manifestation of the Spirit is in evidence.

The consecration or sanctification of the Spirit thus marks the beginning of a new quality of life and relationships in the human community. The Spirit is the creator of the new order of creation in Christ (2 Cor. 5:17). As the spirit/Spirit of *agapē*, the Spirit is both life-force providing motivation and life-principle indicating the ethical response consistent with God's disclosure of love in Christ.[40]

The Spirit of Wisdom. The Spirit is experienced as the *truth* or *wisdom* of God. Paul virtually equates God's Spirit or Mind (*nous*) with the spirit or "mind of Christ" (1 Cor. 2:10-16). He argues that the spirit and wisdom of this age are not only different from but opposed to God's Spirit and wisdom revealed in the crucified Christ. The "unspiritual" person, such as the "rulers of this age" and their followers, cannot comprehend this. Hence, it is the role of God's Spirit to reveal the wisdom of the cross to the church and through the church to the world.

The insight given by the Spirit as the interpreter of God's mind makes possible our understanding of the cross as God's way of salvation (1 Cor. 2:12-13). The Spirit as the knowledge of God teaches us to know the true meaning of life. As the memory of God, it brings to our minds the truly significant "acts of God" in the history of salvation. As the wisdom of God, it guides the church through the ages and across geographical boundaries to maintain the authenticity of the gospel in changing cultures. This latter task is no small achievement! The message itself is historically conditioned, cast in the cultural forms of the first-century Mediterranean world. Yet by the wisdom of God, it continues as a relevant, effective message of salvation.

The Spirit of Power. The Spirit is experienced as the *power* of God (Acts 1:8). Such power overcomes fear and timidity in the face of opposition to the message of the gospel. Accordingly, "boldness" to witness is recognized as the Spirit's presence in the lives of the disciples. This Spirit is also the persuasive power that gives the message its cutting edge (1 Thess. 1:5; 1 Cor. 2:4). It is the power to change lives, to heal bodies and minds, and to bring reconciliation. It is the power of life and light to overcome the powers of evil and darkness, what Paul calls the powers of the air (Eph. 2:2). It is also the "resurrection power," which overcomes death itself (Eph. 1:19-20). The power of God is available to Christians for the continuance of Christ's mission through the presence of God's Spirit in their lives.

The Spirit of Love. The Spirit is also experienced as "God's love . . . poured into our hearts" (Rom. 5:5). This Spirit of love is the spirit of family, giving us a sense of identity and freedom as God's children (Rom. 8:14f.). It is the motivation that prompts us as members of God's family to "walk in love" (Eph. 5:2). Thus, to "walk according to the Spirit" is to walk in the spirit of love.

This life (or walk) in the Spirit is represented everywhere in the New Testament as opposite to a life of self-centered ambition and selfish enjoyment ("the flesh"). Paul wrote, "If we live by the Spirit, let us also be guided by the Spirit" (Gal. 5:25). If we walk by the Spirit, we will not satisfy the desires of the "flesh" (5:16). We may say, therefore, that the Spirit of God is that power and influence of love which constrains us to unselfishness, patience, and forgiveness (Gal. 5:22).

The Spirit of love is also called the "Spirit of freedom" from legalism. The Spirit frees us from the necessity of legalistic codes of discipline to regulate our behavior. To walk in the Spirit means freedom from legal prescriptions because the purpose of God's law is to realize the life of love (Gal. 5:13-14; Rom. 8:1-4; 2 Cor. 3:17-18). This love of God is the very heart and life of the church when it truly exists as the community of the Spirit.

The Spirit of Peace. Finally, the Spirit is experienced as the peace of God which brings order and unity into both the lives of individuals and the life of the church (Eph. 4:1-6). The Spirit of peace is a spirit of humility and service. Indeed, the outstanding characteristic of the Spirit's active presence in the church is unity in the midst of variety (1 Cor. 12:4-7). It is not a spirit of uniformity which inhibits the liveliness of variety, but of joyful service which directs the variety "for the common good."

This Spirit of peace is also a spirit of *reconciliation* and *peacemaking*. This does not mean a Spirit of compromise and relativism. The mark of the Spirit of peace is not compromise, but *meekness*. And meekness rigorously and consistently insists on the justice of God's reign (Matt. 6:33) while submitting itself to God's judgment concerning what is right. Meekness does not equate its own understanding of justice and truth with the righteousness of God and stand above the opponent as a judge. Instead, it takes its place together with the opponent under the judgment of God's Spirit. Meekness therefore attempts in peace to achieve God's justice as disclosed in Christ.

This peace of God is the goal of the church for the world. The church is even now under the governance of the Spirit, and such peace is an anticipatory possibility in its own life.

The Authority of the Spirit in the Church

We see perhaps the most crucial implications of a dynamic equation of the risen Christ to the Spirit when we attempt to discover and locate the source of authority for the church. If the Spirit is in truth the living presence of Christ in the midst of the congregation (Matt. 18:20), how does the Spirit express this continuing authority as Lord of the church and director of the messianic mission?

Ecclesial Patterns. Since the end of the first generation of Christians, the institutional church has carefully contained—and sometimes constrained—prophecy. Both Roman Catholic and Protestant orthodoxies have hesitated to attribute much direct authority to the Spirit. Roman Catholicism tended to restrain the authority of the Spirit by making it an official authority in and of the church. It held that the authority of Jesus Christ was passed on to the apostles and through them to the church in its apostolic succession.

Classical Protestantism has strictly limited the Spirit's authority to the inspiration and illumination of the Bible. Calvin, for example, held that the "prophets and evangelists" mentioned in Ephesians 4:11 were a first-generation phenomenon. The "doctors" of the Reformation church had for all practical purposes taken the place of prophets.[41] Authority was lodged in the Scripture, which, as post-Reformation Orthodoxy came to define it, was verbally inspired and virtually dictated by the Spirit.

Words were carefully chosen to express this relation between Bible and Spirit. The Spirit continues to illuminate the true meaning of the Bible, but this "inward illumination" of meaning was in no way to be confused with "inspiration" or revelation.[42] Further, the Spirit's true interpretation is stated in the creeds of the church. The test of any claim to the Spirit's leading is whether it agrees with the Spirit-inspired Bible and with the creeds.

Rationalistic liberalism, especially in its deistic forms, abandoned all reference to the Spirit as an immanent presence of God. It substituted the rational human spirit as authority both for interpreting the Bible and evaluating its message. The history of liberal theology since the eighteenth century is characterized by a long intramural debate concerning the relation of reason and intuition. This debate has also questioned the possibility of an authoritative word of any kind in religious experience.

None of these traditions in themselves adequately expresses the freedom and authority of the Spirit as Lord of the church (2 Cor. 3:5-6, 17). In each case human definitions and organizations restrict the authority of the Spirit, instead of recognizing it according to the rules of discernment followed in the New Testament church (1 John 4:1-3, 13-16; 1 Cor. 14:29-32).

The Bible, the organized church, and human wisdom all have an important role in helping to determine doctrine and strategy for the ongoing life and mission of the church. But in themselves they are inadequate. This is especially true in the cross-cultural proclamation of the gospel. From the New Testament perspective, the Spirit working through all of these is directly associated with the universalization of the gospel. The same Spirit of Jesus who guided in the first transcultural communication of the message is at work in the mission of Christ today. When the New Testament canon was completed, surely this Spirit did not cease to be the "Spirit of truth" who is leading "into all truth"!

Bible and Spirit in the Church. The relation of the Bible and the Spirit is a vital and mutually interacting one. The question of authority cannot be answered by the simple linear logic of the verbal inspiration theory. Such a position holds that because the Spirit inspired the words and message of the Bible, this inspired book must be the final authority of the church. Rigorously adhered to, this answer in effect takes us back to the Jewish scribal position, which assumed that the prophetic Spirit had been withdrawn from Israel.

The New Testament is the *initial fulfillment* of the promise that the Spirit will lead Jesus' followers into all truth. It is the Spirit-inspired memory, expanded understanding, and witness to Jesus of Nazareth as the Messiah given by the generation that knew him as their earthly leader (John 14:25; 15:26; 16:13). It gives us an authentic and authoritative picture of him as he was understood "in the Spirit" and as that picture emerged in the transcultural preaching of the apostles.[43]

Even though these documents are crucially important as the authentic, inspired record of the incarnation of Jesus, they are culturally and historically limited. They are the *beginning* of the promise that the Spirit will guide into all truth and declare things to come (John 16:13). They share the limitation of the historical Jesus, who was bound by the historical limitation of his hearers. Only the Spirit of the living Christ transcends these historical and cultural limitations and becomes for us the hermeneutical guide for the interpretation and use of Scripture across cultural boundaries. Hence, the Spirit of Christ which inspired the New Testament record remains the living touchstone for truth.

Here again, the church as the sphere of the Spirit must play a key hermeneutical role. It must function as the hermeneutical community, discerning the prophetic voice of the Spirit. But how is the authority and freedom of the Spirit exercised in the life of the church? We do not expect—nor would we accept—newly inspired information about the history of Jesus, such as the Mormons claim. The Jesus of the New Testament proclamation is the touchstone for all spiritual claims.

Neither do we accept prophetic directives which are contradictory to the Spirit of Christ. On the other hand, in the bewildering variation of cultural settings, languages, political situations, and the like, we are not rigidly bound by biblicistic literalism (the "written code") or by dogma, which is a cultural expression of the church (2 Cor. 3:6). Both of these approaches represent a return to "law." And life in the Spirit means freedom from law (Gal. 5:1, 13-14). This freedom of the Spirit is expressed primarily as the word of prophecy in the church.

The word of prophecy does not cancel or negate the written commandment. Instead, it translates the command into dynamic cultural equivalents. Such a prophetic message may be a word of judgment as well as acceptance, inasmuch as it is the contextualization of God's covenant law.[44] We should expect to see the Spirit of prophecy emerge among us with an authoritative word, especially where the gospel is newly proclaimed, or where a culture in which the church is already planted changes radically and rapidly.

The discerning community of the Spirit must recognize and judge such a word. The tests of that authority remain the same as they have always been in the church. The first of these is a clear affirmation of the New Testament Jesus as Lord of the church (1 Cor. 12:3; 1 John 4:2). The second test is that the one prophesying is to bear good fruit (righteous conduct) and be free from ulterior motivation (Matt. 7:15-16; 1 Cor. 13:2). Sectarian prophecies often subtly aim to enhance the status of the leader and are thus disqualified on this point. Also, the prophetic interpretations of "doctors" in the churchly traditions have often compromised the spirit of Christ in favor of political goals of the nation.

The third test is the validity of the prophetic analysis of the present situation and its predictive recommendations. This is the Deuteronomic test; namely, whether what the prophet speaks in the name of the Lord comes to pass (Deut. 18:22). In short, the prophecy must ring true both to the picture of the historical Jesus and to what his Spirit is presently doing. Within these parameters a wide variety of custom, theological explanation, and church practice may be tolerated.

Such authority of the Spirit is given for the present situation. It cannot be infallible, nor can it be passed on from generation to generation in the form of authoritative traditions. It remains an existential authority of the living church that in faith and obedience seeks the wisdom of the Spirit of Christ.

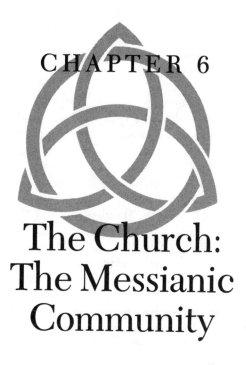

CHAPTER 6

The Church: The Messianic Community

Introduction: The Origin of the Church

Today the word *church* is used loosely to designate any religious body. Some, for example, speak of Buddhist, Hindu, or Jewish churches. But the Christian church did not originate simply as another religious gathering with a newly discovered deity, cult, and moral rules. It began as a messianic movement within Judaism, and insofar as the church has remained authentic, it has maintained this messianic character of movement.

The word *messianic* is often used to describe any zealous charismatic leader who begins a new religious movement. But here again we need to reexamine the meaning of the word in its original Judaic setting. The Jewish messiah was an *eschatological* figure. That is, he was understood to be a savior who would come at the close of the age to correct the injustices of history and usher in the new age. Accordingly, the metaphor used to speak of his coming was the change in political rulers.

When the first disciples called Jesus "Messiah" (Christ), they expected he would immediately establish his new government (kingdom) on earth (cf. Acts 1:6). They expected the end of the old age and the beginning of the new age, with the resurrected "King Jesus" as God's ruler. On the day of Pentecost, Peter called his fellow Jews to join the new messianic community awaiting Jesus' momentary return as ruler (Acts 2).

The newly formed community or "apostles' fellowship" (Acts 2:42) was soon called *ekklēsia*, although we do not know just how or when the term first became attached to them.[1] By the time Acts was written, it was the accepted term to designate each separate Christian congregation as well as the whole movement.

The term *ekklēsia* was taken from the world of Greek politics, where it was used for the assembly of citizens—whether they were called for a meeting or assembled as a mob. The Septuagint (LXX) used it as the translation for the word *qahal* (congregation or assembly) of Israel. From its parallel use in the New Testament, we may conclude that the followers of the Messiah intended to identify themselves with the congregation of faithful Israel who accepted Jesus as Messiah ("the remnant").

When Jesus' return as the messianic ruler of the world was delayed, there was understandably a strong temptation to change the character of the movement. Among the Jewish followers, the temptation was to revert to the old messianic patterns and think of Jesus as an ethical prophet. They would perpetuate his memory and teachings as a sect within Judaism while waiting for the Messiah to come at the close of the age. This Judaistic option died out after the final destruction of the temple by the Romans.

The temptation among the non-Jewish followers was to make the movement into a new mystery religion with Jesus as the mythical savior-god. Such religions were prevalent in the Roman Empire. Their "mysteries" or sacraments were related to the cosmic nature cycle and built on the myth of a dying-rising god. They promised their members that they would share in the secret knowledge and destiny of the god through participation in the cultic ritual of the religion. It was easy simply to make Jesus the object of such a cult, as we see in the Colossian letter, where Paul tries to correct such error.

But the apostolic community resisted these temptations and continued to preach a message of individual and social change (repentance) in anticipation of the final messianic victory. They did not simply help people to adjust to the present evil world as they awaited death and translation into the spiritual realm. They saw themselves as instruments of change, as a *movement* in this present age. Under the authority of Jesus, the returning Messiah, they called all humankind to repentance in anticipation and preparation for his final manifestation. They looked to the future in faith and hope for the culmination of the new age which he had already inaugurated.

We want to look more closely at this new phenomenon in history and at its implications for the church today.

The Church as a Messianic Movement

The Changing Status of "Church"

In tribal and national cultures, religion is simply one aspect of the culture. Religious institutions are part of the political structure. Church and state are not clearly differentiated. Shintoism, which still dominates much of Japanese thinking about religion, is a good example. Shinto, or "the Way of the Gods," is the religious self-expression of the Japanese nation embodying its origin and destiny. Its heroes, sacred objects, famous temples, and the like, are designated "national treasures." Its aim is to promote harmony with the spirit of the nation. It is so thoroughly integrated with the civil and cultural self-image that many Japanese people do not even recognize it as a religion. Even Buddhism, the dominant institutional religion, must bow to the authority of this national civil religion.

We have seen the reemergence of this kind of religion also in Islamic nations. It characterizes Hindu cultures, such as in Nepal, where one is born into the nation, the culture, and the religion. Operating on this principle, Nepal has made it illegal to change one's religious affiliation. The purpose of such religions is to help people adjust and conform to the dominant culture.

Now we come to our point: messianic religion challenges this basic pattern. The apostolic movement emerged as a challenge to the Jewish religious-cultural synthesis as well as the Roman pantheon and civil religion. It offered an alternative community dynamic (*agapē*) and pattern (servanthood) to the social orders in which it lived. It called people to new values, loyalties, attitudes, lifestyles, and goals. It made Jesus the spiritual and political authority for life and called for loyalty to his rule and conformity to his rule and God's will (Phil. 3:20; Rom. 12:2-3).

Over the period of the first 400 years, this movement for *metanoia*, that is, change or repentance, was co-opted by the political authorities and used in the traditional way to support and help unify the empire. The "church" was absorbed into "Christendom" as the spiritual authority for the body politic. When the medieval ideal of a unified "body of Christendom" was shattered, the church in each emerging nation became the religious department of the body politic. As someone once described the Church of England, the church became "Her majesty's government at prayer." Fine lines of organization were drawn to distinguish church and state. But for all practical purposes, the church of Jesus Christ became the churches of the various nations.

During the whole period of this development, there were protests against this co-opting of the church. Believers joined together in voluntary movements free from direct affiliation with and control by the government. The various Anabaptist movements were attempts to reestablish such a "free church" in the messianic tradition. As a result of this history, we have today a multitude of "denominations" which operate as individual churches, each claiming to be the church of Jesus Christ. Against this briefly sketched background we must examine the significance of calling the church a messianic community.

The Eschatological Community

The church is the result and continuation of the eschatological mission of Jesus Christ. When we call the church an "eschatological" phenomenon, we are first locating it in the sweep of history as it moves toward a goal.[2] *Eschaton* means end, as the conclusion of a process—a completion or consummation. Therefore, we may provisionally define the church as *the expression of the new historical possibility "in Christ"—a sign of the coming rule of God. It is an anticipatory representation of the "new order of creation" pointing to the eschaton when all things shall be made new in the consummation.*

Several characteristics are inherent in this definition of the church as eschatological. We can note their significance by contrasting them to mystical (or gnostic) religious organizations. First, the church is a *social community or movement*, not a private spiritual club. It is more than an association of those who enjoy the same private spiritual experience. The church exists as a public community among the various communities of the world, interacting with them. As a community, its focus is upon *ethical* action more than the cultic experience. It emphasizes *personal relations*, not mystical experience or magic.[3] Its highest virtue is love, not knowledge (gnosis). As a movement in history, it is *goal-* or *future-oriented*, committed to working for change toward that goal.

This eschatological character of the church is the theological basis for its mission in world history. The church is not called to be an evangelist to the world because of its superior religious knowledge or philosophy. Nor because of its superior spiritual discipline or ethical accomplishments. Its mission is to bring the people of the world under the authority of the trinitarian God, who is moving all history to its end (Matt. 28:19-20). It is the church's conviction that the plan of God for history has been set forth in Christ and impels it to worldwide mission (Eph. 1:10).

The Community of the Resurrection

The resurrection of Jesus Christ introduced a new era in history and marks the genesis of the church.[4] Jesus anticipated an ongoing movement stemming from his own life and teaching. As both Paul and Peter put it, he is the foundation upon which the "living stones" are built into a spiritual house (1 Cor. 3:10-11; 1 Pet. 2:4-5). But the church as we see it developing in the Acts is clearly a postresurrection movement.[5] Jesus commanded the disciples to wait for "what [the] Father promised" (Luke 24:49). This implies that while the church is the result of his life, death, and resurrection, he did not organize it as part of his ministry.

The disciples recognized that Jesus was Messiah and Lord by virtue of the resurrection. They discovered that his mission of salvation did not end with his death. It was only beginning. They realized that the rule of God which Jesus had announced was still current agenda, and they were to play an integral part in it (Acts 1:3-8; 1 Pet. 1:3). It was this ongoing body of disciples which the Spirit of the risen Christ formed into the "apostolic fellowship" that is the historical beginning of the Christian church (Acts 2:42; 4:32-33). The church was constituted by the presence of the resurrected Christ, and it continues to exist by participation in his life and destiny.

The church has been called, therefore, "the community of the resurrection." In the words of 1 Peter 1:3, it is that body which was given "a new birth into a living hope through the resurrection of Jesus Christ from the dead."[6] Or in the words of Paul, it is that fellowship (koinōnia) of believers who are saved "in hope" (Rom. 8:24). Indeed, Paul wrote to the Corinthians that if Jesus was not actually raised from the dead, then we are of all people most to be pitied (15:16-17). As the community of the resurrection, then, the church is future-oriented. Its prominent characteristic is hope even in the midst of death.

The church lives in the new era introduced by the resurrection of Christ. It belongs to the new age as an anticipatory representation of the new creation order to be consummated in the eschaton. In the midst of the old age, characterized by the reign of death, it lives beyond the domination and fear of death because of the resurrection (1 Cor. 15:54b-57). It lives in accordance with the new possibility of life in Christ (Rom. 6:4).[7] Already it is the beginning of a "new creation" (2 Cor. 5:17).

Put another way, the church lives by a fundamentally different set of realities and possibilities than the societies of "this present age." It honors a different authority, namely, that of the reigning Christ (1 Cor. 15:25-26). It functions from a different motivation and energy. It lives by the rule and authority of the new age which dawned with the resurrection of Jesus Christ.

The Community of the Spirit

Hence, we see that the gift of the Holy Spirit is both the evidence of the new eschatological reality and the guarantee of its future fulfillment. And the "sphere of the Spirit" is a functional definition of the church.[8] Now we must note the converse implications of that statement: the church is the concrete community which gives evidence of the messianic Spirit and the gifts of the Spirit. *The church is the social body or organism that lives and functions by the enabling power and fellowship of the Spirit under the lordship of Christ.* It is precisely the gift of the Spirit which makes the church a sign of the coming rule of God.

What is it, then, that characterizes the church as the community of the Spirit? What are the authenticating marks?

The first mark is *a genuine confession* that "*Jesus* is Lord" (1 Cor. 12:3b, 2 Cor. 3:3-6, 17). The test of genuineness is obedience to his authority (Matt. 7:21). This is the primary and basic evidence. The work of the Spirit is to convince the world of the messianic lordship of Jesus (John 16:8-10). To speak of lordship is to speak of normative authority. The church is that part of the world which recognizes and attempts to live under the authority of Jesus Christ.

A second mark is *freedom from legalism.* The church is that community which lives in the "freedom of the Spirit." Its life together is a life of "faith working through love" (Gal. 5:6b). It is not regulated by the threats implied in religious codes or traditional moral systems. Paul says Christ is the "end (*telos*) of the Law." He means by this that the Mosaic regulations are fulfilled in Christlike behavior (2 Cor. 3:6; Gal. 5:16, 25). In similar words he says that love, the primary fruit of the Spirit, fulfills the law (Rom. 13:8-10; Gal. 5:13-14). In short, the eschatological virtues that mark the church as the community of the Spirit are faith, hope, and love.

The third characteristic is difficult to put into one word, but perhaps the words *openness* or *nondefensiveness* express it. Such a disposition is quite foreign to sinful human community. Jesus' followers are to be "innocent as doves," ready to suffer persecution, and content to be salt and light in society (Matt. 10:16; 5:10, 13-14).

As Aristotle pointed out, the social order at its best is based upon *mutuality* or friendship. Human communities, like individuals, therefore, assume that self-regard and self-defense are basic necessities of existence. Indeed, they fully justify killing another human being if it is in self-defense. Once formed, such a community marks off its boundaries and views the "outsider" with suspicion. It fixes the rules and ideology that define its existence. For its own identity and protection, it assumes a closed, defensive posture. It opens itself to others only when it perceives that it is self-advantageous to do so.

When "churches" adopt such an attitude, they have become spiritually apostate. They, like Ananias and Sapphira, are misrepresenting the Spirit of Christ (Acts 5:3-4). For example, racial and class discrimination stem from fear and are a denial of the Spirit. Religious bigotry and censoriousness "in defense of the gospel" do not display the fruit of the Spirit. Manipulation of individuals through appeals to law and the threat of penalty contradicts the grace of the Spirit.

The open posture is one of "confidence" toward God (*parrēsia*, 1 John 4:17) which comes from intimate acquaintance. It is the stance of trust and acceptance toward others. It is characterized by the "fruit of the Spirit" (Gal. 5:22) and the qualities of love (1 Cor. 13:4-7). It is the action of invitation and of open arms to all who are in need. The open community of the Spirit is a society of peacemakers who "go the second mile," give more than is legally required, and return good for evil (Matt. 5:9, 41-48). This certainly is a new lifestyle or "walk" in the Spirit (Gal. 5:25; Rom. 6:4).

Fourth, the life of the Spirit is expressed in the *worship* of the church. The church's spiritual worship (Rom. 12:1; Eph. 5:18b-20) is an anticipatory celebration of Jesus' victory over death and sin. It is the celebration of hope. Its preaching is the proclamation of the authority of God over his people. Its prayer is that this authority of love will be extended throughout the whole world (Matt. 6:10). Its communion, or Lord's Supper, is the memorial of his sacrificial death and the anticipatory celebration of the eschatological victory feast with the Messiah (Luke 22:18; 1 Cor. 11:26).

Finally, the community of the Spirit is marked by *"gifts of the Spirit"* for the empowerment and guidance of the group (1 Cor. 12:4-7). When Paul introduces the subject of spiritual gifts in his Corinthian letter, he mentions two items especially relevant for the church around the world. First, he says all the gifts (*charismata*) are for the common welfare and witness of the church. Second, he says there are a variety of such gifts, services, and activities (12:4-6). In the following verses he names those gifts the Corinthian church was claiming (12:8ff.).

This suggests that the test for discerning the authentic community of the Spirit is not a literal reproduction of the particular gifts mentioned in the passage. Instead, what counts is evidence that those spiritual gifts are enabling the church to worship and witness in whatever culture it finds itself. The authentic gifts will be recognized by their quality and results. Are they in harmony with the character of Jesus Christ? Do they invigorate, build up, and console the body of believers? And do they convince men and women of Christ's authority? If so, they are gifts of the Spirit of Christ.

The Church and the Churches

All of the many "churches" or denominations today claim to be the church of Jesus Christ. These groups differ widely in doctrine, organization, and ethical convictions. How shall we view this situation theologically? What criteria can we bring to evaluate the claims of individual groups? How can we recognize the church in the world?

One area of difference is their own self-understanding as church. Some view the church simply as a spiritual communion of individuals who share common beliefs. Others view it as the apostolic organization ordained by Jesus himself when he chose Peter to be the first leader. Still others think of it as the congregation of faith where the Word of God is preached and the sacraments are rightly performed.

Still others emphasize the community aspect of the church. They insist it is a community of disciples seeking to discern and live under the authority of Jesus as the Christ. The Anabaptist-Mennonite churches belong to this last tradition. We see partial truth in each of these positions, and each tradition recognizes aspects of the others' understanding. But enough difference remains that they continue to be in competition with each other.

A number of formulas have been suggested through the years for the healing of these divisions. The concept of *denomination*, born in seventeenth-century England, was one of the early ones. It proposed that for the purposes of the state, each named (denominated) group should be recognized as a legitimate member of the church of Jesus Christ and therefore tolerated.

The modern ecumenical movement has insisted that the churches should be united into one body. This would at least help the church carry out its mission to the world and provide for discussing theological differences among themselves. Accordingly, they have attempted to make the simple confession, "Jesus is Lord and Savior," the single requirement for recognition as a legitimate part of the Christian world movement. Even within this broadly defined base, however, unresolvable differences concerning sacramental fellowship and organizational unity have continued.

Evangelicals have demanded greater doctrinal unity based upon the authority of the Bible as God's inerrant Word. In general, they have viewed the true church as a spiritual and theological phenomenon. In practice, they require a confession of new birth and belief in prescribed doctrines. Their attempt to discriminate between doctrinal "essentials" and "nonessentials" allowed a variety of sectarian groups in the movement. They require unity of theological belief patterns while allowing wide latitude in ethical convictions.

While Anabaptist-Mennonites generally confess the evangelical doctrines, their understanding of the church leads them to a different emphasis. They have identified the true church as a *community of faith, discernment, and obedience* to Jesus Christ. The community of faith confesses Christ as Lord and trusts him as Savior. It therefore pledges loyalty to him above all other authorities. As the community of discernment, it gathers around the Word of God under the guidance of the Holy Spirit, attempting to understand God's will for the church today. As the community of obedience, it seeks to follow the example of Jesus in authentic discipleship.

One need not demand perfection before the claims of a group are recognized as genuine. However, we can expect authenticating marks as described above. In summary, these marks are first, a genuine confession of Jesus Christ as he is portrayed in the New Testament. A second mark is the manifestation of authentic characteristics of Jesus himself in the life of the community together and as it faces outward toward the world. The New Testament clearly describes such characteristics as sharing each others' burdens, openness, loving even the enemy, serving those in need, and refusing to compromise with injustice and oppression. A third mark is that the community must give evidence of the life and power of the Holy Spirit as it worships and attempts to carry out the mission of Christ.[9]

The Church and the Rule of God
Interpretations of the Kingdom

Jesus' message was about the kingdom of God, not the church. Except for the two passages in Matthew 16 and 18, the word *church* (*ekklēsia*) does not appear in the Gospels. Conversely, the phrase *kingdom of God* appears rarely in the letters.[10] What is the reason for this rather obvious change of language? Is it a change of focus in the message? Is it a contextual adaptation of language? Does it indicate a basic change in the theological understanding of the apostles? Many answers have been given.

Augustine virtually equated the kingdom and the triumphant church of the early Middle Ages. Alfred Loisy, a modern Roman Catholic theologian, said that Jesus preached the kingdom, but it was the church that appeared. Dispensationalists like Lewis Sperry Chafer taught that Jesus offered the kingdom to the Jews, but when they rejected it, he established the church as an interim arrangement. Classic Protestantism taught that the kingdom is a spiritual reality which will be realized in heaven while the church is its representative here and now.

Millennialism taught that the kingdom now exists with the king (Christ) in heaven. But in one way or another it will be realized on earth in a future thousand-year reign of Christ. Some held that the kingdom will come as a result of the work of the Holy Spirit through the church, and that Jesus will return as the climax of the church's triumph (postmillennialism). Others held that the church would not succeed in ushering in the kingdom. Indeed, that it is not the church's mission to initiate it. Rather, Jesus will return in judgment upon the world systems. He will set up the kingdom and reign one thousand years on earth (premillennialism).

The Kingdom in Biblical Perspective

To answer the questions raised above, we must first try to understand what the kingdom Jesus proclaimed was and how Jesus was related to that kingdom. These are highly controversial questions, as indicated by the above survey. But we cannot simply avoid them for that reason.

I understand the kingdom of God and kingdom of heaven to have the same meaning.[11] *Kingdom (basileia)* does not indicate a political organization exercising power, although it does have political implications. Instead, it points to the authority and power of the ruler—in this case, God. The phrase is better translated, "rule of God." It indicates that rule as it was demonstrated in the life and teaching of Jesus. Jesus' announcement that the kingdom of God has arrived (Mark 1:14) was also the announcement of his own public ministry. His authority to cast out evil powers, to heal disease, to forgive sinful humanity, and to give the new commandment of love, are all manifestations of the authority (kingship, reign) of God. Finally, his resurrection demonstrates decisively the power and authority of God over death.

Jesus' announcement represents a new phase in the history of God's kingdom. Under the old covenant, corporate Israel was God's servant called to proclaim his authority (kingdom). God's kingly authority was not limited to the nation of Israel, but the people had been called to bear special witness to it. According to Isaiah 40, creation itself is the manifestation of God's sovereignty. Yahweh's power over the gods of the nations, which was demonstrated in the Exodus and the ongoing history of Israel, was the evidence of God's rule on earth. And so his *salvation* of Israel and his promised salvation of all nations were often practically equated with his kingdom. God is the one who controls world history, and he manifests his rule in his salvation.[12]

Thus far, biblical interpreters are in general agreement. But concerning the nature and scope of that salvation, there continues to be much disagreement. How is it related to Israel's history, past and future? To the mission of Christ? To the role of the church? Or to world history? While no final definitive answer exists, Christian theology takes its clues from Jesus as the messianic savior who fulfilled the prophetic insight of Isaiah 53. This one will bring forth truth and establish justice among the nations (Isa. 42:1-4).

We need to underscore three things. First, power and authority belong to God. As Messiah, Jesus was the one in whom and through whom that power was expressed. But as he himself made crystal clear, he could do nothing except what the Father gave him authority to do (John 5:26-28). Conversely, this insistence of Jesus strongly emphasizes the point that *Jesus' pattern of saving power is God's kingdom pattern.* We should not expect a reversion to the power of violence to establish the kingdom.

Second, as the Messiah, Jesus was the representative of Israel. The Gospels portray him as a Jewish male who stood firmly in the tradition of the prophets of Israel. They present him as the fulfillment of God's intention for Israel to be God's servant and witness to his kingdom. Both John the Baptist and Jesus challenged their fellow Jews to recognize the new thing God was doing and to obey the call to proclaim and demonstrate God's rule.

When the Jewish leaders failed to recognize Jesus' divine authority and his ministry as the definitive expression of God's kingdom, Jesus said the kingdom of God would be taken away from them and given to another nation producing the fruits of it (Matt. 21:43). He strongly criticized the Jewish teachers because they "lock people out of the kingdom of heaven" (Matt. 23:13).

Third, the church as the faithful remnant of Israel has been entrusted with the role formerly assigned to national Israel. The call which inaugurated the church was a call to repent and to accept Jesus as the true Messiah (Acts 2:36-39). The "keys of the kingdom" have been entrusted to that community which recognizes Jesus as the Christ, the Son of God (Matt. 16:15-20; 18:18). Here *keys* indicates the power to open the doors so all people may enter.

The church, then, is the community which recognizes the power and authority of Jesus Christ as the authentic expression of God's rule in the world. It calls him *Lord, Head,* and *King.* It proclaims that God has given him authority over the lesser powers of this age until death itself is defeated and the kingdom established (1 Cor. 15:24-25; Eph. 1:21f.).

The Church and the Kingdom

The kingdom of God is spiritual in the sense that it is an authority and dynamic from God. But that does not mean it is mystical, heavenly, or private. It is not present as an organized social movement but as a living influence, motivation, and potency in the lives of individuals and social groups. It is expressed in ethical motivation, social actions, and organized movements. We recognize its presence where the power of God defeats the powers of evil.

The church is the primary social agency representing the authority of the kingdom as it was manifested in Christ. Its members are conscious of being in the "kingdom of his beloved Son" (Col. 1:13). The church prays for the kingdom to come on earth (Matt. 6:10). It attempts to express the order of the kingdom in its own life together and to give witness to that order in secular society. It seeks to be God's instrument to move history toward the realization of God's rule in accord with its disclosure in Jesus Christ. As a new social reality in the larger society, it exists and functions as a sign of the present and coming rule of God.

This does not mean the church is God's only instrument. God is not limited to the church any more than he was limited to Israel. Furthermore, the church need not accept cosmic responsibility. It plays a limited role in God's economy as the continuing sign of God's inaugural action in Christ, who even now reigns "until he has put all his enemies under his feet" (1 Cor. 15:25). We need to look at the implications of this concept in more detail.

First, we must note the distinctive nature of the sign which the church raises to the world. It is the sign of the cross and resurrection. The church understands that its King rules from the cross, not as a worldly power, and it obeys his call to "take up the cross and follow him." This means inevitably that the church takes the servant stance of its Master, who was obedient unto death. As the representative of the crucified Christ, it has been given a special vocation: to "overcome evil with good." Where this kind of event is taking place, there Christ is at work in and through his church. There the rule of God is finding expression.

Second, as the continuation of Jesus' inaugural mission, the church by its very constitution is a missionary movement (Matt. 28:19-20; John 15:26-27; Acts 1:8). However, we must take care not to transfer authority for the mission to the church itself. The mission remains Christ's mission, and the Spirit of Christ is the church's resident authority and power. These do not reside only in the organization or offices of the church. This means that the mission must be carefully defined. It must be consistent with the ministry, death, and resurrection of Jesus. In this sense, Paul called the church "the fullness" of Christ (Eph. 1:23).

Further, under the authority of Christ, the church stands in the same relation to the rule of God as did the earthly Jesus himself. His role was to introduce the new era in the kingdom of God. The church is to continue this inaugural role. It is not that Jesus, having successfully inaugurated the rule of God, turned it over to the church to take the next steps of developing and consummating it. The kingdom of God remains in its inaugural stage. And the church continues to spread the message of its advent. Following the example of Jesus, therefore, the church is not to dominate, rule, and judge, but to lead by witnessing to and demonstrating the power of God under the sign of the cross in hope of the resurrection. As the anticipatory kingdom community, it is the salt and light of the world (Matt. 5:13-14), whose goal is the transformation of society under the authority of Christ.

Third, in light of the above, we should not speak of the church as the "agent" of God to build or establish the kingdom. Instead, it is the servant and representative of Christ, who is establishing the kingdom (2 Cor. 5:20). Christ is the "sower" (Matt. 13:1-9). To follow this metaphor, at best the church cultivates and waters the seed which has been planted. The church "receives" the kingdom as a gift of grace, not as the result of works. It prays to "see" the kingdom. It is to "strive first for the kingdom" and to "enter" it. It "preaches" the kingdom and invites others to enter. But the church has no mandate to build, "bring in," or establish the kingdom.

Further, the church must pray that it not become a shut door and stumbling block to those outside its circles who also are looking for the rule of God. In this respect, the church has the same temptation and weakness as Israel before it. Paul warned the Gentile church against pride lest it also be pruned from the Abrahamic vine (Rom. 11:17-21).

We might also note here that Paul foresees the distinct possibility that Israel will one day be restored to the role of kingdom messenger (Rom. 11:1-12).

Finally, the rule of God is the central message and eschatological goal of the church. Paul says the eschatological plan of God has been disclosed in Christ and the church has been given the task of making this plan known to the "rulers and authorities" (Eph. 3:10-11; Col. 1:25b-26). This certainly includes the proclamation of salvation for individuals, but individual salvation should be seen in the context of the coming kingdom. The evangelical message of the church is the announcement that in Christ the reconciliation and healing of human society is possible. All the warring factions of human society are now called to unity in the family of God (Eph. 2:14, 19). For the individual, such a possibility of new community can only mean greater freedom, joy, and fulfillment under the authority of God.

Life and Organization of the Community
Movement or Community?

In sociological terms, the church has the characteristics of both a community and a movement. If we follow the suggestion of Clarence Jordan and call the "kingdom of God" the "God movement,"[13] perhaps we should speak of the church as a working community within that movement. In any case it is important to understand what kind of a community the church is when we consider the questions of organization.

A *movement*, as I have written earlier,

> is not organizationally defined. It gains its character and structure from the purpose for which it exists—its mission. . . . A movement aims to effect changes in the larger social order. It does not exist to perpetuate itself as a movement, but to bring its purposes to realization within the whole social order of which it is a part.[14]

A *community*, on the other hand,

> is a group of people who have formed a pattern of interdependent and reciprocal relationships which aim at enhancing the personal quality of the group itself. What people in community have in common is each other and the mutual enhancement of each person in their life together.[15]

Therefore, when we define the church as a community, we must make certain qualifications. It is a community bound together by the *koinōnia of the Holy Spirit.* It is not simply an association formed to serve the needs of its members. *It is a community whose primary orientation and concern is the God movement.* Its organization and pastoral care of its members are not primarily for the community's self-advancement, but for the advancement of the God movement, or kingdom.

This means the nature of its life and organization will be determined by its understanding of its mission. It is a community gathered for a common mission, with a common loyalty and eschatological goal. That common mission, loyalty, and goal is defined by its "head" and "pioneer," Jesus Christ (Eph. 4:15; Heb. 2:10). That is why we must add the qualifying phrase "of God" or "of Jesus Christ," or "of the Spirit" to the word *community* when we use it to define church.

The New Testament word *ekklēsia* has this same overtone. Some wish to emphasize the holiness of the church and point out that the word literally means "called out." Hence, they have stressed that the church must be separated from the world in character. While this is etymologically correct, the emphasis of the word *ekklēsia* is not on the separateness of the group, but on its being called together for a purpose. The political *ekklēsia* was a town meeting, called to do the business of the larger social group. Similarly, the church as *congregation* meets to do the business of the kingdom of God.

Visible or Invisible?

The question of the visibility or invisibility of the church speaks to the relation of the religious organization called church to the spiritual reality it represents. How is the congregation of imperfect flesh-and-blood members related to the spiritual "communion of saints"? Theologically, the question involves a definition of the nature and source of each person's faith. Practically, it involves the question of church discipline. How shall the congregation deal with the weakness and even obvious indifference and insincerity among its members? Is the church of visible members only the imperfect reflection of the true spiritual body? Shall we therefore indulge its imperfections? Or shall we seek to purge the visible church of obviously insincere members so it may be the true body of Christ? Such questions have framed the issues in the debate about the visibility and invisibility of the true church.

The problem is especially acute where membership in the church is defined by civic and family status. Obviously, not all those born and baptized as infants into a people's or state church are genuine participants in the spiritual reality the church represents. Even in a believers church, there are those whose confession is insincere. Hence, the nature of church membership and the question of discipline ("binding and loosing") are involved in the issue of visibility.

There have been generally three positions on the question.[16] The first two begin with the assumption that the church is a religious organization coextensive in membership with the civic community. The *sacramental*, or Catholic, position holds that the visible church is a sacramental body. Belonging to it means to be joined to the spiritual (invisible) body of Christ. Sacramental participation is the essential element in defining membership of the visible church. Therefore, the church offers its service of priestly mediation for the spiritual benefit of all who will accept.

The *fideistic* (faith), or Protestant, position holds that the "true" church is made up of those who have received the gift of saving faith. These elect ones belong to the spiritual (invisible) body of Christ and are the genuine core of the visible church. Since only God knows the quality of faith, it is invisible to human judgment. The visible church must therefore be satisfied to be an ambiguous body with genuine and counterfeit members intermingled. Consequently, the primary responsibility of the visible church is to nurture faith through preaching and to provide pastoral care for its members.

The *believers church*, or Anabaptist, position suggests yet a third option.[17] The visible church is the congregation of those who give evidence of genuine repentance and sincere confession by their loyalty and faithful obedience to Christ. Although faith is an inward attitude or quality, its genuineness, even in weakness, is visible in its outward expression. It makes no pretension to perfection, but it does recognize a distinction between *weak* faith and *false* or dead faith. Therefore, it defines the visible church as those who have responded to the call of Christ. And it assumes responsibility for the spiritual and ethical discipline of its members.

We should note first that none of the above positions hold that there are two churches, a visible one and an invisible, spiritual one. However, the philosophical assumptions of dualistic supernaturalism which underlie traditional orthodoxy naturally encouraged such a concept.[18] The church with its visible and invisible dimensions is one church. Any visible ecclesiastical body which does not participate in and give evidence of the character of the spiritual body of Christ is not an authentic continuation of the messianic community.

The invisible dimensions of the church may be understood as its faith dimensions. With the physical eyes, we see a religious organization, but with the eyes of faith, we see beyond the social community to the spiritual reality of which it is the *sacrament,* the visible sign. The human organization is not the church by virtue of its perfect character. It is the church by faith, just as each individual is saved by faith. But this does not relieve it of the full responsibility to be a holy, disciplined community.[19]

As the sacrament of Christ's presence, the church is the visible sign of spiritual reality. And for this reason its visible pattern and life are of great significance. Where its visible life contradicts the spiritual character we see demonstrated in Christ and which we understand to be the "fruit of the Spirit [of Christ]," we may legitimately question the claim of any religious organization to be the church of Christ.

The Sacraments. When we speak of the church itself as the sacrament of Christ, we need to relate this to the ceremonies, ordinances, or "sacraments" of the church. These signs, such as baptism, the Lord's Supper, and foot washing, are symbolic expressions of the spiritual nature of the church.

Baptism symbolizes its character as a spiritually cleansed and committed body of those who have pledged themselves to Christ. The *Lord's Supper* symbolizes the renewal of the covenant sealed by the blood of Christ and the continuing participation (*koinōnia*) of the members in the body of Christ. It is the symbol of the body's dependence upon Christ. *Foot washing* is symbolic of the members' willingness to serve and be served by others. It is the symbol of the body's interdependence. Another ceremony—*anointing with oil*—symbolizes the church's faith in God as healer of both spiritual and physical illness. *Marriage* is not exclusively an ecclesiastical ceremony, but within the context of the community of faith, it becomes an expression of the relation of the church to Christ.

Perhaps we should pause here to explain how we have used the words *symbol* and *symbolize* above. A symbol, as Paul Tillich taught us, participates in that which it represents. When we participate in the Lord's Supper, for example, we really do participate in the body and blood of Christ by faith. And we do renew the covenant in his blood. The symbolic act is a representational enactment of the faith reality. We use the word *symbolic* because the ceremonial act is representational. It does not supply or substitute for that which it represents. For example, washing the brother or sister's feet does not supply for *agapē*-ic service. Water baptism does not suffice for the actual cleansing from sin or walking in newness of life.

This distinction is important when we enumerate the visible marks of authenticity in the church. The Protestant tradition has tended to make the ceremonial symbols the focus of visibility in the life of the church. In these ceremonies it holds that the church visibly and audibly confesses its faith and demonstrates to the world its relation to Jesus Christ. The Anabaptist tradition was unwilling to define visibility only in terms of symbolic enactments. It insisted that the ceremonial acts must represent a personal-social reality: a visible reality in the life of the church, celebrating their joint covenant with God through Christ.

We may summarize this visible reality as follows: (1) A mature and voluntary commitment to faith in Jesus Christ as the Lord who saves. Saving faith necessarily involves us in recognizing Christ's authority and submission to his rule in our lives. (2) A willingness to take seriously the teaching and example of Christ for the congregation as these are disclosed in the Bible. This calls for spiritual discernment. It is by no means a literalistic or legal test. As the visible church crosses cultural borders, it must constantly reassess its application of the teaching and example of Christ so its life and witness may continue to be an authentic sign of Christ's presence. And (3) a practicing faith: "faith working through love." The visible test of faith's genuineness is loving obedience to Christ as the messianic head of the church.

Organization and Leadership in the Church

The congregation with its regular weekly meetings is not only the most visible form of the church, but also its constitutive form. The traditional "offices" of the church in its ecumenical form are the projection and expansion of the local gathering. The basic offices of the local and universal (catholic) church are the same: bishop, priest, and deacon—or some variant of this.[20]

Other administrative positions are organizational extensions. As we shall see in the following discussion, these "offices" are both charismatic and functional in character. Our point here is that they grow out of the organized life of the local congregation.

The worldwide (ecumenical) church is more like a network of local centers than a legally defined organization. For practical and historical reasons, "denominational" organizations have formed, but these are not of the essence of church. They are, in fact, presently diminishing in importance. To heal denominational divisions, "ecumenical" organizations have been formed. But these, too, are not of the essence. While organizational union may be good and may reflect the unity of the church, given the organic character of the church and the freedom of the Spirit, formal organization can never define its reality. Even ecclesiastical organizations—such as the Eastern Orthodox Church and the Roman Catholic Church, which claim "universality"—have had to recognize this principle.

Functions of the Congregation. For these reasons, we turn our attention first to the functions of the local congregation when we consider the nature of the church's organization. Patterns of organization and leadership are integrally related to function. They have not been laid down from the beginning as a formal pattern into which the church of all time and cultures must be forced. What uniformity there is in the worldwide organizations of the church, grows out of the unity of its life and mission.[21]

For purposes of analysis, we will divide the functions of the local congregation into internal and external activities. As a community, the congregation must both nurture its ongoing life and serve the purposes of Christ in the larger society. It is the representative of Christ in both its gathered life as community and in its life of service to the world. It therefore needs to be aware of the sacramental character of all its organized life.[22]

The church gathers together for *worship, fellowship,* and *teaching.* In its inclusive sense, *worship* is the service of God (*leitourgia*) and rightly applies to all of the church's activity as it is engaged in serving God. In its more restricted sense, it refers to the congregation's cultic expression of its covenant relation to God. It includes hearing and responding to God's word as a group, praising God for his goodness and sufficiency, acknowledging our sin and weakness, hearing the word of forgiveness, confessing the faith, pledging loyalty to the covenant, and praying to God as a community of his people. Worship first concentrates on the relationship of the community to God and engages the congregation in communion with God.

The purpose of worship is to honor God and to remind ourselves constantly—and the world—that Christ is Lord and that we and all we have belong to God. Worship strengthens the bonds between God and his people. Accordingly, Paul gives prophecy first place in the worship, ahead of speaking in tongues. Prophecy is speaking God's inspired words to the congregation. According to Paul, speaking in tongues is a sign for unbelievers (1 Cor. 14:22-25).

Fellowship, or *koinōnia,* might well be listed as one dimension of worship. It is experienced first as a sharing together in the worship of God. But its expression is extended horizontally in our relation to fellow members of the body. By fellowship we mean the mutual support, admonition, correction, and encouragement we enjoy in the congregation. Fellowship is that sense of caring and being cared for as a comrade in the cause of Christ. It includes activities we sometimes classify as "mutual aid." Listening and responding to sisters and brothers as they express their needs in the gathered community has not usually been included in the regular worship service of the congregation, but it belongs there.

Teaching promotes the continuity of the church's life and tradition. Because the church relies on a written canon for its knowledge of Jesus Christ, teaching has a place of special importance in its life. It seeks not only to understand the text, but to apply it in the contemporary context of the congregation. As a "scribe . . . trained for the kingdom," he or she must deal with both the new and the old (Matt. 13:52). Teaching aims not only at the transmission of information; it also includes admonition and motivation. The apostles were commanded to make disciples and to teach them to do all that Jesus had commanded (Matt. 28:20). The goal of teaching is obedience. Such teaching ought to be a constant part of the gathered activity of the church.

The external functions of the church are *evangelism* and *social witness.* Although individuals are given special gifts for these services, they should first be recognized as functions of the congregation itself. It is an individualistic oversimplification to view the congregation's function as merely inspiring individuals, who then scatter for service in their various secular occupations. The church is not simply a spiritual filling station. As salt and light, the congregation is to be a corporate evangelistic and social witness. Both in its lifestyle and corporate voice as a "secular community of the Spirit," it is to be a sign of the kingdom of God in the midst of the old order. It is to be the community of peace and love.[23]

Evangelism is the spreading of the *evangel,* or good news, about the new thing that has happened in Christ, and the calling of men and women to discipleship. This good news goes forth as the proclamation of the church, not as an individual's private religious discovery. Included in the proclamation is the resurrection of Christ and his continuing presence in the church through the Spirit. Thus the church cannot exclude its own existence from the proclamation. Its call to discipleship is also a call to enter the congregation of believers. On this account, the authenticity of the church as the messianic community is of primary importance in evangelism.

The tradition of revivalism and mass evangelism often overlooked the centrality of the church. The call was to a private experience of salvation by Christ. One can see the extreme effects of such an evangelism in the emergence of "the electronic church," which is not a community, but an aggregate of anonymous individuals. The Church Growth Movement has been a correction in the right direction, but its unhappy separation of evangelizing and discipling still devaluates the congregation's role in evangelism. It is no coincidence that the explosive growth of the early church was directly related to the evangelistic presence of the new apostolic community. Into it women and men were called, irrespective of race, social status, or economic class.

The church's *social witness* must begin in the lifestyle of the local congregation. As Berkhof points out, such a witness is part of the salvation message.[24] The congregation has been particularly remiss in this aspect of its witness. It has usually assumed that the work of social witness and service is the task of individuals working in the context of secular organizations. So individual church members go out into the world to make a civil or political witness. Meanwhile, all too often the congregation itself continues to conform to the offensive social behavior!

In far too many cases, the churches have lagged behind judicial decrees while expecting the courts to enforce *agapēic* justice even in the life of the congregation. The congregation as a local community of salvation must demonstrate the new creation order in its own organized life as an integral part of the salvation message.

The social witness of the congregation to secular society, then, must first take the form of obedience to the gospel standard set by Paul in Galatians 3:26-28. To be "in Christ" means to be in a new social order! The church must function as a "light" to the world (Matt. 5:14). Second, following the example of its Master, the church must be nonconformed to the practices of the world (Rom. 12:2). Noncooperation with evil is fully as important in social witness as cooperation with the good. Such corporate nonconformity will often include congregational protests against evil. The Confessing Church's break with Hitler is one example in modern history where local believers took such corporate protest seriously.

Leadership. Leadership in the church has its own special character. It is a "ministry" and a "gift" (*charisma*) of the Spirit to the church. On the one hand, the church is a family under the headship (authority) of Christ, and congregational leaders are his authorized servants (1 Tim. 4:6). As such, they are to be given respect, submission, and support in their ministry (1 Tim. 5:17). On the other hand, all members are on equal footing as sisters and brothers in a family. Jesus taught his disciples not to call anyone man rabbi, master, or father. He called those who do God's will his brothers and sisters (Matt. 23:8-10; Mark 3:35).

The authority of leaders is a familial and spiritual authority, not political. They are cautioned not to be domineering or dictatorial, but respectful, considerate, patient, reasonable, persuasive, and exemplary (Titus 2:15). The authority of leadership stems from its spiritual and moral character and from its wisdom and experience (1 Tim. 4:12). The church is a *koinōnia*, not a *democracy*. It does not operate by a simple majority vote, but by consensus or the spirit of the meeting.[25] The leaders' role, then, is to enable the congregation to discern the mind of the Spirit. In this role they are more than representatives of the congregation's will. Servanthood does not necessarily mean subservience to the latest congregational survey.

Ministries in the Church. As noted above, there is no universally prescribed pattern of offices for the church in the New Testament. The Ephesians 4:11-13 passage says that the "gifts" given by the Spirit to the church are directly related to the ministry of equipping the members for work in God's service. There is provision for the church's cross-cultural mission (apostles, prophets, and evangelists). "Pastors and teachers" are supplied for ministry to the local congregation. Romans 12:4-8 underscores this relation between function and "gift" when it exhorts the various types of leaders to fulfill their functions with diligence.

It is the continuity of function—not a legal precedent in the New Testament—that has preserved the continuity in leadership roles throughout the history of the church. Therefore, the church should be free to vary the pattern of leadership to meet the changing demands of social and cultural contexts. Historically, it has been free to do this. From its beginning, the church has adapted its organizational patterns to the changing political and social ethos. For example, in monarchical societies it has had bishops. Where oligarchy and democracy have been dominant, patterns of eldership and election of officers have been introduced. The crucial element has been the servanthood character of leadership, not its organizational form.

Women in Leadership Roles. The church has been much slower to live up to its original insight that there is to be no difference in social and legal status between men and women in the church (Gal. 3:26-28). This has been particularly obvious in its rare acceptance of women into positions of leadership. Without doubt this is largely due to the reluctance of Western societies to raise the social and political status of women. Only in the nineteenth century—among independent religious movements like the Salvation Army, Pentecostal Holiness, Seventh-day Adventists, and Christian Science—did women begin to have a role in leadership.

There may seem to be New Testament precedent for denying leadership roles to women. Paul has words, or quotes a statement of others, about women keeping silent in the Corinthian churches (1 Cor. 14:34-35). And the Pastoral Epistles state clearly that women are not to teach publicly or have authority over men (1 Tim. 2:11-12).[26] The basic hermeneutical question in dealing with these passages is whether we are to understand them as universal commandments or as contextual adaptations to the local situation or culture. There is good evidence to think that the latter is the correct understanding.

First, Paul clearly sets forth the gospel principle of equality of the sexes in the church in Galatians 3:26-28. Second, there are examples of women in leadership roles in the New Testament church itself. Priscilla clearly played such a role (Acts 18:2, 18, 26; Rom. 16:3-5; 1 Cor. 16:19; 2 Tim. 4:19). Phoebe was a deacon or minister (Rom. 16:1). Third, Paul himself worked closely with women as "co-workers" (Phil. 4:3) and allowed women to prophesy: to speak God-inspired words for the admonition of the congregation (1 Cor. 11:5). The 1 Corinthians 14:34-35 passage may not refer to the matter of public speaking at all, but to disturbances in the meeting.[27]

In the early and fluid decades of the new movement, women played a significant role in its spread. They enjoyed considerable freedom in the meetings. In societies where women were generally segregated at religious meetings, public scandal may have been the main concern at first. By the latter part of the first century as heresy threatened (1 Tim. 2:11-14; 2 Tim. 3:1-9), *roles* protectively began to harden into *offices*. The cultural patterns of the environment prevailed. We know that the church lost ground in this area of its witness in the following centuries. Women became second-rate members in the church, and the male leaders allowed a double moral standard.

The *gospel* principle of equality in status and position in the church was clearly stated by Paul in Galatians 3:28. It is significant that the principle appears in this proclamation of salvation by grace and Christian freedom to live by a new standard. Unfortunately, the church has never lived up to its own constitutional principle. Therefore, to be faithful to this principle, we need to move away from legalities and return to the major leadership concerns enunciated in the New Testament. These are the concern for order, for genuine spiritual authority, for upholding high ethical standards, and for not causing unnecessary offense in the culture where the gospel is being introduced.

Koinōnia in the Church

Church has usually been associated with the religious institution and its organized rituals and service program. By the fourth century, it was necessary for the properly ordained leaders to be present in order for the church to be gathered. As time passed, church became identified with their official presence. As Cyprian put it, "Where the bishop is, there is the church."

As the congregation became institutionally self-conscious, the concern for proper order and orthodox belief underscored concern for properly ordained leadership. "Apostolic" authority was defined as proper ordination. Only properly ordained leaders could consecrate and dispense the sacraments. And only ordained leaders could define the apostolic faith. Hence, in the process of self-definition and protection against false teaching, *church* came to be defined as the organized religious institution, rather than the messianic movement. This bias has persisted even when the institution was redefined, as it was in the Reformation.

In such a climate of concern, a small informal grouping of believers for Bible study and spiritual discipline became problematic. Without proper authorization and connection to the institution, it was considered schismatic and even heretical. This was especially true where the group assumed the prerogatives of church: sacramental fellowship. The Anabaptists of the Reformation and later Pietist groups experienced the harsh disfavor of the church and eventually were forced out of the institution as heretics. Again, we must note that this bias has continued in modified form in the present. Where leadership is viewed in hierarchical fashion, the ecclesial small group is feared as divisive.

In the mainstream churches, small house fellowship groups, properly contained in and defined by the congregation, are often organized as an incidental part of the program. Their purpose is informal socializing and Bible study. The discernment and decision-making functions of the church are reserved for official committees and councils. Church is identified with the institutional office and program.

However one might rationalize this organization of church, the original genius of the messianic movement did not take this form. In its earliest pattern, it was a network of house fellowships (*koinōniai*) held together by the "apostles' teaching and fellowship" (Acts 2:42). Apostolic recognition of new groups as part of the movement *followed* the initiative of informal lay witness (Acts 8:4-8, 14-17).

We need not copy this pattern exactly, but we should recognize the constitutive elements in it for the definition of the church of Christ.

The church comes into social expression where a group of even "two or three" gathers in the name and spirit of Jesus Christ (Matt. 18:20). It is significant that this sanction of the minimally small number of "two or three . . . gathered in my name" comes in the context of churchly discernment and discipline. Not the size, place, or institutional authorization, but the purpose and Spirit/spirit of the meeting define its churchly character.

Those who define church as a *congregation hearing* the Word of God and participating in the sacraments, emphasize properly ordained teaching and preaching. The size of the congregation is unimportant so long as it can carry out these functions. But where church is defined as a *community of response* to the Word, the size, shape, and character of the group becomes more important. Primary relationships and responsibilities of the members are of paramount concern.

The critical problem of the church today is to preserve the *koinōnia* form of the original movement as a messianic witness. The institutional congregation tends constantly to become another altruistic social organization with its ideology, ritual, and service programs. *The purpose of the ecclesial small group is to help the congregation function as a koinōnia, not a political democracy.* It is the means by which individuals become genuinely involved in the life and mission of the larger body.

Conversely, it can be an effective means by which the larger body carries out its decision-making, pastoral, and evangelistic functions. It can serve as a door into the fellowship of the church. It can foster the personal-spiritual dimensions of the activity and witness of the organization. It can be an instrument of discernment and decision-making. The ecclesial small group should, therefore, understand itself and be understood as the elemental church ("the base church"), not simply as an ancillary program of an otherwise complete organization.

Conclusion

In conclusion, the church has not taken itself seriously enough as God's *messianic change agent* in history. It has too easily limited its mission to that of a religious institution serving the larger political and social order. Although God does not limit himself to the agency of the church, nevertheless he has chosen it as a primary instrument to reveal his plan for human history (Eph. 3:9-11). The church's ministry is robbed of its eschatological, messianic dimensions if it neglects crucial aspects of its witness to God's universal rule and justice (Matt. 6:33) and relegates that sphere to civil and political agencies.

Religious nurture, inspiration of the individual, and maintenance of social morality and family stability are important, but they should not be the primary focus of the church's concern. The church must take seriously its role as *messianic community*, bearing witness to that "eternal purpose that he [God] has carried out in Christ Jesus our Lord" (Eph. 3:11). If it does so, it will need to focus its vision beyond the immediate individual needs of the congregation. Jesus himself recognized that his mission of social and historical realignment would cause disturbance and hardship to some. But he insisted that God's justice must be put ahead of personal and family interests (Matt. 10:34-39).

The sixteenth-century Anabaptist martyrs understood this as they attempted to reestablish the church as a messianic mission, rather than a sectarian unit within Christendom. Thus Menno Simons made "bearing the heavy cross of Christ" a fundamental mark of the true church.

Jesus' demand that his cause be put ahead of father and mother (Luke 14:26) is a hard word. Surely it does not mean that Christians should neglect their responsibility to family (1 Tim. 5:8). But it does challenge Christians to put all of life in proper eschatological perspective. That is the meaning of the command to put the kingdom of God first and to trust that everything else will be added (Matt. 6:19-34). Unless the church actually obeys this crucial commandment, it will fail to live up to its messianic identity.

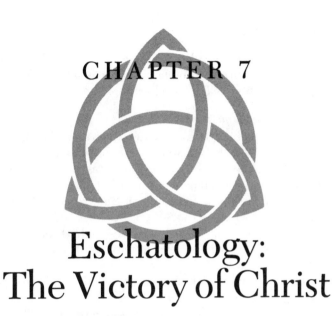

CHAPTER 7

Eschatology:
The Victory of Christ

Introduction

Christian eschatology is an assessment of the movement of history in light of the advent of Jesus Christ. It presupposes that God is "the Alpha and the Omega," the Creator and Consummator of human history. It involves a diagnosis of the human situation based on the revelation of human nature and destiny in Jesus Christ. More narrowly defined, it is a reflection on the consummation of history and human destiny. *Eschaton* means end. It is an account of the hope Christians have in Christ because of his resurrection.

Because of much overspeculation and prediction, eschatology has too often been considered esoteric and relegated to the exotic, along with fortune-telling. Although eschatology is more than the calculated projection of trends, it has more in common with "futurology" than fortune-telling. To make yet another comparison, it is like a medical prognosis based upon a diagnosis and knowledge of the progressive course of a disease and its known remedies. So we will base our picture of the end of history on our understanding of the human dilemma and our faith that Jesus Christ provides the solution for that dilemma.

Many considerations go into the making of an eschatological interpretation. Concepts of time and eternity, presuppositions about the nature of biblical prophecy, understandings of the role and nature of Jesus as the Messiah, and one's hermeneutical method—all these have a direct bearing on the final interpretation. We will therefore look briefly at these presuppositions in our introduction.

Time, Change, and Consummation

The ancients thought of time as a wheel which rotated endlessly. The nature cycle provided the metaphor for temporal movement. There was no eschaton to the circular motion. Time was simply marked off by a sequence of repetitive changes which indicated progression without progress. This is the fruitless, frustrating situation to which the writer of Ecclesiastes speaks when he laments that "there is nothing new under the sun" and "all is vanity" (Eccles. 1). By contrast, biblical time is *historical* time that marks off personal movement based on decision and oriented toward a goal.

An eschaton, or consummation to history, is a distinctly biblical concept. It assumes a beginning and sequential movement toward a goal. Eschaton indicates both a *finis* and *telos*—an end both as the conclusion and purpose to a process. We use the word *chronos* to mark the sequence as a period of time, and we measure such time with our clocks. But the biblical idea introduces another concept of time which the Greeks called *kairos*.[1]

Kairos marks the significant or opportune time (John 7:6-8). It is the time of important events which move history toward its goal. It is the time of the fulfillment of God's promise (Acts 7:17). Israel's Exodus from Egypt and the advent of Jesus were such *kairo*tic moments in history. Paul says Jesus' birth came at "the fullness of time [*chronos*]" (Gal. 4:4). That is, the *kairo*tic moment gave fullness or significance to chronological time. In the words of 1 Corinthians 10:11, Christ's coming marked the "fulfilment [*telē*] of the ages" (NEB). Ephesians 1:10 speaks of the consummating victory of Christ as the "fullness of *kairōn* (times)."

In our modern scientific age, *chronos*, or linear time, marks off the extent of a period of time. This time is a measurement of things in space. We speak of a time-space continuum that we can measure with clocks and calendars. Accordingly, physicists estimate that the universe is about thirteen billion years old. Anthropologists calculate that the present human race (Homo sapiens) has been on the earth for some 350,000 years.

The Bible has relatively little interest in this kind of time. To be sure, the biblical writers keep a chronological record of events, but their concern is not simply with the accuracy of the historical record.

Instead, they are concerned to record the *kairo*tic "acts of God" which give meaning to chronology. As we shall see, their concern was with the consummation or fulfillment of God's purposes in history.[2]

With this difference in mind, we must distinguish between the chronology and the *kairo*logy of future events. Jesus said no one knows the "day or the hour" (chronology) of God's *kairos* (Mark 13:32-33). On the other hand, the apostles assure us that God's *kairos* is always near at hand. This crucial distinction is often overlooked in the discussion of eschatology.

Prophecy and Apocalyptic

Prophecy is often equated with all kinds of prediction from fortune-telling to statistical projections. But the Bible is careful to distinguish it from fortune-telling and speculation based on magical rites. Fortune-telling is based on a concept of fate or luck that is foreign to the biblical concept of prophecy. Time is God's creation, and God is in control of it. Therefore, prophecy is faith's interpretation of history as the acts of the Lord God. The prophet declares "the divinely imparted meaning of history," writes David Napier.[3]

Predictive prophecy is a form of exhortation based not on clairvoyance, but upon moral and spiritual insight. Its predictions are founded on an understanding of God's will and a correct understanding of current events from God's perspective. Such discernment arises from what God has revealed of himself in the past through Moses, the prophets, and Jesus Christ. Thus, the prophets announced God's will for his people and linked their predictions to their exhortations to obedience.

The basic form of the prophetic message is "If you do . . . the outcome will be. . . ." In the context of exhortation, there is promise of blessing for obedience and warning of judgment for disobedience. The prophecy itself does not determine the outcome of events.

The biblical test for truth in prophecy is twofold. First, in line with its hortatory character, authentic biblical prophecy encourages people to honor the God revealed in the historical tradition that culminates in Jesus Christ. Even if a striking prediction comes to pass, the one making the prediction may be a "false prophet" (Deut. 13:1-8; 18:20; cf. Gal. 1:8-9). According to 1 John 4:1-3, false prophets are those who have an incorrect understanding of God's incarnational role in history.

Second, prophecy is integrally related to history. What transpires in history is part of the norm for authentic prophecy. The Deuteronomist puts it plainly: "If a prophet speaks in the name of the Lord, but the thing does not take place or prove true, it is a word that the Lord has not spoken" (Deut. 18:22). Today most Christian prophecies come as interpretations of biblical passages. When such predictions fail to happen, we can safely assume that the interpretation is false. What God has done and is doing in history is crucial for understanding what he will do in the future. Although God is dynamic, he does not change character. Therefore, when predictions about God's future activity contradict his self-revelation in Christ, we can safely ignore them.

Apocalyptic is a specific kind of predictive literature which has a special interest in the end of history. It divides existence into two aeons—the present evil age and the age of salvation yet to come. In this sense, biblical apocalyptic is sharply dualistic. During this present era, God's people must live as "aliens" in a hostile world waiting for a salvation yet to be revealed (1 Pet. 1:5; 2:11-12). As the Noachian flood destroyed the wicked population, so this age will end in judgment and the "new heavens and a new earth, where righteousness is at home" will be ushered in (2 Pet. 3:11-13). Later apocalypticism under the influence of Greek metaphysics tended to change this into a dualism of spiritual (eternal) and temporal (historical) realms.

The historical temporal realm ("this age") is under the immediate—though not the ultimate—control of the powers of evil. Humankind is trapped in slavery to these evil powers. Human history can end only in the escalation of evil and the catastrophic judgment of God upon it. Salvation is understood as the destruction and punishment of evil, both human and demonic, and the final vindication of God's authority and justice. This eschatological salvation will usher in the age of righteousness, when God's Messiah will reign over a new heaven and earth.

Such an apocalyptic view is found both in pre-Christian Judaic and in Christian literature. New Testament apocalyptic continued to use the "wineskins" of Judaic apocalyptic language, but poured new messianic wine into them. Christian apocalyptic in the following centuries often missed the explosive changes implied in this new revelation given in Christ. Jesus was interpreted as the one who came to save humankind from this present evil age, but was rejected by Israel and the bulk of humanity. Consequently, he has withdrawn to heaven, where he now exercises a spiritual reign. At the end of this age he will return in catastrophic splendor as Judge and Savior and set up his kingdom on earth.[4]

Modern Christian apocalypticism has several characteristic features by which one can recognize it. First, it claims to have esoteric knowledge of the end which was revealed to the ancients in a mystery and kept secret until the time of Christ. Second, the knowledge is about the schema of history and about world empires—from Babylon to modern

Great Britain and Russia. A part of this revelation is knowledge of "times and seasons," eras and events, which make it theoretically possible to calculate the chronology of the end. However, a third characteristic is that these revelations are given in the form of symbolic images, allegories, and time equations that preserve the mystery. Finally, its prognosis of human developments is usually pessimistic. Judgment and salvation come only by the sovereign intervention of God.

Both prophetic and apocalyptic approaches appear in the Bible. They are not entirely contradictory, although they do have distinct emphases and in places are difficult to reconcile. In many respects, as John W. Miller observes, apocalypticism is an interpretation and extension of the prophetic literature by Jewish scholars and "wise men" like Daniel (Dan. 1:4), who knew the prophecies only in their written form.[5] Perhaps a brief comparative chart will highlight the differences and similarities.

Prophetic	Apocalyptic
(1) Since God is at work in history (the kingdom of God begun), the prophet attempts to find the meaning of the present situation and predict the outcomes of alternative behaviors.	(1) Since this age is under control of Satan and irretrievably evil (the kingdom of God withdrawn), the apocalypticist dismisses the present and looks forward to a future age for meaning.
(2) The savior comes *within* the boundaries of our human existence with a spiritual and social salvation.	(2) The savior comes *to* the boundaries of our existence and calls the elect *out of* it with a heavenly, spiritual salvation.
(3) Eschatological salvation means *transformation* of the present cosmic system.	(3) Eschatological salvation means judgment, the *destruction* of the present evil system, rescue of the righteous, and a new creation.
(4) The eschaton is the fulfillment of God's creative work.	(4) The eschaton is a cosmic battle entailing the destruction of the old, and re-creation.

Hermeneutical Considerations

When is a prophetic oracle fulfilled? The answer to this simple question is quite complicated by the hermeneutical situation. We do not always know the setting of the original oracle and therefore do not know to what it referred. Further, the local event which was predicted is sometimes given an eschatological slant as an end-time judgment or renewal. This has led to the dual interpretation of some oracles. A simple example of such double fulfillment is Matthew 1:22-23 citing Isaiah 7:14. The Isaiah prophecy undoubtedly had a local reference, and Matthew applies it further to the birth of Jesus. This aspect of interpretation can become complicated, especially with prophecy about Israel's judgment and renewal.

Furthermore, these inspired oracles have been collected, edited, and reported in "books" for future generations, thus removing the prophecies from their original contexts. New significance might have been attributed to the prophecies when they were interpreted for those living in later periods. It is with these recorded prophecies as they have been elaborated in the following centuries that we have to work.

We have already mentioned that apocalyptic is one style of interpreting of the prophetic materials. Daniel 9:2, 24ff., gives an explicit example of how the prophecy of Jeremiah (25:11; 29:10) was elaborated. This apocalyptic elaboration was continued into the New Testament. Such apocalyptic interpretations use highly symbolic—even grotesque—visions which do not give us the kind of literal meanings we value in the twentieth century. Nevertheless, the first-century Christians were satisfied and comforted by such symbolic generalizations about the future. This ought to warn us against literalistic interpretations that provide blueprints of the future.

Apocalyptic aside, the way New Testament writers interpret the written prophecies does not give us a systematic or consistent methodology for understanding them. Passages which originally had no obvious predictive intent are said to be "fulfilled" by contemporary events in Christ's life and ministry. Prophecies about Israel are applied to Christ and said to be fulfilled in him. Some prophecies are given a quite literal interpretation while others are not. Historical passages are given typological and allegorical interpretations and applied to contemporary situations. It is not surprising, therefore, that eschatology has been a highly controversial subject throughout the centuries.

Hermeneutical Schemata. Today interpretative schemes range from the simple denial of a historical consummation to literal calculations and charts explaining how and when it will end. In the early twentieth century at the liberal end of the continuum, the kingdom was construed as values which define the ideal for human society. In more recent liberal theology, the biblical materials are understood as mythical symbols and "mythologized." An "eschatological present" which Jesus introduced and in which Christians now live by faith, is substituted for a future consummation of history. Hence, as Paul Tillich wrote, "It [the *eschaton*] ceases to be an imaginative matter about an indefinitely far (or near) catastrophe in time and space and becomes an expression of our standing in every moment in face of the eternal."[6]

Emil Brunner also recognized the prescientific, mythical character of the apocalyptic symbols in the Bible. But he tried to preserve the biblical concept of a consummation to history. "The Consummation as eternal life is the relationship to God in which we see Him 'face to face': the Consummation as the Kingdom of God signifies the perfection of the relationships between [persons]."[7] He says this consummation of history as the kingdom of God is essential to the kerygma. The end means fulfillment, not only of individual beatitude, but of human society in *agapē*. He does not, however, attempt to imagine the unimaginable and place such a consummation on a chronological continuum.

Neo-evangelical theologians have insisted that the prophetic and apocalyptic language of the Bible must be understood in spatiotemporal terms. The consummation must be understood as a chronological event, even though we do not know when or how it will occur.

The classical models for interpreting prophetic language are cast in *millennial* or *nonmillennial* terms. The millennialists hold that the kingdom of God will be consummated in a literal millennial (1000-year) reign of Christ on earth. They relate the time of Christ's personal bodily return to this reign. Some hold that Christ will come after the millennium (*postmillennialists*) as the grand climax to his present spiritual reign. Others think he will come before the millennium (*premillennialists*) to defeat the evil forces and set up an earthly kingdom. Most taking this position expect the church to be raptured out of the world to escape an intense backlash of evil before the millennial kingdom. Others warn that Christ's return will be after the church endures persecution (posttribulationists). The *nonmillennialists* (or amillennialists) hold that Christ's coming will be bodily and personal. But they do not relate it to a literal reign of Christ on earth. Rather, they hold that his return will usher in the eternal reign of God.

A more recent version of premillennialism introduced in the nineteenth century is called dispensationalism. It is a full-fledged modern version of apocalypticism. It divides world history into eras, or dispensations, in which God deals with humankind according to the principles set forth in each dispensation. The system features an elaborate scheme of end-time events based upon a literal interpretation of the prophetic symbols. Its "any moment" theory stresses the "imminence" of the return of Christ.

The church is in one dispensation, and in a different one is the kingdom, in which Israel is again the central focus. During the present church dispensation, the Spirit of Christ saves individuals through the work of Christ on the cross. But in the future kingdom dispensation, Christ will reinstate the nation of Israel as his people and inaugurate a political reign.

According to the classical orthodox schemata (post-, pre-, nonmillennialism), the church is recognized as the historical expression of the kingdom. The eschatological reign of God is a fulfillment of the lordship of Christ in the church. On the other hand, dispensationalism sees a radical discontinuity between church and kingdom. The church is a spiritual, faith reality, and the kingdom is postponed to a future time. The spatiotemporal consummation is essentially unrelated to the present historical process. It is inaugurated by the violent catastrophic intervention of God.

Hermeneutical Guidelines. Hermeneutical considerations will greatly influence our theological portrayal of end-time events and the consummation of history. None of the above schemata are simply read out of the Bible, although dispensational premillennialism has claimed to be such a literal reading. Our definitions of time and history, presuppositions about the nature of "objective truth," and our philosophy of language all influence our hermeneutical decisions.

First, we should note that history and our modern concept of time are by no means the same. Furthermore, our concept of time and the biblical concept are different. The biblical concept of time is closer to our concept of history. As von Rad points out, the Hebrew concept of linear time developed as a conception of successive and related significant events.[8] Time for them was not a formal concept of an abstract temporal extension in which everything happens. That is a modern "scientific" conception of time. For the Old Testament prophets, time was "filled time" or "historical time."

As we shall be using the term, *history* indicates a temporal chain of significant human action. It is made up of human events—a succession of actions related by the deliberate responses of personal beings.[9] Of course, human events include natural occurrences. But strictly speaking, history, as distinguished from natural change, is the ongoing flow of events as they are experienced and shaped by persons.

The eschaton as described in the Bible is the culmination of such a historical succession. It is marked by cosmic disturbances such as earthquakes and heavenly portents. As the doctrine of creation does not refer to the beginning of abstract time but of human history ("filled time"), so the eschaton is the end of human history and not necessarily of abstract time.

This means that in eschatology we are not speaking of a cessation of the spatiotemporal order, such as the astronomers speculate about. We are speaking rather of the transformation of human existence. We are dealing with human experience and activity in relation to God, not with a theory of the end of the solar system. For example, when the seer of Patmos saw a vision of the moon turning to blood, he was not giving an account of how the earth's satellite will decompose (Rev. 6:12-14). Instead, he was using graphic symbolic portents to describe the fierceness of God's wrath against the systemic injustices of human society.

It is impossible for us to imagine or describe this eschaton of history without using spatiotemporal concepts. But we cannot say with certainty how and when this transformation of our historical existence will intersect with the chronological extension of time. Therefore, our conceptual descriptions must be in figurative language. Eschatology is a philosophy or theology of history, not a scientific explanation of how and when the universe will cease to be.

The biblical concept of eternity is not simply timelessness. It is not the abstract, formal negation of time. If this were the case, as it is in Neoplatonic philosophy, God would be totally removed from time in a static, transcendent existence.

The biblical concept of eternity is expressed with the phrase "into the ages of the ages." This suggests unimaginable aeons of time, such as the "dream time" of the Australian aborigines. This has little relation to clock time, but it does suggest God's everlasting activity and involvement with his universe. Eternity, as Emil Brunner points out, is not the negation of time; it "is full of positive content. Eternity as we apprehend it in faith, is the presence of the self-communicating love of God."[10] From an eschatological perspective, then, eternity is a qualitative concept and indicates the transformation of human existence by the saving action of God in Jesus Christ. John's Gospel says that those who "believe in the Son" already have "eternal life" (3:36).

A second hermeneutical question concerns the "objectivity" of

God's action in history and how we perceive that activity as "truth." Literalists minimize the symbolic character of eschatological language and insist that God's activity must be documentable as empirically supernatural events. These must be observed, verified, and described in literal terms. For example, the creation must be understood as a scientifically verifiable account of the universe's beginning, which can be placed with relative precision on a time chart. Miracles, including Christ's resurrection, must be understood as physical occurrences which can be examined and scientifically documented as history.

Following this logic, eschatological events must also be interpreted as empirical supernatural occurrences which can be located on a time chart of the future. The end of history will happen in a literal succession of natural and political events as described in biblical apocalyptic literature. In other words, such events must be recognizable not only by "faith" but by "sight." Otherwise, they hold, the biblical accounts are not objectively or factually true. And this would place in doubt the actuality of God's work in history.

The concern of literalists to preserve the historical dimensions of eschatology is laudable. The problem is with their conception of how God acts in history. The question is not *whether* but *how* God manifests himself in our spatiotemporal framework. The Bible clearly teaches that God intervenes in cosmic history to create, sustain, guide, and overrule. But the supernatural dimensions of such activity are not available to scientific investigation. To say otherwise is simply a self-contradiction because the scientific method is limited to the empirical. Science can explore and describe the "unusual," the "coincidental," and "not yet understood" causal connections. But it cannot investigate the God-connection.

Perhaps the resurrection of Jesus, which inaugurated the eschaton, gives us our best clue to the nature of future eschatological events. The resurrection narratives give us a two-dimensional report. On the one level, there is simply the report of the mysterious transformation of Jesus' body for which there is only circumstantial evidence. On the other level—the level of historical documentation—they report the consequent experiences of the disciples with the living Christ. Accordingly, we affirm the historical event while we confess the mystery at the core of that event. Exactly what happened and how it happened, we do not and cannot know. How the empty tomb, the appearances of Christ, the spiritual fellowship, and the empowerment were experienced is a matter of historical documentation.

A Christian view of history marks the "beginning" as *creation* by

God. It understands the normative center to be the *resurrection* of Christ. From these events it projects the nature of the eschaton. As neither of the past events in this eschatological projection is fully accessible to scientific investigation and literal description, so we can assume it will be with the consummation. The overwhelming evidence both from the Bible and from science tells us that the "supernatural" element is a faith-perceived dimension of the secular (temporal) order, which, we confess, is also under God's control.

Hence, we should read the apocalyptic descriptions of the end-time events symbolically, not as literal history. We should recognize the visionary prophetic predictions of the end as an interpretative element and not turn them into literal events. Wars, famines, and oppression which are the result of political and economic sin are literal history, but their significance as prophetic "signs" is evident only to faith. Only faith can perceive the reality of God's authority and power moving history toward its end, the consummated "kingdom of God." And eschatology has to do with that kingdom![11]

The great vision of prophetic *hope* pictures the eschaton as that time when God will open everyone's eyes to see that the *faith* reality is indeed the objective reality of history. It will be a time of *epiphaneia* (appearing), when Jesus Christ will be revealed for who and what he truly is. It will be an indisputable manifestation that the God of Jesus Christ is in control and that the *love* manifested in the cross and resurrection of Jesus is the "objective" way of life.[12] We will return to this matter later in the discussion.

Again, God has taken our history seriously. It is his involvement in our history that gives it meaning. This involvement focuses most clearly in God's embodiment in the crucified and risen Jesus Christ. In fact, it is the historical incarnation which necessitates a doctrine of eschatology. In Christ we see the nature and extent of God's plan for human history. We discover that the kingdom of God has cosmic implications which are being worked out through Christ (Eph. 1:10). Therefore, our view of the eschaton must take social history—and not only individual spiritual existence—seriously.

Finally, we must note that the eschaton is the revelation of the same Jesus of Nazareth the Gospels introduce. The Christian insistence on a "bodily personal" return of Jesus underscores this aspect of the eschaton. The final "coming" (*parousia*) is a "return" in the sense that it will be entirely consistent and in character with the historical Christ event. The Christ who comes will be recognizable as the one who has already visited his people. He will not have changed character or be another person than he was. Thus, our interpretation of the symbols of wrath, vengeance, and violence of "the Lamb" must be conditioned by our understanding of Jesus' cross and resurrection.[13]

Jesus and Eschatological Fulfillment
Christ, the Eschatological Transition

The New Testament writers present the Christ event as the fulfillment of God's promised salvation and the inauguration of the final *kairos*. According to Mark's Gospel, Jesus introduced his ministry with the announcement that God's *kairos* has arrived and his rule is about to be inaugurated (1:15). This is clearly eschatological language.

The major thrust of Jesus' message was the kingdom of God. He identified his own authority over demons and sickness as the kingdom, or rule, of God present among the people (Matt. 12:28). He taught his disciples to pray for and seek first the consummation of this kingdom. He rebuked some of his fellow Jews because they did not recognize his ministry as God's *kairos*. The arrival of the kingdom of God in the person of Jesus Christ was the eschatological crisis that ushered in the new era—"the last days."

After Christ's resurrection, the apostles who led the new movement believed they were living in a new era which they referred to as "the last days" (Acts 2:17) and "the ends of the ages" (1 Cor. 10:11). The eschatological *kairos* had come as a surprise. God had "shortened the time (*kairos*)," and they were convinced that the present moment was critical (1 Cor. 7:29; Rom. 13:11). Jesus' coming demanded universal repentance and recognition of the new thing God was doing (Acts 17:30).

The universal note in their preaching—without an accompanying religious imperialism—is new. According to the eschatological oracle of Zechariah, for example, the end time belongs to the victorious Jewish nation (9:1-8; 12:6-8). The pagan nations will recognize Jerusalem as the true center of worship (Zech. 8:20-23; 14:16-19; cf. Hag. 2:6-9). Such a view of God's triumph as a national victory which gives Israel an imperialistic mandate, was strengthened in the time of the Maccabees. The nations of the earth will participate in the final *kairos* only as they recognize God and the authority of Jerusalem.

But the death and resurrection of Christ ended the imperialistic aspect of the vision for the disciples. The new age is to be a time of the gospel breaking down old national and cultural barriers (Col. 1:15; Gal. 3:26-28). Christ's cross and resurrection are to be the means of creating "one new humanity" (Eph. 2:14-15) in which all peoples belong to the one "household of God" (2:19). The salvific reign of God henceforth belongs to all nations. The disciples' commission is to bring them under Christ's authority as fellow disciples (Matt. 28:19-20).

One cannot isolate a single event in Jesus' life as that which inaugurated the new age, but the resurrection is clearly the climax of his earthly messianic mission. As such, it marks the eschatological transition. Paul speaks of it as an anticipation of the final resurrection (1 Cor. 15:20-24). It ends the old era of death. By the same token, it inaugurates the new age of resurrection.

The introduction of the new age of resurrection does not mean that the full eschatological reality is immediately realized. Death is not universally overcome. Instead, the introduction of the new comes as a new historical possibility. Jesus said it begins to grow like a seed that has been planted. It works like yeast placed in dough (Mark 4:26-29; Matt. 13:33). The introduction of the age of electricity did not mean that everyone in the world suddenly had electric lights in their homes. Similarly, the introduction of the new age of resurrection does not mean the immediate conquest of death.

The domination of death and the fear of death ends for those who by faith participate in the death and resurrection of Christ (Rom. 6:4-5). They are able to live a new kind of life in the midst of the old existential order which is even now passing away (1 Cor. 7:31). For them there is already a new order of creation (2 Cor. 5:17). They live with a new hope of the resurrection and can thus live beyond the power and fear of death. In Romans 8:9-11, 19-24, Paul speaks of this as spiritual life in the midst of the old creation, which struggles to give birth to a new thing.[14]

The Kingdom of God

Jesus' eschatological teaching focuses on the kingdom or rule of God "on earth as it is in heaven." Because of its central importance, we need to examine this kingdom truth in more detail. Scholars generally agree that the parables of the kingdom are most likely primary teachings of Jesus. They therefore are a key source in exploring this topic.

In its broadest sense, the *basileia tou theou,* or rule of God, is simply God's sovereignty from eternity to eternity. God is the "Alpha and Omega," the Creator and final Judge. The question is how this is given expression in history. Up to the present, God's sovereignty has not been patently obvious. If God is the "Lord" of history, how and where do we see the manifestation of his rule?

The Jewish rabbis taught that Abraham was the first to make God

king upon earth, since he was the first to recognize the one God as
king. Similarly, the rule of God was made effective in history when Israel accepted the yoke of the law under the Mosaic covenant at Sinai.
Hence, God's reign came to be associated with Israel's political ideal.
God was Israel's king. The rest of the nations were outside his covenant. The nation of Israel was to be God's "servant" through whom he
would establish his rule universally. When this did not happen, the vision shifted to the eschaton. In the eschaton, God's reign would be giv-
en a national expression as the kingdom of Israel under the reign of the
Messiah. Jerusalem would be the world capital and religious center.[15]

Into this historical context, Jesus, and John the Baptist before him,
appeared, saying that the *basileia tou theou* (kingdom of God) was immediately approaching. John announced it as a day of judgment in the
style of the Old Testament prophets. Jesus, on the other hand, saw it as
a day of salvation. What does this mean? What was to be the historical
expression of God's rule?

Jesus' parables give us clues concerning its nature and character. We
will review some of the salient points. First, the kingdom is an earthly
historical phenomenon in which the nations and peoples of the earth
are engaged (Matt. 13:24-30, 36-43). It is not only a spiritual rule in individual hearts. Second, the kingdom is not nationalistic and not exclusively for Israel. It does not result in an imperialistic religio-political institution, but in a great fellowship (Luke 13:18-19, 29). Third, while the
kingdom is a historical and social reality, it is not an ordinarily observable movement or organization (Mark 4:26-29; Luke 17:20). Fourth,
the kingdom is the work of God, not of human religion. It "comes" as
the result of God's intervention, and not of an evolutionary, progressive
movement in history (Matt. 6:10). It is received or entered by faith.

The Sermon on the Mount describes the kingdom's character and
covenant terms. God's justice is at its constitutional core (Matt. 6:33).
The Beatitudes characterize its political stance. Its Torah, or law, can
be summarized in one word: *agapē*. It is based entirely upon unques-
tioning trust in and obedience to God. Its strategy is vicarious servanthood, after the example of Jesus himself. Its king is "the Son of
Man" (Matt. 16:28; Luke 22:30), and its dynamic power is the Spirit of
God.

Such a characterization of the kingdom of God identifies it with the
"kingdom of Christ." This identification of the two kingdoms is supported by the New Testament view that the kingship of Christ, which
began with his baptism and anointing with the Spirit, is the authentic
manifestation of the rule of God (Eph. 1:9-10; 5:5; 1 Cor. 15:24-25;

2 Pet. 1:11; Rev. 11:15; 17:14; 19:6).[16]

In its present stage, the kingdom of God is manifest in the presence and work of the Spirit of Christ. In truth, the gift of the Spirit and the inclusion of the Gentiles in the new covenant are signs of the "last days" (Acts 2:17-21; Rom. 8:23). At present the kingdom of God is experienced by faith as the rule of Christ which is still hidden from the world, as it was in his earthly ministry.

We speak of the rule of Christ as spiritual in the sense that it embodies the authority and power of love, in contrast to the politics of violence, which characterize social and political institutions (John 18:36; Gal. 5:21b-26). This is "the fruit of the Spirit." However, it *is* a historical power and authority and it has a social-political expression. It is the kind of power expressed in the cross and resurrection. For those who would follow Christ, it means servanthood and "bearing the heavy cross of Christ."

The Eschaton *as Kingdom of God*

The eschatological conviction of the church is that the authority of God—God's kingdom, as it was disclosed in Jesus—is the ultimate power in the universe. It will finally be acknowledged openly when Jesus is recognized as "King of kings." God will accomplish his plan for the reunification of the universe through Christ (Eph. 1:10).

The universal rule of God is clearly the goal of history. But it is not clear how Jesus conceptualized the final victory of God's kingdom. He stressed that only God knows the time of the end (Matt. 24:36), and he used current apocalyptic images to speak of it as judgment and salvation. But there is no one standardized picture of the consummation. There are at least four patterns suggested in the New Testament materials.

First, some passages indicate that at the end of world history, the followers of Jesus will be translated into an eternal spiritual kingdom (heaven) prepared for them (John 14:2-3; 1 Thess. 4:17; 1 Pet. 1:4-5; 2 Pet. 1:11). Emphasis in this conception is upon reward in the future state. The righteous enjoy the fulfillment of restored relationship which begins in our earthly life and continues after death (1 John 5:11-12; 2 Cor. 5:8; Phil. 1:23; Rev. 7). On the other hand, those who reject the way of Jesus will suffer God's eternal judgment in "outer darkness" (Matt. 8:12; John 5:29). According to this pattern, the victory of God's reign is beyond historical time as we know it.

The second pattern is a variant of the first. It envisions a new age beyond the present one after the evil of this age has been destroyed. God

will create "new heavens and a new earth, where righteousness is at
home" (2 Pet. 3:8-14; Rev. 20:8—21:5). According to this picture, the
wicked suffer a "second death" (Rev. 21:8) which totally removes them
from the new creation. Again, the theme of discontinuity between this
world and the age to come is emphasized.

A third pattern is extrapolated from the believer's experience of the
resurrection and transformation of the earthly Christ (Rom. 8:11, 18-
25). Those who are already participating in the fruits of the new age in
the midst of the old, endure tension and suffering as they wait for the final transformation. Such transformation will mean life and freedom for
the whole creation, which also "waits with eager longing" for the final
victory over frustration and death. In this model the old age is not destroyed, but transformed. There is continuity in that the struggle of the
world is recognized as "giving birth." And there is discontinuity in that
the transformation or resurrection is totally God's work.

A final conception of the end is the successful completion of creation
according to God's original intention. This is at least implied in the
Colossian and Ephesian epistles. Here the creation is pictured as the
work of Christ. All things exist through him and for him, and he is the
sustainer of all things (Col. 1:15-20). He is the authority above the powers that rule this age, even though they do not recognize him as such.
The church as his ambassadorial community has been given the task of
making his authority known to the "principalities and powers." By virtue of his cross and resurrection, he is the reconciler of all things. He
will bring them to harmonious completion (Eph. 1:9-10; 3:9-12).

According to this last conception, the authority of Jesus is the principle which gives continuity. Because of his death and through his resurrection and exaltation, God gave him authority above every "rule and
authority and power and dominion . . . not only in this age but also in
the age to come" (Eph. 1:20-21). The church is to be "the fullness" of
Christ in this age. Yet the consummation is clearly the work of God in
Christ, not the result of the conquest of the church (Eph. 1:22-23). In
this way the discontinuity between the two ages is preserved.

Since we are attempting to conceptualize the unimaginable, we
should not construe any of these patterns literally or insist on one motif
to the exclusion of the others. They all point to realities beyond our
ability to imagine. They are representations of the different aspects of
the church's hope. They voice the faith conviction that God, who is under, with, and beyond our history, will bring the creative process to a
victorious conclusion after the manner revealed in Jesus Christ.

Eschatology as Futurology

Is there something we should know about the future that is revealed to us in the Bible? There is, but it is not in the form of a calendar of future events, or an assessment of trends as the modern futurologist would make. It has to do rather with the nature of historical-cultural development and human destiny in the light of God's revelation in Jesus Christ. We can best explain this by looking again at the concepts of *chronos* and *kairos*.

The Time of the End

An eschatological view of history makes use of the biblical view of *kairos* as it relates to *chronos*. We may chart that view simply as follows:

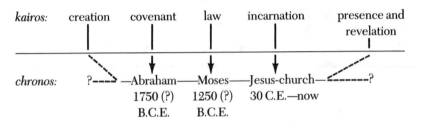

We do not know the precise relation of *kairos*—God's timing—to *chronos*—temporal, or historical time. Only God knows the *time of the eschaton* (Mark 13:32). And so we cannot say on the basis of biblical data that the *parousia*, or coming of Jesus, is *chronologically* near. It is the next kairotic event and it has been introduced chronologically by Jesus. But we cannot presume to estimate its chronological distance from us. This point needs to be made with some emphasis as we near the end of the second millennium and the prophetic calculators begin to whirl.

Jesus clearly said that the chronology of the end events is not a priority for his followers (Acts 1:7). This should warn us against the ever-popular literal attempts to identify dates, places, and nations that will be involved in the "end times." No one could have predicted the time or events of the first advent of Jesus before it happened. Similarly, a blueprint of the future events is impossible. Fascination with eschatological calendars often distracts us from the truly important task of "watching for our Lord's return" (Matt. 24:36-44).

It is important that we recognize the "rule of God" in the *kairotic* moments of our history. Jesus spoke of "seeing" the kingdom (John 3:3) and warned that it is possible not to recognize it even when one sees its manifestations (Matt. 13:13; cf. 5:8).

This relation of *kairos* and *chronos* is also analogous to the relation between God's activity and human activity in establishing the rule of God. God's rule does not come automatically as inevitable evolutionary progress. The events of the past century have put that myth to rest! It will not be effected by human political and scientific institutions, all of which are based on violence and the power of death. On the other hand, it will not be initiated by a sudden intervention from heaven in spite of what happens in human history, as some contemporary apocalypticism suggests. God cannot bring the rule of love to fruition without the willing submission of humans.

Perhaps the organic metaphor of birth, such as Paul uses in Romans 8:22ff., will be most helpful in imaging this reality. Birth does not come because of the struggle and suffering in the birthing process, but it cannot come without it. Birth is the result of the new life God has created, but this new reality can come into human existence only through painful struggle. Movement toward the consummation of history comes through *kairo*tic events which occur in God's timing and by God's power. However, we experience such events as ambiguous and even threatening events in our sinful realm. They occur in the pattern of cross and resurrection, not the pattern of unambiguous, inevitable progress.

The eschatological consummation is a kairotic event which ends history as we know it, perhaps as the bursting of the cocoon ends the life of the larvae. The biblical apocalyptic writers visualized the end of the age as a catastrophic climax of both social events (wars and social chaos) and natural events (earthquakes, drought, and disturbances in the sky). They picture it as a destruction of the old and a recreation (2 Pet. 3:8ff.). In more recent times some have associated it with an atomic disaster. But these events in themselves, occurring as they do in the temporal sequence, do not describe the character and meaning of the kairotic reality.

The New Testament writers use two significant words to describe this reality, the *parousia* and the *epiphaneia* of Christ. The first word means advent or presence. The second means manifestation or revelation. We look forward to the eschaton (*finis*) which will also be a *telos* (goal). It will be a time when the personal presence of Jesus Christ as he was known in crucifixion and resurrection will be made manifest in our world.

This revelation of the Presence will introduce the next stage of God's rule. This much we can say with confidence. But conceptions of this next stage differ widely. Will it be an eternal spiritual existence? Or shall we look for an earthly reign of Christ for a thousand years, or forever (2 Pet. 3:8)? Will it mean a renewal and transformation of the earth and human history with it? Answers to these questions remain unclear.

The "Signs of the Times"

The Bible assures us that the salvation, or rule, of God will come. The question is whether we will recognize and enter it. The manifestation of Christ as the true light and authority in history will come as a surprise even to those who look forward to it. It will come as a shock to those who do not recognize that even now Jesus is Lord of history. Nevertheless, these *kairo*tic manifestations are "signs" which Jesus said his followers should look for. We will recognize them as signs by the Spirit/spirit of Jesus manifest in them because God's rule is identified with the rule of Christ.

Concerning the course of human history, the biblical writers predict that civilization will continue much the same as always. Nations will continue to compete in power politics. Wars and human tragedy will intensify. They hold out little hope for a humanly achieved utopia. For those who do not recognize God's *kairos*, it will seem like everything continues the same as it always has been. In times of turmoil, many charismatic prophets will offer solutions. Some of them will come "in Jesus' name." Therefore, it is imperative for the disciples to recognize false prophets.

The biblical prophets anticipate that toward the end of the age, the pace and scope of human activity will intensify and accelerate. They see this as an intensification of evil and tension, not of goodness and justice. History has fully justified this prediction.

The process of civilization and scientific development has accelerated exponentially! Where eras were once thousands or hundreds of years, we now speak of decades as eras. Incredible scientific breakthroughs have united the world economically and culturally. But this has not led to a new age of peace. Instead, it has led to unprecedented tension and violence with an increased gap between the rich and poor nations.

Furthermore, we are using up the resources that have made life as we know it on earth possible. From the human perspective, the future is still extremely uncertain. The very discoveries that make technical progress possible also threaten human existence. That which gives us control of life also increases our possibility of self-destruction.

Nevertheless, we also see signs of the coming of God's rule. While the church has not been the cause or agent of these developments, it has had a major impact upon the process as salt, yeast, and fire. The aggressive movement to spread the good news of Christ has played a significant role in bringing revolutionary changes in the world. The message of Christ has spread like "a fire upon the earth," and its effects are a sign of the *parousia* of Christ (Luke 12:49-56). There also continue to be many signs that God uses even human wrath to serve his own ends as people struggle to be free from political oppression.

Many have viewed the continuation of the Jews as a people and the more recent reestablishment of the nation of Israel as a clear sign of the eschaton. While the continued existence of the Jewish people is surely a sign of God's faithfulness to his promises, a christological reading of those promises does not suggest that a Zionist state is their fulfillment. Paul indicates that the Jewish people remain in God's purposes. He says their "rejection" is only temporary, that eventually in God's time "all Israel will be saved." When this happens, it will presage great blessing for the whole world (Rom. 11:25ff.).

Dispensational theology connects this promise to a mosaic of other texts and concludes that such salvation means the restoration of Israel as a nation. On this basis they hail the present state of Israel, although still in unbelief, as a fulfillment of prophecy which harbingers the eschaton. The next step is its acceptance of Jesus as its political Messiah. However, little in the salvation offered by Jesus suggests that such a nationalistic state is the goal of salvation history.

Paul's confidence is more likely related to the prediction that the gospel will continue to spread throughout the world before the end comes (Matt. 24:14). The eschatological hope for Israel is that it will recognize the true character of its Messiah as revealed in Jesus. Such a conversion would totally change the character of the Zionist state, which now vehemently rejects the way of peace offered by Jesus. Should that occur, one can hardly imagine the great blessing such a conversion would bring to the world!

The *Eschaton* as Judgment

As we approach this subject, we must remind ourselves that the judgment is a revelation of God's *righteousness*. The final judgment is the eschatological disclosure of God to us. We should be careful not to presume that we know the final verdict of that judgment.

The common concept of the last judgment begins with the idea that we fully know God's standard because we have his *law* revealed in the Bible. Thus we know in advance the verdict and we know the punishment and rewards that will be given. Indeed, in Protestant orthodoxy, the last judgment is a kind of anticlimax! It only ratifies the decision already made at one's death. The hidden assumption, certainly, is that God's judgment is like human judgment. But there are plenty of warnings in the Bible against such an assumption (Isa. 40:14).

The Christian concept of the eschaton as final judgment should be influenced by the new concept of judgment introduced in Christ. In his cross and resurrection we learn that God is not interested in a *quid pro quo* justice. The goal is not to achieve a perfect balance of justice through retribution. The goal is rather the reconciliation and reunification of all things in Christ (Eph. 1:9-10). The cross itself is the judgment of God upon sin, and the resurrection is God's justification—both his own justification (theodicy) and ours.

The cross demonstrates God's inexorable judgment that the consequences of sin is death. In the face of unyielding sinfulness, one cannot avoid death as its intrinsic result—not even God himself. The only way to rectify the sinful situation is through death to resurrection. As we observed in the discussion of Christology, "the final justification of God is not manifested in the last judgment which punishes lawlessness with violent retribution and rewards righteousness, but in the resurrection which overcomes the consequences of sin."[17]

A Hermeneutical Approach

The New Testament uses a variety of metaphors for and descriptions of the judgment of God upon sin and its final consequences.[18] These need to be correlated in a theological statement. But a greater problem than the variety of descriptive New Testament language is the variety of hermeneutical assumptions and theological methods used to portray the final judgment. For example, there are assumptions about the relation of law and grace, love and justice, and about the nature of salvation. And there are differences in approach to the interpretation of the biblical passages themselves.

Several hermeneutical assumptions lie behind this analysis. First, "God is [holy] love" and justice is a subordinate aspect of God's love. Second, grace is not the cancellation of justice (mercy) or the extrinsic satisfaction of justice. It is the ground and intrinsic quality of *God's* justice. God's justice is the formal pattern of God's grace.

I further assume that the metaphorical images and symbolical descriptions of judgment should be interpreted in light of the reality of God's nature as revealed in Jesus Christ, not vice versa. We should not begin an attempt to understand God's judgment with an analysis of metaphorical symbols, such as a king judging his enemies, a shepherd separating sheep and goats, or the wicked being tossed upon the cosmic garbage heap (Gehenna). Nor can we simply reduce the apocalyptic imagery to rational concepts and attempt to create a unified picture. Instead, we must first establish a consistent theological understanding of Scripture based upon the Christ event and its implications. The imagery and symbols ultimately refer to this theological gestalt and must be tested by it. An authentic Christian picture of the final judgment must be consistent with what we know of God as he is disclosed in the cross of Jesus Christ.

In our attempt to understand the eschaton as God's final judgment, we shall be guided by the biblical concept of God's righteousness or justice as his intrinsic goodness and faithfulness through the salvation of his creatures. The final judgment will be the vindication of the "justice of God" ultimately demonstrated in the realization of his righteous purpose in the Christ event. This is indicated in the New Testament statement that final judgment has been put into the hands of Jesus Christ (2 Cor. 5:10; John 5:21-22). Following this lead, we shall begin by examining briefly the biblical concepts of God's judgment and justice.

In general parlance, the word *judgment* implies a critical decision or condemnation based upon law. Thus, the eschatological judgment is viewed as God handing down the final irrevocable legal sentence. Although in many passages the biblical words *mishpaṭ* and *krima* do indicate such a legal condemnation, we must interpret these references against a broader context of usage.

The concept of *mishpaṭ* as God's judgment also implies his creation and rule over his people. Accordingly, his judgment is first his *Torah*, or instruction, for his people's well-being. His judgment is his decision which establishes the true way of life. God's *mishpaṭ* established a relationship between God and Israel in the covenant. Therefore, to give just judgment meant to establish the covenant relationship through the decision and implementation of righteousness.

Further, this *mishpaṭ*, or covenant judgment, establishes a social order which is intrinsically right. God is Creator-Sustainer-Savior. As such his judgment is essential to humanity's life and peace. As Volkmar Herntrich puts it, God's judgments establish a *justitia salutifera* and not a *justitia distributiva* (an order of social health and well-being, not a formal order of distributive justice).[19] Only in that context does God's judgment take on the character of a law or *Torah* by which people can be judged.

When the concept of God as creator and judge are thus held in indissoluble relation, God's judgment is an expression of his essential character. God does not judge by some formal concept of virtue or legal right—a law of distributive or retributive justice. God judges according to the "law" of his own nature, the law of love. The distributive rule is the principle of loving others as oneself. Inasmuch as the Creator's judgment establishes the intrinsic moral order of the universe, it also becomes a word of condemnation to those who refuse to accept it.

In Judaism of the second and first centuries B.C.E., God's legal justice overshadowed the fundamental nature of God's grace. God's law was exalted virtually above God's own person. Writers like Sirach and the author of Wisdom of Solomon said God created the earth for the sake of the Law, or wisdom. God obligated himself to uphold his law with rewards and punishments. And so in Jewish apocalypticism, judgment almost exclusively came to mean condemnation and punishment for the disobedience of God's law.

While the writers of the New Testament do not downgrade the seriousness of God's judgment, they do shift the basis for it from law to grace. The Mosaic Torah already begins this process. God's self-revelation in Jesus fulfills the Mosaic revelation. It actually changes some of the emphases of postprophetic Judaism. This was the meaning of Jesus' words, "You have heard that it was said. . . . But I say to you" (Matt. 5). Although much of the vocabulary from Judaism remains, we must now revise its import in a way consistent with the new revelation of God's character in Jesus Christ.

God's Justice as Fairness

The eschatological question is the question of the ultimate fairness or "impartiality" (Rom. 2:11) of God. It is the Christian conviction that God's agapēic justice will be vindicated in his final judgment. This faith is based upon God's self-disclosure in the cross and resurrection of Jesus Christ.[20] Extrapolating from this, we can offer the following rationale of God's righteousness.

First, the commands of God are *not arbitrary*. The "law of creation" defines the structure and order of existence. It grows out of God's own essential character. This is what we mean when we say God's judgment is intrinsic. Hence, God's law should be understood as a covenant and promise of life and peace (Mal. 2:5). God is not arbitrary in the sense that he does not take selfish advantage of his creatures. His covenant with them is for their good. Even when human infidelity creates a disadvantage to himself, he does not cancel the covenant. It is in the nature of God's essential goodness that he cannot contradict his own nature. He cannot arbitrarily change the rules and he cannot evade the rules for himself while he enforces them on his creatures.

Second, God's justice is *not vengeful*. God is not motivated by resentment. His "wrath" is not retaliatory. His punishment is not vindictive. Although Scripture attributes "vengeance" to God, it also affirms that God's vengeance or wrath is different from human vengeance (Isa. 55:8-9; Deut. 32:35; Rom. 12:17-19), and that human "anger does not produce God's righteousness" (James 1:20). Yahweh's vengeance or vindication is exercised in the public righting of wrong. God's lack of vindictiveness is to be our model for human relationships (Matt. 5:44-45). Vindictiveness or vengefulness by their very definition indicates a change in attitude and a cancellation of previous good will.[21] Such change in God would be a self-contradiction of God's essential goodness.

As a corollary, God's justice is *ultimately redemptive* in intent and purpose. In both the Old and New Testaments, God's righteousness or justice is a synonym for God's salvation or rule. His justice is not a matter of adjudicating a legal balance, but of vindicating the basic goodness and rightness of creation. It is the outcome of his faithfulness to his covenant and assures us of the ultimate establishment of his universal rule.

Finally, we are assured that God deals *with each individual* as a responsible person in his or her historical context. In biblical terms, he "looks upon the heart" and judges according to each person's "works." The word *works* indicates that God judges according to the intrinsic character of the deed, not according to a general law (Rom. 2:11-16). We can be confident that at the last judgment each individual will be fully respected and treated fairly.

We conclude, then, that God acts with absolute consistency and faithfulness to his covenant (James 1:17; Tit. 1:2; 2 Tim. 2:13; Heb. 6:18). Second, God's love will not turn vindictive, but he will not gloss over or indulge evil and sin. (This latter is the basic meaning of *wrath*, as we shall see later.) Finally, God will effectively accomplish his holy purpose in creation. The whole process of history, which has involved so much suffering and injustice, will ultimately be justified by its outcome in the last judgment.

The Wrath of God

The wrath of God is an anthropomorphic expression of God's moral indignation against evil. It indicates his consistent unyielding opposition to evil. We should not understand this moral outrage as spite or retaliation. It indicates rather God's total unwillingness to compromise with or indulge evil. He is adamantly and relentlessly against evil.

Wrath also points to the objective, intrinsic consequences of sin in the created order as God's judgment. The very concept of a rational creation implies an order of existence in which consequences are inherent in the actions themselves. They issue from the action as its innate or natural results. The consequences are not added as an accompanying penalty. For example, war is both wickedness and wrath against sin. It is both sin and punishment for sin. Selfish irresponsibility eventuates in ecological disaster, famine, pollution, and disease. Social revolt is the intrinsic result of oppression and injustice.

Therefore, Paul speaks of the social consequences of lust and impurity as God's abandonment of people to their evil ways (Rom. 1:24ff.). He says the "wages" of sin is death, and that even apart from the knowledge of legal or moral law, death reigned where sin and evil abounded (Rom. 5:13-14; 6:23). In Galatians 6:7 he uses the figure of sowing and reaping. These metaphors all point to the intrinsic consequences of sinful action as God's wrath.

The cross is the supreme expression of the wrath of God against sin and evil. In his identity with God, Jesus expressed God's wrath against sin. He totally refused to compromise with evil to escape the shame and agony of execution. He refused to meet evil with evil to defend himself. Instead, in the spirit of holy love, he prayed for his persecutors' forgiveness (Luke 23:34). From a human point of view, this is a strange wrath, but it is the clearest portrayal we have of the wrath of God. In Revelation 6:16-17 it is called "the wrath of the Lamb."

In his identity with humanity, Jesus suffered God's wrath upon sin. He was so completely "made sin for us" (2 Cor. 5:21) that he suffered the full intrinsic consequences of human hostility and alienation. He experienced them as the abandonment of God. We should not, however, speak of this as a *punishment* by God.

As we said above, our concept of the final judgment must be qualified by this new understanding of judgment as it is revealed in the cross of Christ. The theological significance of the anthropomorphic metaphors of apocalypticism must be determined in light of the revelation of the cross and resurrection. Defined in this way, the parameters of God's wrath are most clearly seen in Jesus.

First, we see God's wrath in Jesus' indignation, in his irrevocable opposition to evil, and in his resolute noncooperation with it. He refused to give it even the semblance of justification in his trial and crucifixion.

Second, God's determination to overcome and destroy evil and death is demonstrated in his resurrection. Also, in the resurrection and glorification of Jesus, we can see God's resolve to reward those who "suffer for doing what is right."

The Final Outcome of Judgment

If we view the final judgment as a revelation of God's righteousness, how shall we understand its outcome? The answer to this question will again depend in part on the hermeneutical approach one chooses. Several possibilities find biblical support. One picture of the consummation follows the basic outlines of Jewish apocalyptic and makes Jesus the conqueror and judge. Apocalyptic metaphors continue to be used to picture the outcomes. These are the destruction and punishment of the wicked, and deliverance and vindication of the elect, the righteous. A second approach, also found in the New Testament, begins with the mission of Jesus to establish the rule of God and sees the eschaton as the victorious conclusion of this mission. It is pictured as victory over death (resurrection) and the reunification of all things in Christ.

With either approach, the primary focus of biblical eschatology is upon the victory of God over death and evil and the establishment of God's rule in creation. One may wonder where individuals fit into this consummation, but hermeneutically that is a secondary consideration. Emphasis is upon the vindication of God and righteousness.

Four alternative scenarios emerge from the various references in Scripture. Each has been championed by some group in the history of the church. The most extensively held is the separation and eternal existence of both the righteous and wicked. The second visualizes the destruction of all evil, including wicked people, and the eternal existence of the righteous. The third speaks of salvation as "conditional immortality." And the fourth anticipates universal restoration of creation under the rule of Christ. We will look briefly at each of these options.

The first alternative picture is based on the texts which speak of "eternal punishment" and "eternal life" (Matt. 25:46). *Eternal (aiōnios)* is read chronologically to mean "everlasting." All the texts referring to "eternal destruction," "resurrection of condemnation" (John 5:29), and "second death" are read in light of this contrast of eternal punishment and reward. Accordingly, the justice of God is vindicated in the everlasting punishment of the wicked in hell and the everlasting reward of the righteous in heaven. Orthodoxy, both Catholic and Protestant, holds that this is the only possible interpretation of the biblical materials. But it is not without its difficulties.

It is questionable whether one should interpret such metaphors as "outer darkness," "the Gehenna [garbage dump of fire]," and "lake of fire" to mean a literal everlasting punishment. This is especially true in light of texts that speak literally of God destroying "both soul and body in hell" (Matt. 10:28), the "destruction of the godless" (2 Pet. 3:7), and "eternal destruction" (2 Thess. 1:9). The question is not merely whether *aiōnios* means everlasting in phrases like "the eternal fire" (Matt. 18:8). The question is how to interpret apocalyptic metaphors.[22] Should they be interpreted literally, or taken figuratively—in this case as a symbol for the extreme seriousness of sin's consequences not only in this life but in the life to come? This, however, is not the most serious difficulty with this position.

The weightier theological problem is that a punitive hell is not a satisfactory solution of the theodicy question. How are we to reconcile the sovereign goodness and power of God with the eternal persistence of evil? The power and right to punish evil cannot vindicate God's goodness. Vengeance and everlasting retribution do not undo or redress the wrong that has been done. Retribution is no substitute for restitution. Furthermore, everlasting suffering unavoidably means that evil in some form continues in the universe. If holy love is sovereign, should there not be a resolution that rids the universe of all evil?

There is no final solution to this dilemma, but if hell and heaven are understood in intrinsic terms, the metaphor is in line with our experience of the nature and consequences of good and evil. The intrinsic reward of love is love itself and the ever-expanding possibility for its fulfillment (heaven). The intrinsic reward for selfishness and hostility is growing alienation and resentful rage, which destroy the soul they feed upon (hell). "The wages of sin"—hatred, fear, deceit, spitefulness—is literally death, both spiritually and physically.

Furthermore, the metaphor suggests that personal existence after death of the body will be in continuity with life in the body. The kind of person we become in this life has significance for the next. The kind of relationships and character we develop now has consequences for our continuing existence. In these terms, heaven is "eternal life"—a life of expanding *agapē*, joy, and peace in the presence of God. Hell is "eternal destruction"—an increasing spiral of alienation, frustration, and restriction of meaningful life.

The second scenario is a variation of the first. Judgment will mean affirmation and reward of righteousness and the destruction forever of evil. That is, there will be no recurrence of sin and evil. This is pictured as the destruction of the old heavens and earth by fire and the creation of new ones in which righteousness dwells (2 Pet. 3:7, 11-13; cf. Rev. 21:1). Also, the wicked people will be destroyed (Matt. 10:28; 2 Thess. 1:9; 2 Pet. 3:7b).

While this explanation is not troubled by the continuing presence of evil in the universe, it fails to account for the staggering loss the Creator sustains in the end. The resolution of the problem is simply an act of destructive power, not one of redemption. However, if the process is one of death and resurrection and the outcome is understood intrinsically, as above, it is consistent with our experience of life in the conquest of death.

When viewed this way, the metaphor speaks to the destruction (or death) of all that is degenerate, and the renewal (or resurrection) of all that still has the potential of life. Destruction and re-creation suggest a new possibility beyond the frustrating power of evil. When read intrinsically, the destruction is not simply an arbitrary act of power. It is the climax of the self-destructive consequence of evil which is, in fact, self-limiting.

The third alternative picture—conditional immortality—does not have a strong explicit basis in biblical texts. It develops from the concept of salvation as life and condemnation as death or "perishing." Heaven is life at its highest potential in the presence of God, opening out on vistas of infinite possibility. This eternal life is possible for all who respond to God's grace. But without recourse to "the tree of life" (Gen. 3:22-24; Rev. 22:19), sinful humanity simply dies. Those who separate themselves from the creative Source of life lose the life God has given to them. They perish.[23]

This view of the judgment is a projection of our experience of sin's progressive blinding and incapacitating effect. Like a narcotic, at first it stimulates and soothes. But in the end, it takes away desire and stimulus to life. Grace, on the other hand, is the influence and stimulus to life and relationship. By its very nature it cannot be forced on anyone. In this view, hell is a self-chosen state of diminishing life and personal relationship which can only end in the "second death." The theoretical possibility of salvation remains open from God's side, but the catastrophic and escalating deterioration of personal vitality leave little room for hope.[24]

Such a picture takes seriously people's decisions for or against God and eternal life as it is revealed in Christ. However, in such a scenario, God's intention for universal salvation is ultimately thwarted by human choice.

The last scenario, called universalism, is a theological construct based upon passages like Ephesians 1:10; Colossians 1:19-20; and 1 Corinthians 15:22-28. (Compare Rom. 5:17; Phil. 2:9-11.) These texts speak of the eschaton as a reconciliation and restoration of all things in Christ, and of Christ's final victory over death itself.

The logic of the position is clear. God is the sovereign power in the universe, his essential nature is love, and his will is that no one should perish (2 Pet. 3:9). If this is so, we can expect that *agapē* love will ultimately triumph over all objections and obstacles. God will accomplish his original intention for creation and he will be vindicated in his creation. The final word of judgment will be a word of *agapē* as displayed in the cross and resurrection. Such *agapē* is not a word of indulgence, but of effective good will determined to overcome the enemy by the intrinsic power of love.

The usual objection to this view is that it does not adequately satisfy the demands of justice. It offers a "cheap grace" to those who reject Christ before physical death. Several observations should be noted in light of this objection. First, such a final transformation will not happen apart from Christ and the way of the cross, the way of suffering love. Here we must recall that the cross is the judgment of God upon sin. All references to universal reconciliation name Christ as the one who judges, reconciles, and transforms.

Second, nothing is automatic or deterministic about the process. No one will be saved without repentance and transformation. No one will be coerced by extrinsic, violent power to submit unwillingly. We are not dealing here with extrinsic concepts of justice, but with the intrinsic consequences of evil.

Third, the tragic consequences of sin will not arbitrarily be canceled. The concept does not imply that an indulgent God will take everyone to eternal bliss when they die in spite of themselves. Death and hell, the consequences of sin, must be overcome before a final verdict is in.

It perhaps is unwise to insist that one or the other of these positions is the only orthodox position. Each makes valid points as metaphors. The same paradox present in the confession of God's sovereignty and human freedom exists here also. God's love will be victorious and his righteousness vindicated, but we can be certain that human cooperation and freedom will not be manipulated.

Death and Resurrection

The word *death* is used in a variety of ways. We need to sort these out if we wish to understand the different things said about death in the Bible. Obviously, it refers to the cessation of biological life and decay of the physical body. This meaning includes "mortality," that is, the state of living with the inevitability of physical death. In this sense, death is simply a constituent factor of creaturehood. This is implied in the Genesis story, which speaks of a "tree of life" in the garden of Eden, from which it was necessary for humans to eat if they were to be immortal (Gen. 3:22). In this sense, sin is not the cause of death. Rather, sin is the cause of humankind's inability to achieve immortality apart from a fearful, painful death. Sin is the cause of the fear of death.

The relation of sin and death is more clearly evident when death indicates separation from the source of life—God. Separated from God, creaturely life must inevitably "perish," since it is totally dependent upon its creative source. Accordingly, in the Genesis account, God warned the human creatures that breaking the covenant would doom them to death (Gen. 2:17). Sin is spiritual suicide. In this sense it is the "wages" and "sting" of death.

A Biblical Perspective on Death

How one views the effects of physical death on a person will depend in large part on how one understands the nature of the self. For example, in naturalism there is no self apart from the biochemical activities of the brain. In some contemporary Buddhist theory, the self is merely the individual expression and activity of the world soul. It is as evanescent as a wave on the surface of the ocean. In either case, death of the body can only mean the extinction of anything which was called self.

On the other hand, the ancient Greek philosophers in the Socratic tradition thought in dualistic terms. They understood the self to be a spiritual substance which they called a *psuchē*, or soul. The human being was described as a combination of physical and spiritual substances. When the physical substance died and decayed, the soul escaped and continued to exist in its own spiritual realm. For Plato, death meant the release of the soul from its physical prison house.

The development of the Christian view was profoundly influenced by the Platonic philosophical tradition. One even sees some development of the concept of human nature in the Bible itself. Already in the New Testament are clear indications that Platonic ideas had been adapted to the basic patterns of the older Hebrew views. For example, resurrection remains the basic category, but it takes for granted the continuation of a personal existence after the death of the physical body. We might describe this as a modified dualism.[25]

According to the Old Testament view, human life is more than a biochemical process. It is a spiritual energy (*nephesh*) from God which expresses itself in and through the physical body (Gen. 2:7). To use contemporary jargon, human beings are a psychosomatic unity. They are better described as "ensouled bodies" than as a duality of bodies and souls essentially independent of each other. Death of the body does not mean freedom or salvation for the soul. Instead, it means diminution of power. The personal energy has no "body" through which to express itself. It is, therefore, like the shadow cast by the body. After death of the body, life continues in an attenuated form in Sheol—a flat, joyless, inactive existence without the body, gloomy and dark (Job 10:21-22), "cut off from the land of the living" (Isa. 53:8). If there is any hope for joyful, meaningful life beyond death of the body, it is hope in God. Therefore, this hope is eventually expressed as resurrection (Dan. 12:2; 2 Macc. 7:29), not as immortality of the soul.

The resurrection of Jesus Christ fulfilled this hope and provided the basis for a new understanding of the meaning of death. First, the resurrection of Christ gave certainty to the hope for a meaningful life beyond death. It assured not the soul's immortality, but the power and faithfulness of God to bring life out of death. Second, it shifted the emphasis away from physical death as the major problem and focused it on spiritual death as the ultimate concern. Jesus' words to Martha, "Everyone who lives and believes in me will never die" (John 11:26), are the reversal of Genesis 2:17, "You shall die."

For Paul also the emphasis shifts. For him the immediate problem is the *fear of death*, which suppresses and debilitates humans, bringing them under bondage to sin. Resurrection for him means a life beyond the power of death, possible because of Christ's resurrection (Rom. 6:5-14). Physical death has lost its "sting" (1 Cor. 15:55-56). It still exists as the frustrating enemy that threatens extinction. But it lost its ghastly power when Jesus called its bluff and won.[26] In this light, physical death becomes a transition, rather than an end to existence. For those who share Christ's life, it becomes a passageway to a higher stage of life.

Following this biblical paradigm of the personal self as a psychosomatic unity, what can we say about the nature and meaning of death in the light of our experience? This remains ambiguous and menacing, but we need to locate it within the context of life.

First, from the temporal perspective, physical death is simply part of the life cycle. It is necessary if births are to continue in our limited universe. Viewed from the physical-temporal perspective alone, death is integral to life. Hence, our emphasis should not simply be on keeping bodies alive, but upon helping people live well so death may come as the fulfillment of life.

We should also observe that a life in unending temporal existence would be meaningless because it would never find consummation. As Karl Rahner has put it, human life itself "strives toward a conclusion to its present mode of existence. Time becomes madness if it cannot reach fulfillment."[27] Life's meaning would be caught in a chain of unending cause and effect, relative to the moment, and ultimately illusory. In such a circumstance, one can begin to understand why the concept of salvation as freedom from the temporal life cycle (*moksha, nirvana*) is so appealing in the major Eastern religions.

Further, we should observe that the meaning of death is closely tied to the meaning of *personal* life. Human life is a life lived in the knowledge of impending death. It is a life in process toward death. We become personal selves in and through the relationships in which we actively participate on our way to die. As an event in the temporal order, then, death is the final act of the individual which completes the definition of his or her life.

Therefore, from the temporal perspective, how one has lived gives meaning to one's death. And how one dies completes and seals the meaning of one's life. Although death remains an imposition, we may speak in relative terms of a good death and a tragic death. For example, martyrdom in a just cause gives meaning retroactively to the life that was sacrificed. By contrast, death by an overdose of drugs adds to the tragedy of the life thus lost. This is at least part of the meaning of the Revelation 14:13 text: "Blessed are the dead who . . . die in the Lord . . . for their deeds follow them." The phrase "in the Lord" describes the life that has been sealed in death.

The "Intermediate State" of the Soul

Death helps to define and seal the meaning of a person's life for those still alive. Yet from the perspective of temporal life, the ultimate significance of death itself is unknown. For example, a sacrificial death points to the significance of that death for those still alive. But it does not indicate the ultimate meaning for the one who has died. While it seals the meaning of a life, it makes that life unavailable to those still living. What does this imply for the one who has died?

Death moves one into a qualitatively different existence beyond the physical and therefore beyond the temporality associated with it. Time is relative to space and movement. We can no longer expect a temporally continuing existence after death, although we have no other conceptual model to work with. But does this necessarily mean nonexistence? May it not also mean translation into another mode of being?

Christian faith opts for the latter alternative. This faith is not sheer wishful thinking. It is based upon the experience of Jesus' death and resurrection. Into the unknown realm of death, we project our own experience of the continuity of the essential self through radical change. The premise for such a projection is the ontological meaning of personhood and the significance of moral decisions.[28]

Lacking any other conceptual model or a biblical term, Christian theology speaks of the time between an individual's death and the universal consummation as an "intermediate state" for the disembodied person. This has led to interminable debate about the status of the soul after death. Is it "sleeping"? Has its life been temporarily suspended as it waits for resurrection? Is it already experiencing the fruit of its previous existence? Is it waiting anxiously for the next stage of its life? The Bible speaks of the soul or person "away from the body" as waiting for the resurrection of the body to complete its destiny. But it also talks of the person or soul already enjoying life with Christ or experiencing the anguish of sin's consequences.[29]

This language in the temporal mode cannot give us a literal picture of the individual's continuing *state of existence* after death. We must distinguish between the conceptual mode of the language and its eschatological content. Instead, it speaks to the eschatological *status* of death and the departed person or soul. It indicates that death itself is not the final consummation. The individual is connected to the whole in such a way that one's life is not fulfilled apart from that of the whole. And yet the individual's destiny is not simply the loss of self-identity and absorption into the undifferentiated whole, as Hinduism suggests. (Indeed, Hinduism sees this not as a consummation, but as the completion of an infinitely long cycle, which repeats itself once the whole is reconstituted.)

Death and the Essential Self

The Bible does not tell us explicitly what happens to the essential self immediately after the death of the body. Perhaps the most difficult aspect of this question is whether physical death permanently fixes one's final destiny. The Bible suggests that physical death itself is a kind of judgment. That is, physical death is part of the consequences of sin. However, it also speaks of death "and *after that* the judgment" (Heb. 9:27, emphasis added).

Roman Catholic theology teaches that the destiny of the individual is sealed in death. But many who are bound for heaven will experience a lengthy period of purgation. Those excluded from heaven will find themselves in a condition morally appropriate to their sin, namely, limbo or hell. Protestant theologians rejected the ideas of purgatory as a temporal extension of penance as well as limbo.[30] They taught simply that death fixes one's eternal destiny in heaven or hell.

The different views among Christians concerning the nature and consequences of death grow out of the variety of metaphors and statements about death in the Bible itself. The New Testament does not offer us a rational analysis of death. Its revelation is given in the context of first-century Judaism and uses first-century conceptual images. Therefore, we must first understand the original meaning of these images. Then we determine how the new context created by Christ's resurrection affects these meanings.[31]

Finally, we need to make a contemporary theological analysis allowing us to understand the original issues and answers and reframe them in the context of our own culture and experience. The biblical materials were not intended to be direct answers to the questions we raise about the nature of the death process and its consequences.

With this in mind, what may we say about the significance of physical death? We have noted that in the biblical view, death does not mean freedom for the essential self, as in Platonic theory. The New Testament nowhere suggests that death itself effects a major character transformation, either into immediate moral perfection or reprobation.

If we extrapolate from our spiritual experience in life, death will be a gracious surprise for those who in solidarity with Christ already know the grace of God. Those who have already found their self-identity in the resurrected Christ and his body, the church, and have tasted the "fruit of the Spirit," might reasonably expect that the trauma of losing the physical body will be minimal. The essential self, the person, who has been formed within the covenant of loving, transparent relationship with Christ, will be sustained in that relationship. This is certainly what Paul implies when he says that even though a disembodied existence is not fulfilling, nevertheless "to be with Christ" in such a state is much better than physical life frustrated by sin (2 Cor. 5:4; Phil. 1:23).

On the other hand, loss of the physical body must be a shocking trauma for those whose meaning in life was limited to satisfying its desires. For the fearful, the deceitful, the hostile, the despairing, the violent, and the self-centered—those living in "spiritual death"—loss of the body is bound to be emotionally painful and disabling. It may be like the painful experience of stepping out of deep darkness into brilliant light. In such a case, the light blinds, and one tries desperately to protect oneself.

To extrapolate further, the sudden loss of the physical body would be a traumatic experience for one whose life had been dependent upon pretense to hide greed and selfish passion. For the body gives both the means to express and the mask to hide one's true thoughts and feelings. To be abruptly and unpreparedly thrust into candid, inescapable relationships where perception is direct, unmediated, and unshielded (1 Cor. 13:12) would be sheer agony. The shock of seeing oneself without a screen, and of knowing that others also see one this way, would be unbearable. To experience the derision, hatred, and loathing—or worse, the apathy, fear, lecherous dependence, and duplicity which one can neither mask nor any longer use for one's self-advantage—would be hell indeed. In such a situation, Sartre's dictum that "hell is other people" would certainly be correct.

Neither the Bible nor our experience of sinful existence give us reason to think that physical death will bring immediate transformation or rehabilitation to the self caught in radical transition. We can only conclude from our learnings in this life that entering physical death will make it more difficult to change, not less. Each time we put off a decisive change, its chance of happening is reduced. Situations of instability and the imposition of radical changes in our life patterns do not make change less difficult. And yet, such violent changes do sometimes shock us into painful reassessment and reorientation of our lives.

The Resurrection

Resurrection is only one of a number of ways in which the New Testament portrays the consummation. It is a pivotal figure and it expresses well the conviction of the New Testament writers that God's victory will be complete in the consummation of all things. It has several advantages as a metaphor to describe the eschaton as an intrinsic outcome of creation and historical existence. For example, it does not make a clean break between the old and the new as does the figure of a fiery destruction of the old and creation of a new heaven and earth (2 Pet. 3:11-13). And it does not have the possible legalistic implications of a final judgment.[32]

First, we should note that in contrast to the concept of immortality, resurrection lays emphasis upon the final victory as the creative act of God's grace. Death can only mean the end of human power and machinations. This theme is played out in every instance of resurrection. It was *God* who raised Jesus from the dead, when he had humbled himself and submitted to death. God the Spirit raises us to "newness of life" if we will die with Christ to the old life (Rom. 6:4). And Christ, as the

executor for the Godhead, finally overcomes death in the consummation of human history (1 Cor. 15:25-26).

Second, continuity between historical and eternal existence is underscored when the consummation is viewed as a raising up of the old
body. This is the significance of "bodily resurrection." The metaphor is
resuscitation of a dead body, but the reality of resurrection far exceeds
the metaphor. The result of resurrection is a "spiritual body" (1 Cor.
15:44). On one hand, it is not a rejuvenation of "flesh and blood,"
which, Paul says, cannot inherit the kingdom of God; change is needed
(1 Cor. 15:50-51). On the other hand, it is not a *de novo* existence for
which the old personal life has little or no significance. When Paul extends the metaphor, he speaks of death as planting a seed which must
lose its physical identity in order to be transformed into new life
(1 Cor. 15:35-38).

Third, resurrection suggests radical change—transformation and
newness. Already in our temporal existence, spiritual identification
with Christ in his death and resurrection means freedom and newness
of life (Rom. 6:5-8). Paul extends this transformation into the eschaton.
The final resurrection will give life to our mortal bodies (Rom. 8:11)
and set our whole body free. In a related passage, where the emphasis
is upon radical change, he speaks of the perishable putting on imper-
ishability (1 Cor. 15:51-53). The "dead," he writes, "will be raised im-
perishable."

Finally, the metaphor of resurrection underscores the completeness
of God's victory over the forces of evil. Resurrection places one beyond
death's power (Rom. 6:9). Death is "swallowed up" by life (2 Cor. 5:4;
1 Cor. 15:54). In all these cases, we should understand death in its
broadest sense as the embodiment of all the frustration and complaint
that accompanies sinful historical existence (Rom. 8:18ff.). Death is the
"last enemy" which Christ must overcome before he turns the final authority over to God (1 Cor. 15:25-28).[33]

Christ's Resurrection and Ours

Paul calls the resurrected Jesus "the first fruits" (down payment) of
the believer's resurrection (1 Cor. 15:23). Faith in a general resurrection did not originate with Christ's resurrection. This was a general belief of Pharisaic Judaism (Acts 23:8), which the disciples of Jesus
undoubtedly shared. But now in the midst of history, these disciples
had already met the resurrected Jesus and confessed his exaltation as
Messiah. This and the living presence of his Spirit in the midst of the
community, became for them the guarantee that God really would ful-

fill his promise of resurrection for all his people (2 Cor. 4:13-14). Jesus' resurrection was the beginning of the end. It not only anticipated the eschaton, it introduced it. And so it became the basis for Christian hope (1 Pet. 1:3).

Furthermore, Christ's resurrection became both the paradigm and the means for the disciples' resurrection. God remains the source of resurrection through the power of Christ's Spirit (Rom. 8:11; 1 Cor. 6:14; 15:22). This resurrection life is already at work in those who are in solidarity with Christ (Eph. 1:19b-20).

But Christ is not only the *means*. He is the "firstborn from the dead" in order that he may be the first of many to follow (Col. 1:18; Rom. 8:29). His life, death, and resurrection become the anticipatory paradigm for all who follow him. This means spiritual and moral renewal after the pattern of Christ even now in our temporal existence. Although the historical resurrection of Jesus is itself mystery, yet it presages the way we shall find victory over frustration and death. It is the Christian's hope to "be united with him in a resurrection like his" (Rom. 6:5; Phil. 3:10-11, 21; 1 John 3:2). Thus, the consummation will mean the completion of what God began in the life, death, and resurrection of Jesus Christ.

Notes

Introduction

1. Menno Simons, who was one of the more conservative Anabaptist leaders, made this point clearly in his argument with Martin Micron. He argues against a statement which he assumed was the doctrine of "the Nicene council, of Athanasius, Erasmus of Rotterdam, Luther . . . and of the most sensible, learned ones." He calls the doctrine "speculation" and says, "Therefore I could wish that the unrevealed mystery were left with God" (Wenger 1956:862).

Chapter 1: Jesus Christ and Theological Reflection

1. Millard Lind has pointed out the weakness of this interpretation of law. He shows how Jesus stands in true continuity with the Mosaic intention. See his perceptive essay, "Law in the Old Testament," in Willard Swartley (ed.), *The Bible and Law*, Elkhart, Ind.: Institute of Mennonite Studies, 1982.

2. *Kainē*, the Greek word for *new*, means new in *kind* as distinct from *neos*, which means new merely in *time*.

3. John Howard Yoder explains this process in his essay entitled " 'But We Do See Jesus': The Particularity of Incarnation and the Universality of Truth" (*The Priestly Kingdom*, 1984:49-54).

4. In *Jesus Christ Our Lord* (1987, rev. 1990), I attempted to give a statement of Christ's person and work that uses the analogy of history and personal being, rather than the analogy of being as static substance. When we think of ontological reality as a dynamic flow of energy which is in constant interaction, it makes sense to think of personal reality as selves in relationship rather than as "souls" or individuated spiritual substances. Although the biblical writers did not think in modern scientific terms, their categories are those of history and personal covenant relationships rather than those of Greek philosophy.

5. As John E. Toews has observed, "At no point in Judaism or the early church does either Son of Man or Son of God connote the humanity or divinity of Jesus, as in the later Christological debates" ("Jesus Christ, the Convener of the Church," Waltner 1990:50.)

In the fourth-century debate with Arianism, theologians stressed Christ's sonship as the "only Begotten Son" to counteract the idea that he was created. He was spoken of as "eternally begotten" (Origin), or as begotten of God in eternity, and therefore of "one substance" (*homoousios*) with the Father.

6. Although the imagery of light and darkness can be found in the Old Testament, its peculiar function in the Johannine writings may have derived from the light/darkness paradigm so prominent in the Dead Sea Scrolls found at Qumran.

7. Jaroslav Pelikan writes, "The primary function of the image in Athanasius was to express the doctrine of Christ, not the doctrine of the Trinity. For this purpose it was well suited. . . . It provided him with a method of asserting the point he never tired of making: that in Christ faith had to do with no one less than God himself, and that therefore the believer could say to Christ, 'In thy light do we see light.' " (1962:72)

8. The word translated *man* is *anthropos* (human), not *anēr* (male).

9. The idea of a *mesitēs* includes the meaning of both agency as well as arbitration. The mediator is a representative and negotiator as well as a reconciler and peacemaker. In the 1 Timothy 2:4-5 passage, "Christ Jesus, himself human [*anthropos*]," is mediator not

only between God and Israel (cf. Moses), but between God, who "desires everyone to be saved" (2:4), and humankind. He brings reconciliation through the mediation of the new covenant. As covenant mediator, he himself is the *antilutron*, the vicarious offering guaranteeing the new agreement between God and humankind. In this sense we may also speak of him as the mediator of the new-covenant image. It is through him as "the human" that the new image of God is effected and communicated to all humankind. It is in him, "Christ Jesus, himself human," that God recognizes his own image and accepts all other humans as in solidarity with that image.

10. Seeberg 1952, 2:65.

11. It is important not to interpret the virgin birth accounts in a way that diminishes the full reality of Jesus' humanity. The accounts were not intended to explain in what sense Jesus is God, but rather how God fully entered our human existence as one of us. He came not as an Athena who sprang fully developed and armed from the head of Zeus, but as a defenseless, dependent baby to be nurtured in a human family.

12. Barth 1957:35.

13. McGinn 1987:64.

14. *Institutes* 2.12.2.

15. *Institutes* 2.12.3. For Anselm "satisfaction" is not punitive, as it was in the writings of Tertullian and later Western theologians. Rather, it was a positive contribution to God in restitution for what humans had denied him. Calvin returned to the penal ideas of Augustine, who followed the Roman law which defined satisfaction as satisfaction of the law's punitive sentence (Franks, 1962:135-137).

16. See Lowell L. Noble, *Naked and Not Ashamed*, Jackson, Mich.: Noble, 1975; also Gerhart Piers and Milton B. Singer, *Shame and Guilt—A Psychoanalytic and Cultural Study*, New York: W. W. Norton, 1971, for further analysis of the concepts of shame and guilt.

17. Waltner 1990:53.

18. Yoder 1972.

19. Weber 1983:103.

20. Modern Western education has equated self-fulfillment with individualistic expression and creativity with a free, unrestrained style. In music, for example, the uninhibited expression of jazz improvisation is equated with creativity. In a discipleship pattern, creativity has the quality expressed by an artist playing one of Mozart's piano concertos. Such creativity is not achieved by rearranging the score, changing the notes, or by an impulsive embroidery of the musical pattern. It comes when the heart and mind of the pianist are finely tuned with the spirit of the composer—where there is oneness of understanding and purpose.

Chapter 2: Revelation: The "Word" That Became "Flesh"

1. Kraus 1990:106-107.

2. Noss 1974:93.

3. Chan 1969:336.

4. Chan 1969:336.

5. For example, some rabbis taught that God wrote the Torah 2,000 years before creation, and on Sinai he gave it directly to Moses, who added nothing of his own genius to it.

6. Buttrick 1962, 3:900.

7. From this perspective, the emphasis upon a supernatural *mode* of revelation in the works of B. B. Warfield, the great Calvinistic champion of an inerrant verbal revelation, seems a little beside the point in spite of all the brilliance of his logic. He attempted to ground the veracity of the message in its supernatural modality and inerrancy. He has many articles on the subject, but see "The Biblical Idea of Revelation," in Craig 1948:71-104.

8. Gerhard von Rad thinks the category of ecstasy is too limited and rigid to describe the prophetic process. They were not ecstatics in the sense of ceasing to have a will of their own and being under complete control of external forces. He points out that the

phrase "the Lord said to me" indicates their clear self-conscious reception of a message which they must accept responsibility to deliver (1965:59ff.). John W. Miller makes the same point (1987:24-25).

9. Kraus 1990:35.

10. Pannenberg 1977:112, 193, 246, *et passim*.

11. Brunner has emphasized this point in his *The Divine-Human Encounter*, a translation of *Wahrheit als Begegnung* by Amandus W. Loos (1943).

12. Karl Barth spoke of God as the "Wholly Other" who makes himself available to us in revelation. Helmut Thielicke spoke of him as "trans-subjective," a reality outside or beyond our own subjectivity. He is not the projection of our own subjectivity, as the mystical experience might imply.

13. Brunner stressed the "I-Thou" communication that calls for a response of faith-obedience. Karl Barth pressed this idea of self-revelation even further. He insisted that revelation is the disclosure of God's own presence among us (*Dogmatics* 1956, I, 2:181ff.). He emphasized that in revelation, God himself comes to us in experiential form. He presents himself to us in a historical mode so that he is really experienced in the happenings of history. In revelation we are dealing not just with ideas, religious concepts, or ethical commands. We are dealing with God's own self.

One is reminded in these discussions of the Reformed concept of the "real presence" of Christ in the sacrament. When Barth speaks of the revelation of the Holy Spirit at Pentecost, he says it is a matter of affirming that the crucified and resurrected Jesus is now truly present "in the Church of Jesus Christ and in the faith in Jesus Christ" (1936, I, 1:380). In the same way he affirms God's real presence in his self-revelation.

14. Barth 1936, I, 1:360.

15. Brunner 1947:73, 99; Brunner 1951:59.

16. Brunner makes this same general point, but with a slightly different emphasis. "Jesus Christ is the 'Word' of God; it is therefore impossible to equate any human words, any 'speech-about-Him' with the divine self-communication. Jesus Christ Himself is . . . the decisive self-communication of God, is a Person, a human being, the man in whom God Himself meets us" (1950:15-16).

17. Thus Calvin says that the manifestation of God in nature speaks to us in vain. "It is therefore in vain that so many burning lamps shine for us in the workmanship of the universe to show forth the glory of its Author. . . . But although we lack the natural ability to mount up unto the pure and clear knowledge of God, all excuse is cut off because the fault of dullness is within us" (*Institutes* 1.6.14-15).

Brunner has taken essentially this same position. "Original" or "primal" revelation is only one half of the truth for biblical revelation. The other half is "original sin." Neither of these is "historical." They are simply the presupposition of the biblical concept of revelation; namely, that humans are responsible for their sin because of the revelation implied in the creation of humanity in the image of God. Only the historical self-revelation of God in the biblical tradition is salvific (*Revelation and Reason* 1946:262ff.; *Dogmatics* 1950, 1:17).

The problem here lies in the rather arbitrary distinction between the "primal word" and the "historical word." It is precisely this sharp dualistic distinction between creation and redemption, nature and grace, an ethic of justice and love, and salvation as a spiritual or social experience, that has given us the problem. We may make these distinctions for theoretical analytical purposes, but in the reality of our experience of God's self-revelation, they are merely aspects or dimensions of the saving revelation of God's own self.

Christ is clearly identified with both the primal and historical word in the Gospel of John and the letters of Paul. He is the Word of creation which has now become the "embodied Word." *And in both manifestations he is the Word of "grace and truth."*

18. Pp. 142-146, 151f., 156ff.

19. *Institutes* 1.6.1. Compare article 1.1 of the Westminster Confession. "Although the light of nature, and the works of creation and providence, do so far manifest the good-

ness, wisdom, and power of God, as to leave men inexcusable; yet are they not sufficient to give that knowledge of God, and of his will, which is necessary unto Salvation" (Schaff, *Creeds* 3:600). Karl Barth includes a comprehensive survey of the historical developments in his *Dogmatics* 1936, I, 1:284-291.

20. *Institutes* 1.5.14-15; 1.6.1.

21. Barth 1956, I, 2:280ff.

22. Barth 1956, IV, 1:483f.; 1961, IV, 3:135-65. See also Berkhof 1985:51, 83-84.

23. The two names most often associated with this view are Karl Rahner and Raimundo Pannikar. Rahner developed the concept of "anonymous Christians," and Pannikar spoke of "the cosmic Christ in Hinduism."

24. Weber 1981:210.

25. The position of Reformed orthodoxy is clearly represented in the works of B. B. Warfield, who wrote, "These two species or stages of revelation have been commonly distinguished from one another by the distinctive names of natural and supernatural revelation, or general and special revelation, or natural and soteriological revelation. Each of these modes of discriminating them has its particular fitness and describes a real difference between the two in nature, reach or purpose. . . . The one is addressed generally to all intelligent creatures, and is therefore accessible to all men; the other is addressed to a special class of sinners, to whom God would make known His salvation" ("The Biblical Idea of Revelation," in Craig 1948:74). This is simply a logical extension of the general doctrine of election and limited atonement.

26. Although von Rad is making a slightly different point, he underscores this concept of the sufficiency of each "word" of God through the prophet when he writes that the word is the complete word of God for the person to whom it was spoken. He adds, "At different times and to different people the prophet takes different ways of saying the same thing" (1965:88).

27. The biblical account testifies to the unity of revelation in a number of ways. In the Old Testament the basic category for God's saving revelation is "covenant." It is recorded that God made a covenant with Adam (the human race at its origin) and renewed it with Noah (the new beginning of humankind). The covenant with Abraham was to be a means of blessing for all nations. All these covenants precede and prepare the way for God's special covenant with Israel. Indeed, the Genesis account is a kind of preface to the covenant through Moses.

In the New Testament Luke traces Jesus' genealogy to Adam. This suggests he is the culmination not only of Jewish history, but of all human history. John quotes Jesus as saying that Abraham rejoiced in anticipation of his day (8:56). Paul states that God has always had only one standard of salvation; namely, that which was revealed in Jesus Christ (Rom. 2:11-16; 3:25b-26). But John's statement (1:1-14) is perhaps the clearest of all. First he says that the world was created by God's self-communication (1:1-3). Then that the Word as life was the light of humankind (1:4-5). This Word enlightens everyone born into the world. Indeed, the Word has always been in the world, even when it was not recognized (1:10). And this self-same Word was embodied in Jesus (1:14).

28. To speak of the Jesus of history as normative does not necessarily imply that all revelation has ceased or even that general revelation—revelation outside the perimeters of the church—has come to an end. Indeed, the promise of a final manifestation and saving presence of Christ in the *eschaton* suggests otherwise. *General* revelation is not to be understood as a historical stage that ends at the incarnation. Only its normative status is altered. And *special* revelation is not henceforth canalized or channeled only in the church—through an ongoing infallibility (Roman Catholic) or through the production of new scriptures (Mormon). *Special* is now defined as the normative Word which continues to be spoken in and through the Spirit of Christ, who is not confined to the Hebrew-Christian tradition of revelation (John 3:5-8). The scriptural witness to Jesus remains an effective instrument, but not master, of the Spirit, who reveals the "word of Christ" to human hearts in saving power.

The final salvation-revelation lies ahead at the end of history, but we are assured that the Jesus who will then be universally manifested will be none other than Jesus of Nazareth. Thus the two streams of historical revelation represented in Hebrew-Christian history and world history outside that cultural tradition continue to flow side by side. But Jesus Christ is the normative disclosure for both. The Christian "hope" is that they will be brought together in him.

29. In Romans 2 Paul says those who "do instinctively what the law requires," even though they do not know "the law," may find themselves excused when God judges the secrets of the human heart "through Jesus Christ" (2:14-16). Further on, he says that Gentiles who are inwardly or spiritually "Jews"—that is, those who are within the pale of saving revelation—have "praise . . . from God" (2:28-29). Such argument clearly implies that the God of grace revealed in Jesus Christ can save those who stand outside the Hebrew-Christian revelation and are ignorant of it. However, this does not become an excuse for evangelical inactivity. Rather, it is precisely the self-revelation of God's true nature and intention in Christ that compelled Paul to share the good news.

30. This is one of the erroneous linguistic theories lying behind the doctrine of scriptural inerrancy. The definitive exposition of the inerrancy doctrine by Hodge and Warfield was based squarely upon the Scottish commonsense philosophy, which held that meaning somehow lies in the words themselves. This philosophy has given rise to a variety of "literalist" canons of interpretation, and it continues to be an ingredient in the "contextualization" debate in Evangelicalism.

31. Following this analogy, Luther also made a distinction between the Old and New Testaments. The Old, he said, was the written word. The New is the living voice. In this he was no doubt alluding to Paul's distinction between the covenants in 2 Cor. 3:3-6. There Paul speaks of the new as a work of the Spirit in the heart, and not of words or letters written on stone tablets.

32. Weber 1981:228.

33. B. B. Warfield took a different tack. He argued that the clearest, most direct supernatural revelations were the oracular disclosures, which he called "the naked messages of God" (Craig 1948:85). This was his primary model for all revelation. However, he freely admitted that not all the Bible had this direct modal character of "revelation." That is where the doctrine of "inspiration" became important. *Inspiration* is the work of the Holy Spirit in the hearts, minds, mouths, and hands of the writers of Scripture, which made their words "the oracles of God" ("The Oracles of God," Craig 1948:351ff.). Inspiration guaranteed the inerrant veracity of the words of the Bible, and in effect gave them the perfect character and quality of revelation. Although he rejected the concept of dictation, except in the case of oracles, he said that verbal inspiration in effect made the words of Scripture the words of God.

Such a position can be defended only on the presuppositions and definitions of a rationalistic concept of language and truth, a point which Warfield recognized and acknowledged. In this respect he once called Augustine "a flaming rationalist." The late Francis Schaeffer was aware of this rationalistic base and defended it. C. F. H. Henry also makes the case for such a rational position in his magnum opus, *God, Revelation and Authority* (6 volumes). But most fundamentalists and neofundamentalists apparently think they are defending a simple biblicism.

This position is not biblically defensible, nor is it adequate as an empirical theory of language in the West. Furthermore, it is not serviceable in the missionary task of taking the gospel message across cultures to Asia and Africa. It simply does not lend itself to the task of what Paul Hiebert calls "critical contextualization" of the biblical message (*International Bulletin*, 11 [no. 3, 1987]: 104-112).

34. The question of biblical interpretation has become crucial for Mennonites and for fundamentalists in general during the past quarter century of rapid social change. Many beliefs and practices which had been based on a simple literal interpretation and application of Scripture have been radically changed, but an adequate methodological rationale for the changes has not been articulated. Recently, several good books on methodology have been published by Mennonite authors. Note, for examples, Perry Yoder's *From*

Word to Life (1982); Willard Swartley's *Slavery, Sabbath, War, and Women* (1983); and Paul M. Zehr's *Biblical Criticism in the Life of the Church* (1986). These books deal with method and critical presuppositions, but they do not speak explicitly to the theological framework for interpretation.

35. Pannenberg 1977:132.

36. Pinnock 1984:62.

37. We are not challenging their canonicity, but simply establishing a hermeneutical norm. Sometimes this point has been made by speaking of a "canon within the canon." Already in the Reformation, Luther spoke clearly on this point and did not hesitate to designate the "chief books of the New Testament."

38. Swartley gives examples of how these passages are interpreted from "hierarchical" and "liberationist" theological perspectives (1983:164ff.).

39. I dare to make this kind of distinction in spite of the fact that Paul begins the exhortation in 1 Corinthians 11:3 with an analogy based upon the relation of Christ and God. Paul is clearly arguing his case in the immediate cultural context of thought and practice. In his argument he uses rabbinic interpretation of Old Testament passages, current concepts about angels, and contextual cultural practice. But note in verse 11 how he modifies his own rule that "the husband is the head of his wife," stated in verse 3, with the qualification, "in the Lord."

My point is not to discount the validity of his theological argument and application in his first-century context. I simply distinguish these kinds of passages from those that bear more immediate witness to Christ and the implications of revelation received through him. Our original point was that not all passages have a uniform significance as witness to the self-disclosure in Christ. Paul himself apparently indicates his awareness of this difference when he clinches his point by appealing to church tradition rather than the original revelation in Christ (v. 17).

40. I am indebted to Fr. Michael Cook, who in turn gives acknowledgment to Norman Perrin, for this careful analysis of the nature of the biblical reports (1981:22).

41. Kern Trumbath has suggested that we differentiate between *Bible*, which designates the sixty-six books, and *Scriptures*, which designates the authoritative norm for the church. He points out that only those who have been saved by God's inspired work claim that the "Bible" is "Scripture." He adds, "The Bible is inspired precisely because it has served as the vehicle through which God has inspired Christian salvation within them" ("Biblical Inspiration and the Believing Community: A New Look," *Evangelical Quarterly*, July 1986:250-251).

42. Klaassen 1981:87.

43. The question whether inerrancy as a technical concept can be attributed to the Reformers of the sixteenth century is hotly debated. It is especially difficult to attribute it to the Anabaptists. They undoubtedly held to a high view of scriptural authority, but inerrancy as we know it today did not develop until somewhat later. We do not see much evidence of it in early writings. Their view of Scripture must be understood in light of the following: (1) their rejection of scholastic assumptions and methodology, (2) their renewed emphasis upon the Holy Spirit as the continuing dynamic and enlightener, (3) their emphasis upon the church under the guidance of the Spirit as the hermeneutical community of discernment, and (4) their clear differentiation between the authority of the Old and New Testaments. These emphases do not flatly contradict the concept of inerrancy, but they do point toward a different rationale. It is significant that the later movement did not make much of an appeal to the arguments of Protestant Scholasticism. Only much more recently has the issue entered the Mennonite church under the impact of fundamentalism. See my article, Kraus 1967:309ff., and Paul M. Zehr 1986.

44. This position, given its definitive American formulation by the theologians of "old Princeton," is still the position of fundamentalists and neofundamentalists. More recently renewed doubt has arisen about the adequacy of the theory, both as a descriptive rationale or an apologetic for the Bible's authority. See, for example, Clark Pinnock, *The Scriptural Principle* (New York: Harper & Row, 1984). We should note that this doubt is not

new in evangelical circles. Men like James Orr and E. Y. Mullins, both of whom wrote articles published in the original volumes of *The Fundamentals*, had such reservations even though they held to high views of Scripture.

Chapter 3: God the Parent-Creator as Father of Jesus Christ

1. Kraus 1990:42f.

2. Kraus 1990:157f.

3. Kosuke Koyama has given us a subtle critique of modern idolatry as it has been evidenced in Japanese cultural forms. See his *Mount Fuji and Mount Sinai: A Critique of Idols* (Maryknoll, N.Y.: Orbis, 1985).

4. Not all Buddhism is theistic, but the Amida figure functions as a high God of grace in the Japanese tradition. Especially the name of Shinran is associated with a concept of grace that has been compared favorably to that of Martin Luther.

5. The Oomoto religion is one of the so-called new religions which emerged in Japan during the nineteenth century. Its originator, Nao Deguchi, was a poor peasant woman who was seized with prophetic charisma by the creator god, Konjin. Konjin told her that his place as the original creator had been usurped by lesser gods and that now he had come to restore the right order in the universe. This was a direct challenge to the sun goddess, Amaterasu, who was the emperor's ancestor. By implication it was also a challenge to the imperial concept of the "divine nation." While Oomoto religion emerged from within Shinto, it has taken an ecumenical stance and has attempted to unite the religions of the world under the rule of the creator god.

6. Biblical scholars differ in their views of the originally intended meaning of the name given in Exodus 3. Four different possible meanings are indicated. Theologically, all four are significant and true to the biblical and Christian view of God. (1) "I AM WHO I AM." This means God is not to be identified with any of the known deities of the nations, such as Egypt or Canaan, or with any of the tribal deities of their ancestors. He is the one who names himself. (Compare Acts 17:23-24, where Paul uses "unknown god" as the way to introduce the "God who made the world and everything in it.") God cannot be named by human knowledge. He cannot be known "in himself," that is, examined by the processes of human science and reason. Or, in the vocabulary of the Bible, God cannot be "seen." He can only be "heard."

(2) "I AM THE LIVING GOD" (compare Matt. 22:31-33). Translated this way, the meaning would be that the true God is not created by humans like idols. He lives and is present and able to rescue Israel. He has not forgotten his promises to Abraham, and he is there to fulfill them. (Note verses 16-17.) This underscores God's faithfulness and dependability as the God of covenant.

(3) "I WILL BE WHO/WHAT I WILL BE." God is the God of history as well as of nature. He is not bound up with the cycle of nature—a notion which was fundamental in animism and idolatry. God is free to act according to his own nature and will. He can respond in freedom as a person. Thus God will be known by his acts in history. He is the God who delivered Israel out of Egypt; the God who raised Jesus from the dead. The biblical writers constantly identify God as the one who has done and will do significant things in their history. (Compare, for example, Isa. 46:11; 49:22-23; Jer. 16:21; Ezek. 5:13-17.)

(4) "I CAUSE TO BE WHAT IS." That is, "I am the Creator God." As sovereign of the universe, *God* is in control, not fate or *karma*. Compare the Greek myth that even Zeus, the father of the gods, is finally subject to Fate.

7. It is the province of a Christian philosophy of religion to offer evidence from human reason and experience for this faith assumption with which we begin.

8. To see the significance of this, we need only compare it to the mythology of a nation like Japan. The *kami* are the gods of Japan. The original formation of primeval substance was lost in the mists of antiquity. The powers who were responsible for it are unknown. The creation—or better, procreation—of the earth as we know it began with the creation of the Japanese islands and people. Thus Japan is a "divine nation." Norinaga Motoori

(1730-1801), the well-known Shinto philosopher of the eighteenth century, wrote, "Indeed, our country being literally the homeland where the Sun Goddess was born, is destined to be the great center of all other nations. . . . More important is the heritage of the imperial family, which is destined to survive uninterrupted for generations until the end of the world" (*The Great Asian Religions* 1969:297). Thus it is understandable that he questioned whether anyone but a Japanese could worship the *kami*.

In contrast to this, the biblical story does not have Canaan as the original land. Israel was not the original people. Elohim was not originally an Israelite god. Indeed, even when God is known by the name Yahweh, he does not belong to Israel. Israel is his servant to the nations (Exod. 19:5-6). Elohim/Yahweh is the God of all the earth. And he has made covenants with all nations (cf. Gen. 9:8; Acts 17:26). Accordingly, humankind is bound into one family under the covenant of life and peace which God has made with them.

9. Conzelmann says, "Judaism has no epistemological reflections about God and the makeup of the world. It has no concept of nature except for what it takes over from the Greeks (Philo). . . . The factors in the idea of God are: the creation and guidance of the world, the election of Israel, the giving of the law. Israel has experienced God's guidance (leading, punishment, reacceptance) in its history and can draw the appropriate conclusions for the present" (1969:13).

10. Both Karl Barth and Emil Brunner emphasized the "Lordship of God." To say that God reveals himself as Lord means that God in his freedom reveals himself as the ultimate authority for humankind. "Revelation," wrote Barth, "is the revelation of lordship, and at the same time of the Lordship of God. . . . 'God reveals Himself as the Lord' means that He reveals what only He Himself can reveal, [namely,] Himself" (*Dogmatics* 1936, I, 1:352-353). Barth's specific point here is that God's lordship means that we must accept his self-revelation for what it is and not usurp his authority by trying to reason out what he *must* be from the perspective of human logic. In other contexts, Barth stresses the "utter superiority" of God's authority over humanity—an authority "in distinction from all other authorities" (*Dogmatics* I, 1:441).

Brunner observes that "the translators of the LXX were strictly accurate when they unhesitatingly rendered the Name of Yahweh by the title of 'Lord.' The Lordship of God implies two things: (1) God is Subject: addressing us, making Himself known to us. . . . (2) God meets us in revelation as the unconditioned Subject in such a way that He claims us unconditionally for Himself; thus He meets us as Absolute Lord" (1950, 1:138, 139, 141).

11. In the Greek language, both *kurios* and *despotēs* are used of those in positions of power and authority. Both have the power to command. However, *kurios*, the word used almost exclusively in the LXX and New Testament, puts emphasis upon the legitimacy of the authority or power. "One may sum up the whole development by saying that *kurios*, originally the one who is fully authorized and has the legal power of disposal, did not contain the element of arbitrariness which so easily clung to *despotēs*." (See *kurios* in TDNT, 3:1046.)

12. Jeremiah gives a devastating description of the impotence of idols, which were made by the goldsmith (10:3-16). He concludes, "There is no breath (*ruakh*) in them" (10:14). He insists that they did not create the heavens and the earth and prophesies that they will perish from the earth (10:11). Compare similar denunciations in Isaiah 46:5-11; 48:3-5; and Habakkuk 2:18-20.

13. Paul uses the Greek word *nous* to translate the Hebrew *ruakh* in Romans 11:34 and 1 Corinthians 2:6, where he is alluding to or quoting Isaiah 40:13.

14. Aulén 1960:102.

15. Brunner 1950, 1:158.

16. According to the ancient Zoroastrian and Manichaean religions, good and evil, light and darkness, were in eternal struggle. In Greek mythology, even Zeus, the father of the gods, was not all-powerful over Fate. In Japanese Shinto, there are many evil *kami* as well as good ones. And there seems to be no resolution of the problem of evil. The prob-

lem seems rather to be viewed as continuity of existence. In Amida Buddhism, on the other hand, universal enlightenment or Buddhahood is the final resolution through the grace of Amida.

17. Berkhof 1986:41ff.

18. In 1 Corinthians 8:4-6 Paul states that idols have no existence, and at the same time he recognizes their power over those who think they do. He says there are many "gods" and "lords" recognized by people of the world, but for Christians there is only one "God, the Father," and one "Lord, Jesus Christ." Further, this one God is the Creator from whom and for whom all things were created, and the Savior through whom they continue to exist. This is a crucial passage for understanding Paul's approach to missionary activity in polytheistic cultures.

The setting for this passage is the superstition that the idols may have real existence. Paul does not discuss how we may discriminate idolatrous from authentic authority. But his words, "for us . . . one Lord, Jesus Christ," suggest that Christ is the criterion. What meets the test of his *agapēic* standard is authentically divine.

19. The Bengali reformer, Chaitanya (1485-1527), who established the Bhakti cult of Krishna, taught that love for Krishna and Krishna's love for the devotee is the highest spiritual relationship. He described this relationship as a mutual erotic passion between Lord Krishna and Radha, his consort in lovemaking. In practice, the relationship was expressed in the contemplative worship of the image of Krishna and in singing his praises. Such erotic imagery is quite different in both concept and religious practice from the biblical concept of God's *agapē*. See R. G. Nath's, "A Survey of the Chaitanya Movement," in R. C. Majumdar, ed., *The History and Culture of the Indian People*, vol. 4 (Bombay, 1964).

20. Nygren 1953:726ff.; Aulén 1960:113f.

21. Sallie McFague simply accepts Nygren's definition of *agapê* as love without consideration of value and insists that an erotic element is needed to create value. She writes, "It [*eros*] implies that the world is valuable, that God needs it, and that salvation is the reunification of the beloved world with its lover, God" (1987:131). But when she speaks of the world as "God's body" and of God as "Lover" of his body, she introduces a narcissistic note into the metaphor.

22. Aulén 1960:118.

23. See Aulén 1960:110.

24. Kraus 1990:164-165.

25. Belief in the doctrine itself was considered necessary to salvation in earlier orthodoxy. The so-called Athanasian Creed from the fifth or sixth century states this explicitly: "(1) Whosoever will be saved, before all things it is necessary that he hold the Catholic Faith: (2) Which Faith except every one do keep whole and undefiled, without doubt he shall perish everlastingly. (3) And the Catholic Faith is this: That we worship one God in Trinity, and Trinity in Unity" (Schaff 1877, 2:66). Today many evangelicals hold, rather, that it is necessary to believe in the God who is witnessed to in the trinitarian doctrinal statement.

26. Brown 1906:160.

27. Craig 1952:22.

28. Weber 1981:351.

29. Clarke 1898:172-174.

30. McGinn 1987:266f.; Seeberg 1952, 1:232.

31. The major leaders of the Anabaptists all used trinitarian language. Dirk Philips' writings are quite orthodox. See for example, "The Church of God" (Williams and Mergal, eds., 1957:237-240). Ridemann's "Confession of Faith" follows the Apostles' Creed in a thoroughly orthodox way. For example, "We have said and acknowledge that God is one. . . . Therefore we acknowledge also his Son who was in the Father before the world was made" (1950:22).

Marpeck's language is thoroughly trinitarian, but his interest lies primarily in the full humanity of Christ as the true Son of God. For example, from his tract on *The Humanity of Christ* we read, "This Son of Man . . . is appointed a Lord and Ruler of all things; yes indeed humanity is taken up into God the Father and God the Father into the Son, who from eternity has been one essence, Spirit, and God" (Klassen & Klaassen 1978:508).

Menno also wrote a *Confession of the Triune God*. He confesses the unity and Trinity of God in traditional language, but he hesitates to use terms like *substance* and *persons*. He prefers simply to confess the incomprehensible and ineffable spirituality of the one eternal God, who exists as Father, Son, and Holy Spirit. He refers to the "true divine being, Jesus Christ, whom the fathers have called a *person*" (italics mine; Wenger 1950:492). His hesitancy to call Christ in "His eternal divine Being" a "person" stemmed from his understanding of person as a separate being "seated next to God from everlasting" (1950:861). Compare Keeny 1968:95-96.

32. The Japanese language, with its preference for more concrete modes of expression, has a particularly difficult time labeling the concept. *Sanmi-ittai* translates rather literally as, "three ranks of being or status in one body." While one must guard against the suggestion of multiplicity of deities in a polytheistic culture, neither do we want to indicate hierarchical ranking within the Godhead.

33. McGinn 1987:288.

34. Henry's monumental work on revelation, *God, Revelation and Authority* (Word, 1976-1979), everywhere presupposes the triune essence of the Godhead as both the ground and content of inerrant, propositional revelation. However, he does not discuss it except to criticize Barth's doctrine as inadequate and to insist on the essential deity of Christ both as preexistent and incarnate Logos. The "multipersonal Godhead is an irreducible aspect of New Testament revelation" (III, 2:204).

Donald Bloesch gives a clear, concise discussion of the doctrine under "The Sovereignty of God." His emphasis is upon the dynamic freedom of God as personal being. "The doctrine of the Trinity is not an explanation but a definition of the being of God and the life of God" (1978:37).

35. Manschreck 1965:16-17.

36. Wenger 1956:496-97.

37. Reinhold Seeberg has observed that for all its brilliance and subtlety, Augustine's doctrine of the Trinity "exerted but slight influence on practical piety" (1952, 1:240). A quite effusive spirituality was developed around the symbol, but it was not ethically developed to the same extent. Emphasis was placed on substance (*ousia*) as the ultimate unifying nature of Deity rather than on personal-ethical character. Quite in contrast to this, Menno's consuming passion was upon practical, ethical spirituality.

38. Barth 1936, I, 1:403.

39. Barth 1936:402.

40. Barth 1936:412-413.

41. Buttrick 2:434.

42. Millard Lind has suggested that *Father* is a "secondary image" for God in the Old Testament. It is used less than a dozen times of Yahweh as the Father of Israel. On the other hand, the *Elohim* of the nations around Israel are freely pictured as generative fathers. Fatherhood in Paul is generally by adoption. Even in Israel, it was associated with covenant adoption rather than mythical birth. In personal conversation, Lind has suggested further that perhaps it was only after the mythical sexual allusions were thoroughly eliminated that Jesus could make the parental image of Father central. See also John W. Miller, *Biblical Faith and Fathering: Why We Call God Father* (Paulist Press, 1989).

43. Wilson-Kastner 1983:28.

44. McFague 1987:99.

45. I have used the pronominal form, *he*, as an inclusive, gender-undetermined personal pronoun. I have referred to Deity exclusively as *God* because *she* and *Goddess* are still gender-specific at this point of usage and thus no improvement over *God* and *he/him*, which do have some history of indefinite-gender personal use. I have chosen to do this in the interests of *not* specifying gender for the Deity.

46. Perhaps we should speak of God with adverbial qualifiers such as *motherly, father-*

ly, friendly, and *loving,* rather than in gender-specific metaphors such as *Father, Mother,* and *Lover.* Obviously, this will require some adaptation in the liturgical aspects of the church's life. For example, in the West we might address God as "Dear Heavenly Parent." In Japan the problem of such metaphorical language is exacerbated by the distinct traditional roles and attitudes attributed to father and mother and by the Shinto concept of the gods as ancestors.

47. What Paul Hiebert says about the problem of contextualization in foreign cultures applies equally to our own when radical shifts require change. See "Critical Contextualization," *International Bulletin of Missionary Research,* July 1987:104ff.

48. Robinson 1973:221-222.

49. Tillich 1951, 1:147-148; cf. 83ff.

50. Both *dikaios* and *dikaiosunē* began as terms to define the customarily proper and legally right conduct. In the Old Testament, right is embodied in the law of Moses. In the New Testament, Jesus Christ embodies it, especially in his sacrifice on the cross. Gottlob Schrenk says that the concept of *dikaios* in the New Testament is largely determined by the Old Testament. But it supersedes it and gives it a new emphasis. In the New, the "justice of the One who is absolutely righteous is demonstrated in the atoning sacrifice of Jesus" (Kittel 2:188).

51. I have dealt with the definition and characteristics of *agapē* at more length in *Jesus Christ Our Lord* (1987, 1990:75n, 142ff., 164-166). See also the chapter, "The Spirit of Love," in Kraus, *The Community of the Spirit* (1974).

52. Weber 1981:438.

Chapter 4: Humanity in the Image of Christ

1. Kraus 1990:97.

2. Kraus 1990:187ff.

3. Wenger 1954:73ff.

4. This is the way most tribal definitions of humanity are constructed. People of the tribe are human by virtue of being the offspring of the tribal god. Others outside that relationship are less than human.

5. Some interpret "according to their kind" as a scientific statement that the species are fixed and that further development of animal and plant life is impossible. This interpretation is highly questionable. The statement is simply the nontechnical way of saying that God created the various kinds of animals. The New Revised Standard Version now translates the phrase simply as "of every kind" (Gen. 1:11, etc.).

6. When evolutionary theorists speak of the *origins* of the universe and humankind, they have gone beyond the domain of science. They have become philosophical speculators. Some forty years ago, Lecomte Du Noüy, the famous French biologist and author of *Human Destiny,* wrote, "It is impossible nowadays to imagine how evolution began. Was there an initial cell? Or, as seems plausible to admit, did amorphous living matter precede the first cells? We do not know" (Du Noüy 1947:57-58). Again he says, "We cannot conceive this process [biological evolution of humans] except as the result of a long evolution: but we can only surmise, not prove it, and the whole process escapes us completely" (Du Noüy 1947:97).

More recently, Earl Hanson in his preface to a textbook on evolution, wrote, "Strictly speaking, natural selection says nothing directly about the nature of living things or where they came from in the sense of the origin of life" (Hanson 1981). Even as I write this footnote, scientists are preparing to launch the Hubble telescope into space to peer 15 billion light-years into space, which means 15 billion years into the past. Their great hope is to find out more about the origin of the universe. But even so they point out that they still will only be observing light that is one or two billion years on this side of the origin!

The Bible's concern is with the origins and the meaning of human existence, to which science cannot speak. When fundamentalist theologians insist on a literal scientific interpretation of the Genesis accounts, they are making the Bible pronounce on issues outside its intended meaning.

7. Wingren, a Swedish theologian, expanded on the christological approach of the late Bishop Aulén (1960:52-57). He argues that a correct christological approach does not displace the first article of the Apostles' Creed with the second. Rather, the disclosure in Christ (incarnation) fills out the original meaning of creation. He writes, "The Creator who lets man live and who thereby creates him, creates him in His image (Gen. 1:26f.), and this image in which every man has been created is Jesus Christ, who is 'the image of the invisible God, the firstborn of all Creation' (Col. 1:15). The 'new man' whom the believer in Christ 'puts on' (Rom. 13:14; Gal. 3:27) is Christ Himself. This is what God the Creator intended man to be in Creation. To become like Christ, therefore, is also to conform to God's will in Creation and to receive 'life' (cf. Col. 3:10; Eph. 4:24). These many New Testament passages about the 'image' and 'likeness' are marked by their reference both to Christ and to the believer. They have undoubtedly derived their form from the important Old Testament passages on Creation in Gen. 1:26, and are fully comprehensible only in light of this passage" (1961:35).

8. From the Apocrypha, note 2 Maccabees 7:28: "I beg you, my child, to look at the heaven and the earth and see everything that is in them, and recognize that God did not make them out of things that existed. And in the same way the human race came into being."

9. The setting for these words is a Sabbath healing. Jesus thus declares that the Mosaic Sabbath does not mark the cessation of God's creative work, but that he himself is the continuation of the redeeming-creating work of God.

Gerhard von Rad deals with the intertwining of the themes of creation and redemption in his article, "The Theological Problem of the Old Testament Doctrine of Creation," in Anderson's *Creation in the Old Testament*.

10. John A. Hutchison has written, "The biblical view is notable for the absence of any trace of body-soul dualism. Man is an integral and indissoluble unity, more readily described as an ensouled body than a duality of soul and body. His life as a whole is the creation of a good God" (1956:83-84).

11. See also the discussion further below, "Death and the Essential Self," in chapter 7.

12. The command given to Adam (humankind) and to no other creature establishes their freedom, as Westermann points out (1974:89). It sets the conditions and limits of the creature's response. Freely chosen obedience would have established and expanded human freedom, whereas a choice not to obey also established but greatly limited human freedom. The command is the reverse side of God's promise. The required response sets the conditions and limits of the creature's existence in love.

13. See Kraus 1990:178.

14. The account uses the plural, "Let us make humankind in our image." There is a long history of interpretation of this passage which takes this plural as an implicit reference to the Trinity of God's being and suggests that in some sense humans correspond to that Trinitarian being. It seems more likely, however, that the reference is to God as the gracious heavenly Ruler surrounded by his heavenly court—those beings who already shared his image, and like himself were personal beings (Job 1:6; 1 Kings 21:19; etc.). On earth humankind, "made a little lower than the angels," joins this great heavenly entourage.

15. There is a general agreement between biblical and systematic theologians that *image* does not refer to some particular element or aspect of human nature. Westermann says the account is "not a declaration about man but about the creation of man. . . . The meaning must come from the Creation event. What God has decided to create must stand in a relationship to him." Adam and Eve are creatures "that correspond to him[self], to whom he can speak, and who can hear him" (1974:56). He gives a brief history of exegesis of the passage on pages 57-59, and a more extended one in his commentary on Genesis 1-11 (1984:147-155). See also my *Authentic Witness* (1979:81ff.) for backgrounds in Greek and modern thought.

Barton Babbage, an evangelical scholar who gives an excellent review of the contemporary theological discussion on the subject, summarizes the position of T. F. Torrance as follows: "Thus the *imago Dei* is not a doctrine about man's being in himself; it is rather an acknowledgment that he depends entirely upon the will of another" (1957:16). Torrance is following Barth, who spoke of the image as an *analogia relationis*, and an "analogy of grace." Babbage sums this up with the phrase, "a saving, dynamic relationship of faith" (17).

See also Roop 1987:321-323: The image of God distinguishes humankind from the (other) animals. The image of God refers to the bodily form and the spiritual attributes. There is an emphasis on our relationship with God and each other, and to human responsibility under God to manage the world for the benefit of all life on earth.

16. When the image is identified with a spirit or mind (*nous*) in the Greek sense, it becomes a spiritual part of the human being. Traditional Christian theology has adapted the biblical concept of image to the Greek psychological model. Thus, rather than humans being *made in God's image*, humans have the *image in themselves*. According to the Greek model, which many Christians adapted for their own use, the spirit is essentially divinity. The immortal spirit-reason is joined to a fleshly body to make a human being. In the Christian modification of this, the image is the rational spirit bestowed by God and is usually associated with God's breathing life into Adam (Gen. 2:7).

17. Karl Barth is the source for contemporary christological definitions of humanity in the image of God. His opening proposition in *Dogmatics* III, 2:208, states, "As the man Jesus is Himself the revealing Word of God, He is the source of our knowledge of the nature of man as created by God" (3). Later in the same volume he says Jesus' humanity must be defined as "fellow-humanity" and as a humanity for his fellow humans. It is this nature of his human existence that teaches us what humanity in the image of God means (206ff.). "Therefore, as we turn to the problem of humanity, we do not need to look for any other basis of anthropology than the christological. On the contrary, we have to realize that the existence of the man Jesus is quite instructive enough in this aspect of the question of man in general."

This principle of interpretation has been affirmed from a variety of theological positions. In 1965 Kenneth Cauthen, a contemporary American theologian, wrote, "The important point here is that the *Logos* who was the agent of creation is present in the manhood of Jesus of Nazareth. Thus, the pattern and meaning of the divine purpose and activity everywhere expressed in the cosmos are decisively disclosed in a particular person and event" (Cauthen 1965:39).

18. "Man Created in God's Image," quoted by Shaw 1953:108.

19. Westermann 1974:61. Von Rad speaks of it as a "formula of approbation" (1972:61). Irenaeus (c. 130-200), a bishop and theologian in Asia Minor, spoke of Adam as "yet an infant," and as "making progress day by day, and ascending toward the perfect[ion of God]" (*Adversus Heresies*, 4.38.1, 3). Against the perfectionism of the Gnostics, he viewed humankind even yet as looking forward to maturity (4.37.7).

20. Ulrich Luz in an article, "The Image of God in Christ and Mankind" (*Concilium* 1969:80-92), concludes that Paul speaks of "natural man" bearing the image of God only in 1 Corinthians 11:7. He says *man* here means male. He also says the references to Christ as the *eikōn* of God apply to the resurrected heavenly Christ, not the earthly Jesus. "To say that Christ is the *eikōn* of God does not mean that he is the embodiment or true face of the humanity which God created in Genesis 1; it means that Christ, in an exclusive sense, is the one who reveals God to the world" (84).

I would agree that the *eikōn* passages do not primarily elucidate anthropological insights. I also agree that they refer most directly to the risen glorified Christ and that the *eikōn* becomes primarily a soteriological concept. But Luz has too rigorously excluded any other possible reference. His basic approach is to interpret the sayings as products of "pre-Pauline 'enthusiastic' communities," and he pays little attention to the Pauline text itself.

For Paul the risen glorified Christ is the crucified Jesus. Indeed, it is precisely the Jesus who submitted fully to the Father's will who is "glorified," who becomes the "image and reflection of God." Thus the earthly Jesus and anthropological insights are not to be excluded.

The relation of the image to salvation is obvious. Salvation is our restoration in—or our stage-by-stage creation in—the image displayed in Jesus Christ. See Kraus 1990:194-198.

21. Brunner 1951:59.

22. Westermann 1974:90-91.

23. The movement in this passage from "form of God" to "form of servant" to "highly exalted," is sometimes described as a parabolic movement. We should not read this as movement from political authority based on divine power to humiliation of human servanthood, and then reinstatement to divine kingly authority. The exaltation is the enthronement of the Servant Messiah. The name "above every name" that is bestowed upon him is the name of Servant. Therein is God glorified.

24. Paul Jewett, who teaches at Fuller Theological Seminary, discusses this issue with clarity in his review of Barth's and Brunner's positions (*Man as Male and Female* 1975:29ff.).

25. Even in 1 Corinthians 11:2-16, where he elaborates a hierarchical relationship as the natural order, Paul honors this principle. The "in the Lord" (11:11) relationship modifies this hierarchy by recognizing male-female interdependence and complementarity. This principle is carried further in Galatians 3:27-28 and Ephesians 5:21.

26. I owe this general classification to S. J. De Vries. See his article, "Sin, Sinners," in Buttrick 1962:362.

27. "In such a universe," says Mary Douglas, the British anthropologist, "the elemental forces are seen as linked so closely to individual human beings that we can hardly speak of an external, physical environment. Each individual carries within himself such close links with the universe that he is like the center of a magnetic field of force.... Physical forces are thought of as interwoven with the lives of persons. Things are not completely distinguished from their external environment" (1979:81, 89).

28. In Japan, for example, the Shinto rites are based largely on this principle. See the ritual prayers from the *Engi Shiki*, which are dated about 927 C.E. (Chan 1969:264-265).

29. Prohibited conduct is spelled out in traditional terms: covetousness, attachment to false views, falsehood, harshness, unlawful injury to another, adultery, etc. These pollute individuals. Proper disciplines must be followed to cleanse oneself. The *Laws of Manu*, which prescribed the rules for medieval Hindu society, illustrate this pattern. For example, one rule (11:257) reads, "If a man [of caste] is polluted by one of the great sins, he should live with cows for a year controlling his mind, studying sacred texts, taking the name of God and repeating it constantly. He should live only by begging. Then he will be purified" (Chan 1967:61).

30. Chan 1969:61.

31. Walter Gutbrod puts it well when he says this of the postexilic period: "Observing the Law does not create the relation to God; it keeps the people in this continuing relation, e.g., 2 Ch[ron]. 33:8. In fact, however, the emphasis and concern rest increasingly on the second aspect, so that everything depends on observance of the Law.... The Law takes on increasingly independent significance" (Kittel 4:1043). During this era, particularly in the first centuries B.C.E. and C.E., emphasis on separatism from pagans seems to have dimmed some of their best insights into the nature of covenant law. This resulted partly from the stress of political domination and religious persecution.

In his essay, "Some Theses Toward a Theology of Law in the New Testament," John E. Toews views this assessment as "a polemic against Judaism" and argues that the kernel of covenant law was not lost (*The Bible and Law* 1982:43-64). See also E. P. Sanders' *Paul and Palestinian Judaism* 1977: esp. pp. 426-428. While these theses are a proper corrective, they are somewhat overstated.

32. "It was St. Paul who roused the Adamic theme from its lethargy; by means of the contrast between the 'old man' and the 'new man,' he set up the figure of Adam as the inverse of that of Christ, called the second Adam.... At the same time, the figure of Adam ... was personalized on the model of the figure of Christ, to which it serves as contrast" (Ricoeur 1967:238).

33. The association of this chaos with a precreation "fall" of Lucifer (Isa. 14:12) is a

speculation that fits the Babylonian account better than the biblical one. In any event, there is no hint that an opposing force such as Lucifer had anything to do with the creation.

34. Paul Tillich defined the Fall in philosophical terms as the "transition from essence to existence." He said this was not an event in time and space. When he was criticized for making creation and fall coincidental, he replied that "original sin" is not a "structural necessity." He explained that "theology must insist that the leap from essence to existence is the original fact—that it has the character of a leap and not of structural necessity. In spite of its tragic universality, existence cannot be derived from essence" (1957, 2:44). He described it as a state of "estrangement."

35. "Even under the lordship of *sin* and *death* his nature is still human nature and so is the image and likeness of what it will be under the lordship of *grace* and *life*" (Barth 1956:48).

36. There is a clear pattern of thought development concerning the devil in the Old and New Testaments. Even though Babylonian influence is obvious, one can make a case for a parallel between a growing consciousness of the seriousness and pervasiveness of evil and the increasing identification of Satan as the personification of evil. In the New Testament, Satan emerges as the full personification of evil and opposition to God. Thirty-three times he is called *Satanas* (adversary), thirty-two times *diabolos*. Once he is called Belial, or worthless one.

37. By *story* I do not mean to indicate that it is untrue. It is symbolic and it presents a much larger and more profound truth about human nature than a purely literal interpretation could ever render.

38. These theologians used 1 Timothy 2:14 with a vengeance as the official interpretation of the Genesis 3 account. One should note, however, that the Timothy text is not offered as an inclusive exegesis of Genesis, but only as an incidental reference to buttress the author's admonition. Nowhere else in the New Testament is it suggested that the woman actually bears more responsibility than the man for what happened.

39. Ricoeur 1967:255.

40. I have discussed the soteriological issues at length in chapters 11 and 12 in *Jesus Christ Our Lord* (1987,1990:187ff.).

Chapter 5: The Holy Spirit as the Spirit of Christ

1. The biblical words *ruakh* and *pneuma* and the Latin *spiritus* have multiple meanings, but as a rule they mean wind, breath, life force, or living person. Thus *ruakh* is the breath of God which animates our animal bodies (Gen 2:7; 6:17; 7:15; Ezek. 37:5ff.). God is called Spirit in the sense of being a living person. The *pneuma* in humans is the inner personal life force. When the Hebrews thought of God's Spirit as wind, their image was of a mysterious force which might bring either good or ill fortune. For example, it was the wind that drove back waters of the Red Sea (or Sea of Reeds) and dried the land so they could escape from Egypt. But again, the same hot, dry wind sometimes dried up the crops and brought famine.

The wind, of course, is atmospheric *movement*. The more comprehensive metaphor of atmosphere in which we live and breathe seems also to be implied in the Pauline metaphor, "in the Spirit." But in contrast to the Greeks, who tended to be more pantheistic (Acts 17:28), the Hebrews of the Bible preferred the concept of movement—the action of God (Acts 2:2). God as Spirit is a transcendent creative, personal power manifesting himself in our dimension of existence. God is not an animistic or pantheistic power immanent in the universe.

2. Berkhof 1986:331.

3. The language used to describe the Spirit in the Bible is often impersonal because the Spirit is so closely associated with the *activity* of God. Metaphors like "filled with" and "poured out" are impersonal metaphors of substance, not personal metaphors of presence. The Greek word *pneuma* is grammatically of neuter gender. Today it often seems more natural to use the neuter *it* rather than *he* or *she*. However, inasmuch as the

Spirit is identified with the *personal* presence and activity of God, a personal pronoun or the name should be used. Note how the NRSV handles this problem in Rom. 8:16: "that very Spirit" for "the Spirit itself."

The recent feminist insistence on using the feminine pronoun for the Holy Spirit raises a problem of another kind. It is true that the Hebrew word *ruakh* is grammatically feminine. And the *ruakh* of God is closely associated with Wisdom, which has a feminine persona. It is also quite proper to disassociate our concept of God from purely male imagery. But rather than introducing feminine terminology which has the same drawbacks as masculine terminology, we need a personal pronoun that can supply for both sexes equally.

G. W. H. Lampe gives an excellent summary of the work of the Spirit in the Old Testament in his *Interpreter's Dictionary of the Bible* article, "Holy Spirit" (Buttrick 2:626-30).

4. One should not overemphasize the discontinuity between the way the Old and New Testaments speak about the Spirit and his work among God's people. However, there is some noticeable variation. Some interpreters have emphasized the differences in the Spirit's mode of operation, calling special attention to the New Testament metaphors of baptism and filling. A careful survey of the language of both Testaments, however, will hardly substantiate a sharp modal distinction. Yet there is heightened awareness of and intimacy with the Spirit which followed from the disciples' experience with Jesus, but modal designations remain much the same.

5. If this sounds strange to our contemporary ears, compare Acts 8:26, 29, and 39, where an angel and the Spirit appear in the same role.

6. There is a multifold element indicated in the personal unity and the universal sovereignty of the biblical God, but it is witnessed to in quite other terms. For example, God is both transcendent and immanent (Eph. 4:6). He is the sender and the one sent, the lover and the one loved, the one who not only *is* (the Greek concept), but who *was* and is *becoming*.

7. Hendry 1965:24-25.

8. Scott 1929:153, 258. Both of these theologians are attempting to say what the creeds said with *substance* and *persona*, but in language more in touch with modern thought patterns. Hendry qualifies the "identification," or sameness as God, with an adjective of action. Scott in effect says "equivalent but not the same as." That is, the Spirit is God, but God is more than the Spirit.

9. "When we cry, 'Abba! Father!' it is that very Spirit bearing witness with our spirit that we are children of God" (Rom. 8:15-16). The Spirit speaks through the disciples in witness. In connection with that witness, it convicts and convinces the world of Jesus' lordship (John 15:26; 16:7-9). The Spirit is the source of our life in Christ and "bears fruit" in human attitudes and actions. Thus we recognize the Spirit as that divine personal reality in our experience of Christ, alive and at work among us.

10. See Kittel 6:385.

11. The references to the Spirit in Luke 11:13 and 12:10, 12 are words of Jesus in which he makes statements about the future rather than about his own power or authority. The Holy Spirit in these cases seems to take on Jesus' postresurrection identity. In 12:10, by way of contrast to the Matthew and Mark parallels, Luke seems to distinguish clearly between "Son of Man" and "Holy Spirit," anticipating a situation such as we see in Acts 4:3ff. and 8:14-24. The passage in Luke 10:21ff. is intriguing but enigmatic.

12. Berkhof has noted this dual relationship of Jesus and the Spirit in the New Testament materials. He writes, "There is not only a relationship of sequence. In the New Testament the relationship between them is presented in two ways. On the one hand the Spirit creatively precedes; he is greater than Jesus and controls him. Jesus is the work of the Spirit. On the other hand the Spirit is the work of (the risen) Jesus, interpreting Jesus and being ruled by him" (1986:329). However, Berkhof's point is slightly different from mine. He says the first emphasis is the ground for a Spirit Christology in which Jesus is viewed as the incarnation of the Spirit (330).

13. According to Matthew 3:13-17 and Mark 1:9-11, Jesus had a vision of the Spirit's

descent. He heard the words of assurance that he was the messianic Son. These accounts give no report of others sharing the vision or audition. John's Gospel, however, tells of the event from the Baptist's perspective. The Baptist sees the Spirit and bears witness that Jesus is the one who will baptize with the Holy Spirit and fire (1:31; cf. Matt.3:11; Mark 1:8).

14. In Matthew 10:1, Mark 3:15; and Luke 9:1, Jesus himself gives "authority over unclean spirits" or "demons" to his disciples. This certainly is none other than the power and authority of the Holy Spirit over evil spirits. It is an anticipation of the postresurrection gift of the Spirit. In both cases the Spirit's power and authority are identified as coming from Christ himself.

15. Baillie 1948:145.

16. This baptism with the Spirit is not a special second experience, as in the Holiness-Pentecostal tradition of a "second blessing" or in the fundamentalistic sense of a second step which follows "receiving Jesus as Savior." In the Lucan and Pauline materials, it is the experience which stamps converts as bona fide members of the new body of Christ (Acts 2:38; Rom. 8:9b; 1 Cor. 12:13).

17. This is an amazing transition and not at all to be taken for granted. Perhaps the nearest parallel is the experience of the Buddha's followers. They were convinced he had found the way to enlightenment and continued devoted to him. But even so, there was no sense of continuing dynamic presence. In the modern case of Gandhi, the movement rapidly fell into decay because "Bapuji" was no longer present, and no one could take his place.

18. The word *allos* (another) suggests that Jesus himself fulfilled this role in the first place. Now it will be played by another one of the same identity. Compare 1 John 2:1, where the heavenly Christ is also called *paraklētos*—or mediator—for us in the Father's presence. If there is any distinction to be made, the *paraklētos* of John 14:16 is at work in and with us (cf. Rom. 8), while the *paraklētos* of 1 John 2:1 is *pros ton patron*, with the Father (Kittel 5:800ff.).

19. Moule 1978:39.

20. In the "Farewell Discourses" of John 14–17, Jesus speaks of the Spirit as "another Advocate" who will always be with them (14:16-17). In the next verse John represents Jesus as saying, "I am coming to you." In this same place Jesus speaks of the "Advocate" as the "Spirit of truth," who will lead them into all truth. The Spirit is thus identified with Jesus, who declared in verse 6, "I am the . . . truth." In this Gospel, the Spirit is sent by the Father at Jesus' request and in "Jesus' name." Yet it also says that Jesus himself sends the Spirit (14:26; 15:26; 16:17). In 14:27 the Spirit's presence with the disciples is the gift of Christ's peace. In 20:22 the Spirit is the breath of Christ's life in them, giving them his authority to forgive sins.

Reflecting such language, George Hendry wrote, "The Spirit is the true vicar of Christ, Christ's alter ego, and was known as such in the Church by the fact that he was encountered in the same role of Lord (*kurios*) as Christ himself had been" (1956:65).

21. See Gal. 4:6; Rom. 8:9; Phil. 1:19. Compare Acts 16:7; 1 Pet. 1:11. The latter passage even refers to the Spirit which inspired the Old Testament prophets as the "Spirit of Christ."

22. These are misunderstood when they are taken analytically. Note how he speaks of participation in the Spirit producing the mind of Christ (1 Cor. 2:15-16). He parallels *power of the Spirit* and *power of our Lord Jesus* (1 Cor. 5:4). Note also the parallelism in 1 Cor. 6:11, "the name of the Lord Jesus Christ and . . . the Spirit of our God."

23. Barth goes on to note, "What is involved is the participation of man in the word and work of Christ." This is an important aspect pointing to the difference between Christ and the Spirit. We will look at this under the heading, "The Spirit and the Church." Here our point is that the Spirit continues the mission of Jesus the Messiah rather than inaugurating one of his own.

24. Scott 1929:144.

25. "The Spirit is fundamentally the power which sets a man in God's saving work in

Christ, thus taking him out of his own control, making impossible any trust in his own *sarx* (flesh) and yet also opening him for a life in *agapē*" (Kittel 6:432).

26. Kittel 6:433, slightly altered.

27. Hendry 1965:41.

28. *Dogmatics* 1962, III, 2:12.

29. "The Holy Spirit in the New Testament sense is the presence of God which bears witness to, and makes effectual, the historical Christ as a living personal presence. The operation of the Holy Spirit is necessary for the Word about Christ to become the Word of Christ for us, and for the Word of Christ to become the Word of God" (Brunner 1962:12).

30. Today in ecumenical circles there is renewed emphasis on a "trinitarian" activity of God. This view, in effect, affirms God's presence and saving activity outside the bounds of the faith community—even outside the perimeters of biblical religion. The church's vocation is associated with the explicit witness to Jesus as a unique savior while recognizing a saving revelation of God in many religious and social justice movements which have no direct relation to him. This view holds that to limit the Spirit to the church would greatly curtail the activity of God in the world. Thus it asserts a trinitarian freedom of God's Spirit to work when, where, and how he will.

This emphasis on the freedom of the Spirit to be present throughout the world may be a necessary corrective to the tendency to equate *church* with the ecclesiastical organizations of Christendom. But it often insists on recognizing a trinitarian activity of God that manifests itself outside the church in un-Christlike revolutionary violence and morally ambiguous demands for justice in the name of the biblical God. It thus reintroduces the worst aspects of tritheism at the practical level. Such theology confesses the Spirit's freedom from ecclesiastical structures. But by implication it also introduces a serious ambiguity into the definition of the Spirit's character and role.

31. In the one passage which speaks most clearly about the Spirit's work in the world, the role is defined as "advocate" for the claims of the historical Jesus—the Jesus of the cross and resurrection. As the "prosecutor," he will make a convincing case against the wise and powerful of the world. He will prove that Jesus' way is right, that the real sin is unbelief, and that the standards of judgment which the world applies are themselves under judgment (John 16:8-11). In somewhat the same vein, Paul speaks in 1 Corinthians 1:18—2:16 of a "demonstration of the Spirit and of power" in contrast to the wisdom and power of this age. This is the Spirit which also defines the perimeters of the church.

32. Barth 1949:138.

33. Newbigin writes, "It [the church] is both the first-fruits and instrument of God's gracious election, for His purpose is precisely the re-creation of the human race in Christ. In the same way the life of the visible Church is the reality within which alone the doctrine of the Holy Spirit is to be understood" (1954:114). This placing of the church within the universal mission of Christ as the context of the Spirit's activity is clearly in line with the New Testament.

Moltmann makes this same point. "It is not the church that has a mission of salvation to fulfill to the world; it is the mission of the Son and the Spirit through the Father that includes the church, creating a church as it goes on its way. It is not the church that administers the Spirit as the Spirit. . . . The Spirit administers the church" (1977:64). He goes on to point out that this positioning of the church within "the history of the Spirit" does not limit the Spirit to the church, but it gives the church a perspective from which to recognize "the saving efficacies of the Spirit outside the church" as "signs that the Spirit is greater than the church and that God's purpose of salvation reaches beyond the church" (65).

34. In the letters, the word *ekklēsia* replaces the more Hebraic term *basileia tou theou*. Both terms stem from political usage and carry implications of a social movement.

35. The phrase occurs in Phil. 2:1 and 2 Cor. 13:13. It has been variously translated, but the basic grammatical question is whether to take it as an objective or a subjective genitive. Schweizer concludes that it is best understood as an objective genitive, but that

it should be interpreted as that fellowship in the church which is given by the shared Spirit (Kittel 6:434).

We might note here that the metaphor of God or Spirit living in "God's temple"—the church (1 Cor. 3:16)—is not really a contradiction of this social concept of the Spirit. The Spirit of the group was enshrined in the temple, which objectified the sacral identity of the group.

36. In the early church, this notion of infusion gave rise to mythological concepts of "holy" water and bread as the mysteries of the Spirit. And produced the thought of holy offices actually constituting the church.

37. A subjective image of spirit as corporate reality survives in the language of highly individualistic societies of the West in such phrases as *group spirit, the spirit of the meeting,* or *the spirit of the law.*

38. C. F. D. Moule comments, "The phrase in 2 Cor. 13:13 commonly rendered 'the fellowship of the Holy Spirit' probably does *not* mean the community created and vitalized by the Holy Spirit. *Koinōnia,* the word translated 'fellowship,' is constantly misconstrued in Christian devotional writing, as though it were a concrete noun, 'the fellowship.' It is not. It is an abstract noun meaning 'joint participation,' 'sharing.' Certainly, that joint participation in the Holy Spirit does lead to fellowship; but the fellowship is the result. The cause is the joint sharing in the Spirit" (1979:75-76).

Participation in the group manifestations of the Spirit's presence and power marked the origin of the church in the first instance. According to Luke, such participation continued to be the authenticating mark. At crucial points the manifestations which had characterized the Pentecost experience were repeated where the new stage of development needed apostolic authentication. See Acts 8:14-16; 10:44-48; 19:1-7.

39. The phrase "lie to the Holy Spirit" is literally "falsify the Holy Spirit" (*pseusasthai se to pneuma to hagion*). Ananias was not simply deceiving men and women through misrepresentation and pretense; he had tried to "lie . . . to God" (Acts 5:4).

40. The gift or "baptism" of the Spirit is not necessarily marked by a special emotional experience or "sign." One may, and indeed should, expect an appropriate emotional response to the new depth of reality God's Spirit brings into our lives. Certainly we feel thrill and elation with great music, or emotional animation with a loved one's presence. We should expect no less when the new experience of *koinōnia* in the Spirit of Christ becomes reality for us. "Joy in the Holy Spirit" (Rom. 14:17) is a characteristic sign of the new life in the Spirit (Acts 2:46b-47). Joy and hope are the special work of the Spirit in the life of the individual and the church (Gal. 5:22; 1 Thess. 1:6; Rom. 15:13).

41. *Institutes* 4.3.5ff.

42. According to the Westminster Confession, the "inward illumination" of the Scripture is necessary for a "saving understanding" of it. There are no "new revelations of the Spirit" (art. 1). The Spirit makes the "ministry, oracles and ordinances of God" in the church effective (art. 25). Thus the continuing work of the Spirit in the church in no way goes beyond the final word of Scripture. "The Holy Spirit speaking in the Scriptures" is the "Supreme Judge" in all religious controversy (art. 1).

43. The New Testament is already a *contextualized presentation* of the gospel in a Hellenistic setting. It presents both a record of the historical Jesus Christ and the implications of his life, death, and resurrection as they were spelled out in the life and witness of the church. *In the generic sense, it is prophecy vouchsafed to us by the Spirit and authenticated in the life of the early church.*

44. This is the major concern of Millard Lind's article, "Refocusing Theological Education to Mission: The Old Testament and Contextualization," which was originally published in *Missiology: An International Review* 10 (1982) and reprinted in his collected essays (1990:38-53).

Chapter 6: The Church: The Messianic Community

1. The first group that formed after the day of Pentecost was called "the apostles' . . . *koinōnia,*" or fellowship (Acts 2:42). Those who did not join the movement called them

"the way," or sect (9:2; 19:9). A few years later in Antioch, the disciples were called *christianoi* (Christians) or partisans of the Christ (Messiah). The earliest attested usage of *ekklēsia* for the followers of Jesus is found in the first Pauline letters. Here it is used to mean both the whole messianic movement and its separate congregations. Apparently both *synagogue* (James 2:2, Greek text) and *ekklēsia* were used in the early years to designate Christian (or Christian-Jewish) congregations, but later the synagogue became exclusively Jewish and the *ekklēsia* Christian.

The English word *church* and the German *Kirche* come from the Greek word *kuriakos*, meaning "belonging to the Lord." They tend to identify the church with the "Lord's house" or the meeting place on the "Lord's day" (Rev. 1:10). For a definitive survey of this data, see K. L. Schmidt's article on *ekklēsia* in Kittel 3:501-536.

2. Contemporary theologians use the term *eschatological* in a variety of ways. Evangelicals in the revivalist tradition mean the continuing expectation of an imminent return of Christ and end of the world. They attempt to keep that expectation alive through preaching and teaching on the subject of eschatology. Liberals in the Ritschlian tradition define *eschatology* as the philosophy of history. They believe there is progress and meaning in history. The "eschatological" ideal is a historical goal toward which the church should work with optimism. Theologians like Bultmann have spoken of the eschatological moment as one of existential confrontation with the crucified Christ. Eschatological living demands that we decide for Christ as God's judgment and salvation of history. More recently, Moltmann has defined the eschatological stance as living by hope in the God who raised Jesus from the dead (Rom. 8:24).

3. Bultmann has characterized the church as "the eschatological Congregation" and says that its very existence belongs to "the eschatological salvation-occurrence." But one is disappointed when a few paragraphs later he says, "The eschatological Congregation takes its purest form from time to time in the *cultic gathering* in which Christ is confessed as Lord" (1951:308, emphasis mine).

4. I am using this concept of a new era in much the same way we speak of the introduction of electricity or the explosion of the atom bomb as the beginning of a new era. Although the new era potentially changed the whole world scene, many people have continued to live in the old era without the benefits of electricity.

5. The language of Ephesians 2:20 suggests either that the apostles themselves are the foundation (NRSV) or that they laid the foundation (NEB). In 1 Corinthians 3:10ff., Paul speaks of laying the foundation. If the foundation is "Jesus Christ," Paul has laid that foundation. In any case, the apostles are credited with the actual formation of the organized church based, of course, on Jesus Christ and empowered by the Spirit of Christ.

6. Schmidt makes this same point, approaching the concept from the opposite direction: the church was not created by the "enthusiasm of pneumatics and charismatics." He writes, "The new thing about the *ekklēsia tou theou* . . . is given with the fact that a specific number of selected disciples of Jesus experienced the resurrection of Jesus Christ from the dead and received special authorization thereby" (Kittel 3:507-508).

7. As Bultmann rightly notes, the "in Christ" formula in the writings of Paul, "far from being a formula for mystic union, is primarily an *ecclesiological* formula. It means the state of having been articulated into the 'body of Christ' by baptism" (1951:311).

8. See chapter 5.

9. Menno Simons lists the marks of the true church in his "Reply to Gellius Faber." To Luther's mark of (1) "unadulterated, pure doctrine" and Melanchthon's (2) "Scriptural use of the sacramental signs," he adds (3) "obedience to the Word," (4) "unfeigned brotherly love," (5) a confident confession in the face of persecution, and (6) bearing the "pressing cross of Christ" for the sake of his testimony and Word (Wenger 1956:739-743).

10. The term *kingdom of God* or *kingdom of Christ* appears several times in Acts (1:3; 8:12; 14:22; 19:8; 28:23, 31). After that it appears in the early letters of Paul (1 Thess. 2:12; 2 Thess. 1:5; Gal. 5:21; 1 Cor. 4:20; 6:10; 15:24, 50), once in Romans 14:17; Ephesians 5:5; and Colossians 4:11. James 2:5 refers to the kingdom which the poor

inherit—a rather obvious reference to Jesus' teaching and ministry. Floyd Filson concludes, "These facts show that the church had no intention of abandoning Jesus' message or distorting its basic meaning" (1956:107).

11. By and large, Matthew's Gospel prefers *kingdom of heaven*, while Mark and Luke use *kingdom of God* in parallel references. No doubt *kingdom of heaven* is a pious circumlocution to avoid needless use of God's name (cf. Dan. 4:17; Ps. 11:4; Exod. 20:7). The distinctions insisted upon in dispensationalist theology seem forced and are unnecessary to explain the different usage.

12. See Gerhard von Rad's *Old Testament Theology* (volume 2) for an excellent discussion of these themes. The chapter on Deutero-Isaiah is of particular significance. See also G. Ernest Wright, *God Who Acts* (London: SCM, 1952).

13. Jordan, who was deeply immersed in the civil rights movement as a committed, scholarly Christian, used the term "God Movement" in his paraphrase of the New Testament called *The Cotton Patch Version*.

14. Kraus 1974:27.

15. Kraus 1979:121.

16. Emil Brunner, who says the concept of a visible church distinguishable from the invisible church "is wholly foreign to the New Testament," gives a good explanation of how the distinction developed from Augustine onward. He himself holds that "there is . . . only the one ekklesia, which is at the same time spiritual and invisible (intelligible to faith alone) and corporeal (recognizable and visible to all)." The true church, he says, is a visible sociological community that exists as a "fellowship," rather than an "association," as defined by sociologists (*Dogmatics* 1962, 3:27-33).

17. Donald Durnbaugh has popularized the term *believers church* as a further refinement of the concept of *free church*. He explains that he uses the apostrophe after the plural form "purposely to emphasize the communal and collective quality of belief, in opposition to the individual alone." While I agree fully with his intention, unfortunately the apostrophe usually indicates ownership. I have therefore omitted it. The term *believers church* covers more than Anabaptists. However, Durnbaugh's own definition, which I accept, is drawn directly from the Anabaptist ideal (1968:7, 32-33).

18. Otto Weber admits that the concept of an "invisible church" is difficult, but he adds, "Nevertheless, the old term is still important as a signal. It implies that the Community is never established out of itself, never out of its form, nor out of its number, nor out of the 'world.' It is 'visible' not only in terms of its appearance but also of its essence. There is no ideal image of the Community hovering over it somewhere. But it is neither exhausted nor submerged into its tangibility, which includes then its tangible questionableness, disorder, and impoverishment of form" (1983, 2:545-546).

19. See Marlin Jeschke, *Discipling in the Church: Recovering a Ministry of the Gospel* (Herald Press, 1988).

20. This is reflected most clearly in the organization of the Roman Catholic Church, which is self-conscious about the organic unity and organizational structure of its local and universal expressions. It suggests an organic rather than an organizational relation of the local congregations to the whole.

21. Attempts to establish an "episcopal," "presbyterial," or "congregational" order on the basis of New Testament precedent are a thing of the past. Contemporary New Testament studies have shown that already at the beginning of the church, different patterns of local organization existed and that organization changed as the historical situation changed. The organization reflected in the Pastoral Epistles, for example, is not the same as that of the early chapters of Acts or the Corinthian letters.

22. The concept of the church as a sacramental body had been defined differently in the history of the church. According to the traditional Roman Catholic concept, the clerical office is sacramental and constitutes the essential church. The clergy are empowered to consecrate the sacraments in the ongoing life of the church. The Protestant tradition identifies the concept largely with the idea of the "communion of saints," the spiritual presence of Christ in the world. In the Anabaptist-Mennonite tradition, the congregation

as the *koinōnia* of Christ is the visible sign of his rule in the world. Thus in its total life together as the "body of Christ," it is sacramental. And the "sacraments" of baptism and the Lord's Supper are referred to as ordinances or ceremonies in the sacramental life of the church.

23. Kraus 1974:63-96.

24. Berkhof 1986:373ff.

25. Consensus does not mean full unanimity on all details of a proposal. It indicates group solidarity, general agreement, and willingness by all to move ahead, even if some uncertainty remains. It also implies sensitivity to the opposition and willingness to take them seriously, even if they are in the minority.

26. The immediate interpretation of 1 Timothy 2:11-14 is simple, but how it fits into the larger New Testament picture is not clear. If it is from the hand of Paul himself, he must have rather drastically changed his mind over the years. It simply does not fit with his earlier posture toward women speaking in the public assembly (1 Cor. 11:5) and with his close association with women as fellow missioners (Phil. 4:3). The letter assumes an official structure in the church organization—bishops, elders, deacons—which we know to be a development beyond the period of the 60s and 70s, when Paul was most active. Chapter 3:11 seems to assume that the diaconal ministries are appropriate for women, but they are not to be teaching or preaching elders (5:17) or bishops (3:1ff.).

When we ask how this applies to the church universal, we must consider two questions. First, are the episcopal structure and "offices" reflected here to be universally applied in the church? We have generally replied in the negative. We have followed the earlier precedent of leadership on the basis of gifts and calling. Second, in light of the obvious variation in New Testament teaching and usage on the subject, we must ask whether the flat denial of teaching and leadership positions to women in this case is not contextually conditioned.

The injunction is obviously the most severe of any in the New Testament against the use of women in leadership positions. This and the general tenor of the whole letter suggest that the writer is dealing rigorously with a contemporary error concerning male-female relations in society (perhaps Christian gnosticism). Apparently, uneducated women in the church were accepting and promoting false doctrine. If so, the text should be seen in its environmental context as a local corrective, not as a universal dictate for the church.

27. The obvious conflict between this text and chapter 11 has led to a number of suggestions for resolving the ambiguity. Some think the words forbid any public teaching, as in 1 Timothy 2:8ff. They suggest it was inserted into Paul's text at a later period. There is some slight textual evidence for this. Others take the position that the injunction is not against orderly prophesying, but against disorderly interruption during the meeting. Disorder seems to have been a problem at Corinth. Another possibility is that Paul is quoting statements with which he does not agree, as in 1 Corinthians 6:13a and 7:1b.

Chapter 7: Eschatology: The Victory of Christ

1. Greek philosophers also used the word *kairos*, but they associated it with fate as in "the fateful moment."

2. The Hebrew concept of time and eternity was not analytical or philosophical. Time is the sequence of activity that stretches back into the unknown and unimaginable past (eternity past) and will presumably continue for ages to come (eternity future). Paul can speak of the *chronois aiōniois*, eternal times (Rom. 16:25; cf. 2 Tim. 1:9). See "Chronos" in Kittel 9:592-93 and in Cullmann, *Christ and Time* (Westminster, 1950, chaps. 1-6). Between the "eternal" past and future is the observable, remembered past, the present, and the hoped-for future generations (history). Creation is the beginning of this historical or remembered time. The final "day of the Lord" is the end of the future time. This history is divided into eras marked by significant events in remembered history (*kairoi*), such as the call of Abraham, the deliverance from Egypt, and the reign of David. Viewed in this way, time is simply a segment of eternity.

God is in eternity (the heavens) in the sense that he comprehends the whole. He knows the end from the beginning. He is not limited by or dependent upon time. He does not "need time" to do something like we do. He merely says the word and it is done. This does not imply that God cannot act in our dimension of time. He is Lord of time.

3. "Prophet, Prophetism," Buttrick 3:896ff.

4. Since the early 1970s, biblical scholars have given renewed attention to the apocalyptic literature of the first and second centuries B.C.E./C.E. See, for example, James Barr, "Jewish Apocalyptic in Recent Scholarly Studies," Rylands University Library of Manchester, Autumn 1975; John J. Collins, *The Apocalyptic Imagination: An Introduction to the Jewish Matrix of Christianity*, New York: Crossroads, 1984.

Klaus Koch in *The Rediscovery of Apocalyptic* (SBT, 2/22; Naperville, Ill.: Alec R. Allenson, 1975), lists the following eight characteristics of biblical apocalyptic: (1) urgent expectation of the end of earthly conditions in an immediate future; (2) the end as cosmic catastrophe; (3) periodization and determinism; (4) activity of angels and demons; (5) a new salvation which is paradisal in character; (6) manifestation of the kingdom of God; (7) a mediator with royal features; and (8) *glory* as a catchword.

5. John W. Miller 1987:288. Gerhard von Rad (*Old Testament Theology*, 2:99-125, 301-315) and Martin Hengel (*Judaism and Hellenism*, 1:175ff.) offer varying accounts of the origins of apocalyptic and its relation to classical prophetism. *Paul Hanson, The Dawn of Apocalyptic* (Fortress, 1979) deals with the historical and sociological roots of Jewish apocalyptic eschatology. Compare his distinction between the prophetic and apocalyptic (pp. 11-12) with the chart in the text below.

6. Tillich 1963:395.

7. Brunner 1962, 3:440.

8. Von Rad 1965:100ff.

9. Few evangelical scholars have dealt directly with the concept of history. The chapter by Earle E. Cairns' in *Contemporary Evangelical Thought* (C. F. H. Henry, editor, 1957:181-211) is an exception. He defines written history as "the interpreted reconstruction of man's socially significant past activities which is based on organized data gathered by scientific techniques." He then argues that historical interpretation should therefore include philosophical or theological consideration as well as scientific analysis. With this I fully agree. However, his implication that God's activity in history is certifiable by scientific methodology is debatable. Apparently this leads him to assume that the Bible is an objective (scientific?) historical record, and its eschatological predictions should be read literally.

In a more recent volume, Stephen Travis offers a different approach which takes the multidimensional character of historical events more seriously. See *I Believe in the Second Coming of Jesus* (Eerdmans, 1982). See also my discussion of the nature of history in *Jesus Christ Our Lord*, 52-53.

10. Brunner 1962, 3:377.

11. In more technical terms, we should interpret the *historical* predictions—apocalyptic and otherwise—as "objective-subjective" data (Kraus 1990:52ff.).

12. Thomas Finger wrestles with this same problem and suggests a slightly different approach. He affirms that the "bodily" return of Christ will be a "spatio-temporal event." He then attempts to bring such an event into line with a "modern scientific view of things." He argues that while science cannot anticipate such an event and the world transformation which it implies, nevertheless it can provide a model for our imaging it. (See Finger 1:164-167.)

13. The idea that Jesus will return in a quite different character at his second appearance is common. For example, in a sermon entitled "Perfect Justice," preached in 1970 on "The Hour of Decision," Billy Graham said, "The gentle Jesus of Nazareth will become the mighty Lord and Judge who with flaming fire will take vengeance on those who have rejected him (2 Thessalonians 1:8)." The language of the Thessalonians passage, which is extremely graphic, is taken as the vengeance of human justice, not as the inexorable passion of God's love.

14. C. H. Dodd emphasized the present reality of this eschatological vision. He interpreted the resurrection of Christ and the coming of the Spirit as the realization of the promised new age—"realized eschatology." See his *Parables of the Kingdom* (Nisbet, 1935).

15. Kuhn, *Basileus*, Kittel 1:573. He notes further, "Expectation of the Messiah King . . . develops out of the originally secular expectation of an Israelite king who will revive the monarchy in all its greatness and restore the splendor of the idealized Davidic kingdom. This hope became a hope for the end of the age. It is not, therefore, eschatological in the strict sense. The coming of the Messiah precedes the eschaton in Jewish thinking" (p. 574).

16. Some theologians distinguish between the two kingdoms. They hold that the kingdom of God is his eternal sovereignty and the kingdom of Christ is his spiritual reign in the church or his messianic reign which will be concluded with the close of history. While individual texts such as 1 Corinthians 15:25 may be read this way, the theological and ethical implications of such a bifurcation throw doubt upon normativeness of God's self-disclosure in Christ. It inevitably implies a subordinationist Christology and suggests a difference in character between the two kingdoms.

17. Kraus 1990:152.

18. A number of metaphors for the judgment have been taken from the sheepfold (Matt. 25:32-33), the farmer winnowing his grain from the chaff (Matt. 3:12; 13:40-42), the fisherman sorting his catch (Matt. 13:47-50), the judge giving a sentence (1 Pet. 4:5), and the victorious king judging and punishing his enemies (Rev. 6:10, 15-16). But such metaphors do not provide a criterion of judgment. Criteria mentioned are works of conscience which recognize the intrinsic law of God (Rom. 2:14-16), care of the poor and helpless (Matt. 25:31ff.), recognition of Jesus as the true revelation of and way to God (John 14:6), and faithfulness and self-denial in the service of Christ (Mark 8:34-35). On the other side of the coin, there are sharp warnings against an insincere profession of loyalty to Christ and his way (Matt. 7:26-27).

The vocabulary of the letters changes somewhat, but the basic criteria of judgment remains the same. For Paul the broad criterion is being "in Christ" and manifesting the "fruit of the Spirit [of Christ]." "Holiness," a life of moral integrity after the example of Christ, is held to be essential. This may also be referred to as "putting on Christ" or "walking in the Spirit." All of these reflect a genuine orientation of life (repentance) toward Christ, the crucified and risen Savior. This is made possible by his Spirit at work in the believer. The shorthand word for all of this is *faith*.

19. Kittel 3:926.

20. This was Paul's implicit conclusion as he struggled with the problem in Romans 9—11. Some Jews based their salvation and righteousness exclusively on the Mosaic covenant. They felt that Paul's message of salvation by faith in Jesus as the Messiah outside the Mosaic covenant made God arbitrary and untrustworthy. Paul's reply is based on the assumptions of his critics. He does not give an analytical ethical defense. His argument is basically as follows: (1) Humans, both Jews and pagans, are truly blameworthy and have created a situation in which even God's *agapē*ic justice appears ambiguous. (2) God's mercy and justice are not arbitrary. He does not accept Jews and reject Gentiles on the basis of their religious classification. All will be judged by their "deeds" (Rom. 2:6). (3) God's final solution is salvation and righteousness "by faith," because it is not possible by human achievement. (4) Beyond this, God's ways are inscrutable (11:33).

21. Even if one makes a case for the moral legitimacy of revenge as a response to the violation of God's right as Deity, the basic nature of the vengeance as a conditioned negative response remains. Therefore, we must understand those passages like 2 Thessalonians 1:7-9 as strictly anthropomorphic imagery.

22. *To pur to aiōnion* (the eternal fire) in Matthew is quite obviously a metaphorical reference to the *tēn geennan tou puros* (the hell [Gehenna] of fire), the garbage dump of Jerusalem in the valley of Hinnom, which smoldered endlessly. Compare the phrases in Matthew 18:8-9. Whether this is the origin of all the apocalyptic references is not cer-

tain. Fire also has the symbolic meaning of purification through the destruction of contaminating elements (Mal. 3:2-3).

23. *Apollumi*, the verb used in John 3:16 and 2 Peter 3:9, in the middle voice means ruin, loss, perishing. It suggests a self-inflicted process, or at least a process for which one is responsible. The word thus carries the concept of intrinsic consequences.

24. This is the view of John R. W. Stott, of C. S. Lewis in his *The Great Divorce*, and of F. F. Bruce in his foreword to Edward Fudge's *The Fire That Consumes* (1982:vii).

25. While death for Christians does not mean immediate consummation or resurrection, it does mean that the person lives with the Lord (1 Thess. 5:10; cf. 2 Cor. 5:8-9; Phil. 1:23; Rev. 7).

26. While death remains the enemy "as a part of the world's paradigm which is passing away, it loses its power to impel or to negate one's energies. It has lost its ultimacy" (Lloyd Bailey, 1979:91).

27. Rahner 1978:271.

28. The Hindu, or naturalist, model of death's effect is based upon a quite different ontological assessment of personhood and its moral significance. In the Christian view, the essential self develops an identity throughout a lifetime of personal relationships. It has ontological significance. One may describe it phenomenologically as a developing "body" of attitudes, feelings, responses, and beliefs which defines itself in personal relationships. It is what Paul refers to as the old and new way of life (Eph. 4:22-23). For behaviorists, whether of the naturalist or Zen Buddhist variety, these are simply activities that cease with death.

29. Paul speaks of the state of the self after death as being "away from the body," and "naked," without a body (2 Cor. 5:8, 3). In such a state it is waiting to be "clothed" in the resurrection. Rev. 6:10 speaks of the souls of the martyrs under the altar waiting for vindication. But Jesus told the thief on the cross that he would be in "Paradise" that very day (Luke 23:43). In the parable of the rich man and Lazarus, both are said to be reaping the rewards of their respective lives (Luke 16:22-23). The language of death as sleep (Acts 7:60; 1 Cor. 15:18, 20; 1 Thess. 4:15) suggested to the ancients that death is not the extinction of life, but the cessation of bodily activity and availability. Life beyond death would be analogous to life in dreaming. Thomas Finger, following the lead of Oscar Cullmann, concludes "that the dead in Christ are in some passive state. Perhaps not wholly unconscious. It may well approximate pleasant dreaming" (1985:141). See also *Cullmann, Christ and Time* (Westminster) 1950:231ff.

30. "Limbo is, according to Roman Catholic theology, that place where the souls of unbaptized infants go. Not having received sanctifying grace, and so dying in original sin, these infants do not suffer the pains of hell. But on the other hand, they are excluded from the perfect joy of the beatific vision" (Harvey, 1964:146). In Jewish writings of the second century B.C.E. and later, there are references to a segregated Sheol (Buttrick 3:655).

31. The New Testament does not speak explicitly to whether physical death fixes one's final destiny. The metaphoric and parabolic materials from the Gospels are largely from rabbinic origin, and the rabbis did not all hold the same views. Some thought of punishment after death (*hadēs*) as purgative. (For a source of ideas on purgatory, see 2 Macc. 12:45; cf. Matt. 12:32.) Most thought the punishment was limited in duration—at least for Jews (2 Esdras 7:76ff.). These ideas were based upon a legalistic definition of sin and its consequences. Thus, while the New Testament writers continue to use such apocalyptic figures as a heuristic strategy, we must ask what changes in their meaning are implied by the radical rejection of rabbinic legalism. According to Paul's gospel of grace, God does not assign penalties according to our concepts of legal guilt. If this is so, how shall we conceptualize the consequences of sin at the moment of death?

The New Testament does not hold out explicit hope for a reversal of judgment after physical death. But what is the implication of 1 Corinthians 15:29; Ephesians 4:8-10; 1 Peter 3:18-20; Revelation 22:2?

32. The *eschaton* is spoken of in a variety of ways throughout the New Testament. It is

destruction and new creation, renewal and recreation, and reunification in Christ. It is the "manifestation and presence" of Christ, the return of Christ to set up his kingdom. These should not be understood as a series of events in temporal sequence, but as a series of complementary metaphors or symbols describing what from a temporal-physical perspective is indescribable. Different writers of the New Testament prefer different symbols. *Resurrection* is a favorite of Paul.

33. The New Testament concept of the relation of resurrection and judgment is difficult to discern. Paul views resurrection as God's final victory in and for the saints. That which was introduced in Christ's resurrection and continued by the Spirit in raising us to newness of life, will be consummated by God in the final resurrection. He is not explicit about the relation of resurrection and judgment. Two passages speak of a resurrection of all human beings—both "those who have done good . . . and those who have done evil" (John 5:29; Acts 24:15). One passage speaks of the resurrection of the just (Luke 14:14). Revelation 20:4-5 presents an apocalyptic scenario with two resurrections—one before the millennial reign and another after it. Following the second resurrection there is judgment.

It is difficult to draw hermeneutical conclusions from this data. Does Paul's failure to mention the resurrection of the wicked imply they have simply perished? Or does it imply they have been judged and doomed to remain without bodies? See 2 Thessalonians 1:9-10. Do John's terms, "resurrection of life" and "resurrection of condemnation," speak of two resurrections? Or do we have a single resurrection issuing in both eternal life and eternal death?

In John, judgment belongs to the Son of Man. He will ultimately judge all humankind—both those who have already died as well as the generations from the time of Jesus to the end of the world. This corresponds to Paul's conviction that judgment has been handed over to Christ. As I have already suggested, one should not use the apocalyptic images to chart a temporal sequence of events in the consummation.

Bibliography

Anderson, Bernhard W., ed.
  1984 *Creation in the Old Testament.*
    Philadelphia: Fortress Press.

Augsburger, David W.
  1986 *Pastoral Counseling Across
    Cultures.* Philadelphia: West-
    minster Press.

Aulén, Gustaf
  1960 *The Faith of the Christian
    Church.* Philadelphia: Fortress
    Press.

Babbage, Barton
  1957 *Man in Nature and Grace.* Grand
    Rapids: Eerdmans.

Badham, P.
  1976 *Christian Beliefs About Life After
    Death.* Library of Philosophy of
    Religion. New York: Barnes and
    Noble.

Badham, Paul and Linda Badham, eds.
  1987 *Death and Immortality in the Re-
    ligions of the World.* New York:
    Paragon House.

Bailey, Lloyd R.
  1979 *Biblical Perspectives on Death.*
    Philadelphia: Fortress Press.

Baillie, D. D.
  1948 *God Was in Christ.* New York:
    Scribner's Sons.

Barth, Karl
  1936 *Church Dogmatics*, vol. I, 1. Ed-
    inburgh: T. & T. Clark.

  1938 *The Knowledge of God and the
    Service of God According to the
    Teaching of the Reformation.*
    London: Hodder and Stoughton.

  1956 *Church Dogmatics*, vol. I, 2. Ed-
    inburgh: T. & T. Clark

  1957 *Christ and Adam: Man and Hu-
    manity in Romans 5.* New York:
    Macmillan.

  1960 *Church Dogmatics*, vol. III, 2.
    Edinburgh: T. & T. Clark.

  1960 *The Humanity of God.* Rich-
    mond, Va.: John Knox.

Berkhof, Hendrikus
  1986 *Christian Faith: An Introduction
    to the Study of the Faith*, rev. ed.
    Grand Rapids: Eerdmans.

Berkouwer, G. C.
  1962 *Man: The Image of God.* Grand
    Rapids: Eerdmans.

Bloesch, Donald G.
  1978 *Essentials of Evangelical Theolo-
    gy*, vol. 1. New York: Harper.

Bright, John
  1967 *The Authority of the Old Testa-
    ment.* Nashville: Abingdon Press.

Bromiley, Geoffrey W.
  1979 *Introduction to the Theology of
    Karl Barth.* Grand Rapids:
    Eerdmans.

Brown, William Adams
  1906 *Christian Theology in Outline.*
    New York: Scribner's Sons.

Brunk III, George Rowland
  1987 *The Christian's Future.* Scottdale,
    Pa.: Herald Press.

Brunner, H. Emil
  1943 *The Divine-Human Encounter.*
    Philadelphia: Westminster Press.

  1947 *Man in Revolt.* Philadelphia:
    Westminster Press

  1950 *The Christian Doctrine of God
    (Dogmatics*: vol. 1). Philadel-
    phia: Westminster Press.

1951 *The Scandal of Christianity.* Richmond: John Knox.

1952 *The Christian Doctrine of Creation and Redemption* (*Dogmatics*: vol. 2). Philadelphia: Westminster Press.

1962 *The Christian Doctrine of the Church, Faith, and the Consummation* (*Dogmatics*: vol. 3). Philadelphia: Westminster Press.

Buttrick, George Arthur, ed.
1962 *The Interpreter's Dictionary of the Bible.* Four volumes plus supplement (1976). Nashville: Abingdon Press.

Calvin, John
1960 *Institutes of the Christian Religion.* Library of Christian Classics, 20-21. Philadelphia: Westminster Press.

Carson, D. A. and John D. Woodbridge, eds.
1986 *Hermeneutics, Authority and Canon.* Grand Rapids: Zondervan (Academic Books).

Cauthen, Kenneth
1965 "Christology as the Clarification of Creation," *Journal of Bible and Religion* 33, no. 1 (AAR).

Chan, Wing-Tsit, et al.
1969 *The Great Asian Religions: An Anthology.* Toronto, Ont.: Collier Macmillan Co.

Charlesworth, James H.
1983, 1985 *The Old Testament Pseudepigrapha,* volumes 1 & 2. Garden City: Doubleday.

1988 *Jesus Within Judaism: New Light from Exciting Archaeological Discoveries.* New York: Doubleday.

Clarke, William Newton
1912 *An Outline of Christian Theology.* New York: Scribner's Sons.

Conzelmann, Hans
1969 *An Outline of the Theology of the New Testament.* New York: Harper & Row.

Cortes, Juan B., and Florence M. Gatti
1987 "On the Meaning of Luke 16:16," *Journal of Biblical Literature* 106 (no. 2): 247-259.

Coward, Harold
1985 *Pluralism: Challenge to World Religions.* Maryknoll, N.Y.: Orbis Books.

1988 *Sacred Word and Sacred Text.* Maryknoll, N.Y.: Orbis Books.

Craig, Samuel G., ed.
1948 *The Inspiration and Authority of the Bible by Benjamin Breckenridge Warfield.* Philadelphia: Presbyterian and Reformed Publishing Co.

1952 *Biblical and Theological Studies by Benjamin Breckenridge Warfield.* Philadelphia: Presbyterian and Reformed Publishing Co.

Cullmann, Oscar
1950 *Christ and Time: The Primitive Christian Conception of Time and History.* Philadelphia: Westminster Press.

Dickson, Kwesi A.
1984 *Theology in Africa.* Maryknoll, N.Y.: Orbis Books.

Driver, John
1986 *Understanding the Atonement for the Mission of the Church.* Scottdale, Pa.: Herald Press.

Du Noüy, Lecomte
  1946 *Human Destiny*. New York &
    London: Longmans Green.

Dunn, James D. G.
  1980 *Christology in the Making*. Phila-
    delphia: Westminster Press.

Durnbaugh, Donald F.
  1968 *The Believers' Church: The Histo-
    ry and Character of Radical Prot-
    estantism*. Scottdale, Pa.: Herald
    Press.

Filson, Floyd V.
  1956 *Jesus Christ, the Risen Lord*. New
    York: Abingdon Press.

Finger, Thomas N.
  1985 *Christian Theology: An Eschato-
    logical Approach*, vol. 1; 1989,
    vol. 2. Scottdale, Pa.: Herald
    Press.

Friedmann, Robert
  1973 *The Theology of Anabaptism*.
    Scottdale, Pa: Herald Press.

Fudge, Edward William
  1982 *The Fire That Consumes: A
    Biblical and Historical Study of
    Final Punishment*. Houston, Tex.:
    Providential Press.

Hanson, Earl
  1981 *Understanding Evolution*. New
    York: Oxford University Press.

Hanson, Paul
  1979 *The Dawn of Apocalyptic: The
    History and Sociological Roots of
    Jewish Apocalyptic Eschatology*.
    Philadelphia: Fortress Press.

Harvey, Van A.
  1964 *A Handbook of Theological
    Terms*. New York: Macmillan.

Hendry, George S.
  1956 *The Holy Spirit in Christian
    Theology*. Philadelphia:
    Westminster Press. (Revised,
    1965, London: S.C.M. Press.)

Henry, Carl F. H.
  1976-1979 *God, Revelation and
    Authority*, 4 volumes. Waco,
    Tex.: Word Books.

Henry, Carl F. H., ed.
  1957 *Contemporary Evangelical
    Thought*. Great Neck, N.Y.:
    Channel Press.

  1962 *Basic Christian Doctrines*. New
    York: Holt, Rinehart, and
    Winston.

Hick, John H.
  1976 *Death and Eternal Life*. San
    Francisco: Harper & Row.

Hodge, Charles
  1895 *Systematic Theology*, 3 volumes.
    New York: Scribner's Sons.

Hutchison, John A.
  1956 *Faith, Reason, and Existence: An
    Introduction to Contemporary
    Philosophy of Religion*. New
    York: Oxford University Press.

Jeschke, Marlin
  1988 *Disciplining in the Church:
    Recovering a Ministry of the
    Gospel*. Scottdale, Pa.: Herald
    Press.

Jewett, Paul K.
  1975 *Man as Male and Female*. Grand
    Rapids: Eerdmans.

Keeney, William Echard
  1968 *The Development of Dutch
    Anabaptist Thought and Practice
    from 1539-1564*. Nieuwkoop: B.
    De Graaf.

Kittel, Gerhard, ed.
  1964-1967 *Theological Dictionary of
    the New Testament*. Ten
    volumes. Grand Rapids:
    Eerdmans.

Klaassen, Walter, ed.
  1981 *Anabaptism in Outline: Selected
    Anabaptist Sources*. Scottdale,
    Pa.: Herald Press.

Klassen, William, and Klaassen, Walter, eds.
1978 *The Writings of Pilgram Marpeck*. Scottdale, Pa.: Herald Press.

Knitter, Paul
1985 *No Other Name?* Maryknoll: Orbis Books.

Koontz, Gayle Gerber & Willard Swartley, (eds.)
1987 *Perspectives on Feminist Hermeneutics* (Occasional Papers, no. 10), Elkhart, Ind.: Institute of Mennonite Studies.

Kraus, C. Norman
1967 "American Mennonites and the Bible," *Mennonite Quarterly Review*, October 1967.

1974 *The Community of the Spirit*. Grand Rapids: Eerdmans.

1979 *The Authentic Witness*. Grand Rapids: Eerdmans; and Scottdale, Pa.: Herald Press.

1990 *Jesus Christ Our Lord: Christology from a Disciple's Perspective* (rev. ed.). Scottdale, Pa.: Herald Press.

Lampe, G. W. H.
1977 *God as Spirit*. London: Clarendon Press.

Lind, Millard C.
1990 *Monotheism, Power, Justice: Collected Old Testament Essays*. Elkhart, Ind.: Institute of Mennonite Studies.

Manschreck, Clyde, trans. and ed.
1965 *Melanchthon on Christian Doctrine: Loci Communes* (1555). New York: Oxford University Press.

McFague, Sallie
1987 *Models of God: Theology for an Ecological, Nuclear Age*. Philadelphia: Fortress Press.

McGinn, Bernard, and John Meyendorff, eds.
1987 *Christian Spirituality: Origins to the Twelfth Century*. New York: Crossroads Publishers.

Miethe, Terry L. (ed.)
1987 *Did Jesus Rise from the Dead? The Resurrection Debate*. San Francisco: Harper & Row.

Miller, John W.
1987 *Meet the Prophets*. Mahway, N.J.: Paulist Press.

1989 *Biblical Faith and Fathering: Why We Call God "Father."* Mahway, N.J.: Paulist Press.

Moltmann, Jürgen
1977 *The Church in the Power of the Spirit*. New York: Harper & Row.

1981 *The Trinity and the Kingdom: The Doctrine of God*. San Francisco: Harper & Row.

Morris, Desmond
1967 *The Naked Ape: A Zoologist's Study of the Human Animal*. New York: McGraw-Hill.

Morris, Leon
1972 *Apocalyptic*. Grand Rapids: Eerdmans.

Moule, C. F. D.
1979 *The Holy Spirit*. Grand Rapids: Eerdmans.

Newbigin, Lesslie
1954 *The Household of God*. New York: Friendship Press.

Noss, John B.
1974 *Man's Religions*, 5th ed. New York: Macmillan.

Nygren, Anders
1953 *Agape and Eros*. Philadelphia: Westminster.

Ogden, Schubert M.
1982 *The Point of Christology*. New York: Harper & Row.

Packull, Werner O.
1977 *Mysticism and the Early South German-Austrian Anabaptist Movement 1525-1531*. Scottdale, Pa.: Herald Press.

Pannenberg, Wolfhart
1977 *Jesus—God and Man*, 2nd. ed., tr. by Lewis Wilkins and Duane Priebe. Philadelphia: Westminster Press.

Pelikan, Jaroslav
1962 *The Light of the World: A Basic Image in Early Christian Thought*. New York: Harper & Row

Pinnock, Clark H.
1984 *The Scripture Principle*. New York: Harper & Row.

Pittenger, Norman
1980 *After Death—Life in God*. New York: Seabury.

Preus, Robert D.
1970 *The Theology of Post-Reformation Lutheranism: A Study of Theological Prolegomena*. Saint Louis: Concordia.

Rahner, Karl
1963 *Theological Investigations*, vol. 2. London: Darton, Longman and Todd, New York: Seabury Press.

1978 *Foundations of Christian Faith*. New York: Seabury Press.

Ramm, Bernard
1983 *After Fundamentalism: The Future of Evangelical Theology*. New York: Harper & Row.

Ricoeur, Paul
1969 *The Symbolism of Evil*. Boston: Beacon Press

Ridemann, Peter
1950 *Account of Our Religion, Doctrine and Faith* (1565). Trans. by Kathleen Hasenberg. Suffolk, England: Hodder and Stoughton, and The Plough Publishers.

Robinson, John A. T.
1950 *In the End, God....* London: James Clarke & Company.

1973 *The Human Face of God*. Philadelphia: Westminster Press.

Roop, Eugene F.
1987 *Genesis* (Believers Church Bible Commentary). Scottdale, Pa.: Herald Press.

Russell, D. S.
1964 *The Method and Message of Jewish Apocalyptic 200 B.C.-100 A.D.* Philadelphia: Westminster.

1978 *Apocalyptic: Ancient and Modern*. Philadelphia: Fortress Press.

Sanders, E. P.
1977 *Paul and Palestinian Judaism*. Philadelphia: Fortress Press.

Schaff, Philip
1877 *Creeds of Christendom*, 3 vols. New York: Harper Bros.

Scott, C. A. Anderson
1929 *Christianity According to Saint Paul*. Cambridge: University Press.

Seeberg, Reinhold
1952 *Textbook of the History of Doctrines*, 2 vols. Grand Rapids: Baker Book House.

Shaw, J. M.
1953 *Christian Doctrine: A One-Volume Outline of Christian Belief*. London: Lutterworth Press.

Smith, Huston
1987 "Is There a Perennial Philosophy?" *Journal of the American Academy of Religion* 55 (no. 3).

Stendahl, Krister, ed.
1965 *Immortality and Resurrection.*
New York: Macmillan.

Swartley, Willard M.
1983 *Slavery, Sabbath, War, and
Women: Case Issues in Biblical
Interpretation.* Scottdale, Pa.:
Herald Press.

Swartley, Willard M., ed.
1982 *The Bible and Law* (Occasional
Papers, no. 3). Elkhart, Ind.: Institute of Mennonite Studies.

Tillich, Paul
1951 *Systematic Theology*, vol. 1. Chicago: University of Chicago
Press.

1957 *Systematic Theology*, vol. 2. Chicago: University of Chicago
Press.

Torrance, James B.
1987 "Authority, Scripture and Tradition," *Evangelical Quarterly,*
July, 245-251.

Travis, Stephen H.
1982 *I Believe in the Second Coming of
Jesus.* Grand Rapids: Eerdmans.

Visser't Hooft, W. A.
1948 *The Kingship of Christ.* New
York: Harper.

1963 *No Other Name: The Choice
Between Syncretism and
Christian Universalism.*
Philadelphia: Westminster Press.

Von Rad, Gerhard
1962 *Old Testament Theology*, vol. 1.
New York: Harper & Row.

1972 *Genesis: A Commentary.*
Philadelphia: Westminster.

Waltner, Erland, ed.
1990 *Jesus Christ and the Mission of
the Church: Contemporary
Anabaptist Perspectives.* Newton,
Kan.: Faith and Life Press.
Herald Press.

Weber, Otto
1981, 1983 *Foundations of Dogmatics,*
2 vols. Grand Rapids: Eerdmans.

Wenger, John C.
1950 *Doctrines of the Mennonites.*
Scottdale, Pa.: Herald Press.

1954 *Introduction to Theology.*
Scottdale, Pa.: Herald Press.

Wenger, John C., ed.
1956 *The Complete Works of Menno
Simons,* trans. by Leonard Ver-
duin. Scottdale, Pa.: Herald
Press.

Westermann, Claus
1974 *Creation.* Philadelphia: Fortress
Press.

1984 *Genesis 1-11: A Commentary.*
Minneapolis: Augsburg.

Williams, George H., and Angel M.
Mergal, eds.
1957 *Spiritual and Anabaptist Writers.*
Philadelphia: Westminster Press.

Wilson-Kastner, Patricia
1983 *Faith, Feminism and the Christ.*
Philadelphia: Fortress Press.

Wingren, Gustaf
1961 *Creation and Law.* Philadelphia:
Muhlenberg Press.

Wolff, Hans Walter
1974 *Anthropology of the Old
Testament.* Philadelphia: Fortress Press.

Yoder, John H.
1972 *The Politics of Jesus.* Grand
Rapids: Eerdmans.

1984 *The Priestly Kingdom: Social
Gospel as Ethics.* Notre Dame,
Ind.: University of Notre Dame
Press.

Zehr, Paul M.
1986 *Biblical Criticism in the Life of
the Church.* Scottdale, Pa.:

General Index

Index of Persons

Scripture Index

The Author

With his wife, Ruth, C. Norman Kraus served under Mennonite Board of Missions in short-term assignments and for seven years in Asia and Australia (1980-87). During this time he wrote *Jesus Christ Our Lord*, subsequently revised (Herald Press, 1987, 1990), which prepares for the more general discussion of theology in *God Our Savior*.

For a long period Kraus served on the overseas committee of the Mennonite Board of Missions and for five years on its health and welfare committee. He has gone on teaching missions to churches in India, Indonesia, the Philippines, Taiwan, Hong Kong, Australia, and various East African countries.

Kraus has taught at the following seminaries in Asia: Serampore (India) Theological College (1966-67); Union Biblical Seminary (1983) in Pune, India; Eastern Hokkaido (Japan) Bible School (1981-86); and Baptist Theological College of Western Australia (1987).

Prior to this recent assignment in Japan, Kraus was a professor of religion and director of the Center for Discipleship at Goshen (Indiana) College. He was also book review editor of the *Mennonite Quarterly Review*. A student of both Anabaptism and Evangelicalism and its origins, he is the author of *Dispensationalism in America* (John Knox, 1958).

A native of Newport News, Virginia, Kraus earned graduate degrees from Goshen Biblical Seminary, Princeton Theological Seminary (Th.M.), and Duke University (Ph.D.). Aside from numerous articles, he is also the author of *The Healing Christ* (Herald Press, 1971), *The Community of the Spirit* (Eerdmans, 1974), *The Authentic Witness* (Eerdmans, 1979), and the editor of *Evangelicalism and Anabaptism* (Herald Press, 1979).

In 1950 Kraus was ordained as a minister in the Indiana-Michigan Mennonite Conference. He has moved to Virginia, where he is a member of the Park View Mennonite congregation and for a year was interim pastor of Community Mennonite Church, both of Harrisonburg, Virginia.

At present Norman and Ruth are at home in Harrisonburg, where he is continuing his writing.